Macroeconomic
Theory

The Irwin Series in Economics

Consulting Editor   LLOYD G. REYNOLDS
Yale University

Macroeconomic Theory

WILLIAM R. HOSEK, Ph.D.
Associate Professor of Economics
University of New Hampshire

 1975

RICHARD D. IRWIN, INC.   Homewood, Illinois   60430
Irwin-Dorsey International   London, England   WC2H 9NJ
Irwin-Dorsey Limited   Georgetown, Ontario   L7G 4B3

© RICHARD D. IRWIN, INC., 1975

All rights reserved. No part of this publication may be reproduced, stored in a retrieval system, or transmitted, in any form or by any means, electronic, mechanical, photocopying, recording, or otherwise, without the prior written permission of the publisher.

First Printing, January 1975

ISBN 0-256-01669-0
Library of Congress Catalog Card No. 74–12922

Printed in the United States of America

*To Jeanette, Sibyl Gwynne,
and Marissa Jean*

Preface

IN THE nearly 40 years since the appearance of John Maynard Keynes' *General Theory of Employment, Interest and Money* considerable refinements have been made in Keynes' basic model. A major function of any textbook is to survey the state of the arts in its field and in attempting to fulfill that function this book reviews the contributions of both theoretical and empirical research to the theories that underlie the components of aggregate demand, the money market, and the labor market.

More importantly, modern macrotheory describes a general equilibrium system (highly aggregated, to be sure) consisting of three major markets, the product, money, and labor markets. Unfortunately, many textbooks discuss macroeconomic policy in the context of only the product market (the "Keynesian Cross") or only the product and money markets (the IS-LM model). The labor market and the determinants of aggregate supply are usually treated separately and are not integrated into the full model. Part Two of this book seeks to overcome this by combining and analyzing the three markets prior to the discussion of policy. In this way fiscal and monetary policy can be discussed simultaneously (and their relative effects compared) without implicit reference to basic relationships hidden in later chapters. Moreover the linkages among all three markets become important in transmitting policy changes. Early introduction of the concepts of the aggregate production function and labor market also gives the student time to become familiar with ideas that appear again in the discussion of economic growth and the recent approaches to macroeconomic disequilibrium.

Unemployment is built into the model by a simple device, well established in Keynesian literature, the rigid nominal wage rate. While recent writers (Robert Clower and Axel Leijonhufvud, for example) dispute that Keynes made this assumption, it is part of Keynesian literature. For purposes of this book it may be treated simply as one of several possible conditions that keep the labor market from clearing at full employment. Used in the context of the basic model of this book, it permits the student to analyze the effect of policy on unemployment and the trade-off between the price level and unemployment. The more recent theories of unemployment also have their day, but at another point in the book (Chapters 16 and 17).

The basic model development of Part Two is preceded, in Part One, by an introduction which establishes the framework for the model. It identifies the major sectors, the markets in which they interact and the flows and linkages among them. Part One also deals with the measurement of macroeconomic variables and includes a discussion of the neglected flow of funds accounts.

Part Three deals with advanced developments in the theories of the components of the basic model. In the belief that economics is an empirical science, the results of empirical as well as theoretical research are discussed. Major developments in money supply theory have taken place over the past decade, placing the money supply process on the same level as discussions of consumption, investment, and money demand. Consequently a separate chapter is devoted to money supply theory. The implications of all these developments, together with a second look at stabilization policy, are discussed at the end of Part Three.

The balance of payments, instability and growth, and inflation being major policy concerns, Part Four contains special chapters on international economics, dynamics and growth, and inflation. Balance of payments analysis is handled by building the conditions for external equilibrium into the basic model. Current controversy over the stability of the Phillips curve is covered in the chapter on inflation. Finally current developments in disequilibrium macroeconomics and the challenge of radical economics are covered in the last chapter.

Controversy permeates macroeconomic theory. Where appropriate, disputes are identified and (hopefully) both sides are presented. References to the dispute between fiscalists and monetarists, for example, are scattered throughout the book. The student is frequently cautioned against assuming that macroeconomic theory is a polished field in which no further research is necessary. From the student's perspective, facility with graphs and minimal algebra are all the technical skills necessary to understand most of the material in the book. The chapter on dynamics and growth is a necessary exception.

The book profited substantially from the many comments and suggestions provided by Karl Asmus, Alan Pankratz, Lloyd Reynolds, Dennis Starleaf, Dwayne Wrightsman, and many graduate and undergraduate students at the University of New Hampshire. Any errors that remain in the book are my responsibility.

Last, but hardly least, many thanks for typing go to Becky Childs and Elaine Vachon, and especially to my wife, Jeanette, who spent many hours transcribing my garbled tapes.

December 1974   WILLIAM R. HOSEK

Contents

part one
The Nature and Measurement of Aggregate Economic Activity

1. Introduction   3

    Purpose of Macroeconomic Analysis. Overview of the Economy: *Sector Classification. Sector Interrelationships. A Simplified Framework.* Institutional and Behavioral Assumptions. Plan of the Book.

2. Measurement   19

    National Income Accounting: *Income. Expenditure. Conceptual Problems.* The Flow-of-Funds Accounts. Other Indicators.

part two
Macroeconomic Analysis of a Closed Economy

3. The Basic Model: Aggregate Demand   37

    The Components of Aggregate Demand: *Consumption. Investment. Government Expenditures on Goods and Services.* A Simple Model of Income Determination.

4. The Basic Model: The Money Market   49

    The Demand for Money. The Supply of Money. The Money Market and Aggregate Demand.

5. The Basic Model: Aggregate Supply   61

    Aggregate Supply. The Labor Market. The Complete Basic Model.

6. Operation of the Model — 71

Autonomous Changes. Adjustment Mechanisms. Financing Autonomous Spending. An Alternative View: Velocity and the Equation of Exchange. Appendix A. Appendix B.

7. Stabilization Policy: A First View — 92

The Goals of Policy: *Unemployment. Price Stability. Economic Growth. Balance of Payments. Role of the Policy Maker.* The Tools of Policy. Some Illustrative Policy Changes. Relative Impact of Fiscal and Monetary Policy.

part three
Further Sector Analysis

8. Consumption — 113

The Absolute Income Hypothesis of the Basic Model. Alternative Income Concepts: *The Relative Income Hypothesis. The Permanent Income Hypothesis. The Life-Cycle Hypothesis.* The Role of the Interest Rate. The Role of Wealth. Related Empirical Studies. Some Implications. Appendix: *The Scatter Diagram, Freehand, or "Eyeball" Method. The Method of Least Squares.*

9. Investment — 135

The Hypothesis of the Basic Model. The Stock Adjustment Approach: *The Crude Accelerator. The Neoclassical Approach. The Role of Liquidity or Internal Funds. The Role of Expected Profits.* The Special Case of Investment in Inventories. The Empirical Evidence.

10. The Labor Market — 148

Labor Demand. Labor Supply. Appendix.

11. Money Demand — 160

Issues in Money Demand. The Definition of Money. Some Theories of Money Demand. Related Empirical Studies.

12. Money Supply — 182

The Money Supply Framework: *Balance Sheets of the System. The Money Supply Identity.* Money Supply Theory: *The Currency Ratio. The Time Deposit Ratio. The Excess Reserve Ratio.* One Application: *A Money Supply Liquidity Trap?* Related Empirical Studies.

13. Stabilization Policy: A Second View   197

Policy Effectiveness: The Empirical Evidence on the Form of the Basic Model: *The IS Schedule. The LM Schedule. The Problem of Stability in the Model.* Measuring Policy Changes: The Indicator Problem: *Appropriate Indicator Qualities. Possible Fiscal Policy Indicators. Possible Monetary Policy Measures.* The Strength of Policy: *The Transmission Mechanism. The Lag in Effect.* Policy Proposals.

**part four
Special Topics**

14. International Economics   217

The Foreign Sector and the Basic Model: *The Balance of Trade and Aggregate Demand. The Capital Account Balance and Other Items.* Balance of Payments Accounting: *The Current Account. The Capital Account.* Determinants of the Components of the Balance of Payments: *The Influence of Income. Influence of Relative Prices. The Influence of Relative Interest Rates. The Influence of Exchange Rates.* External Equilibrium and the Basic Model: *The IS Curve with the Addition of the Balance of Trade. The External Equilibrium Function.* Policy Issues: *Analysis of Policy Effects. Use of Nonmarket Changes.* A Caveat on Partial Equilibrium Analysis.

15. Dynamics and Growth   240

Static and Dynamic Analysis: *Some Concepts. Plan of the Chapter.* Dynamics without Growth. Economic Growth: *Some Terms and Definitions. A Simple Growth Model. The Neoclassical Approach.* Sources of Economic Growth. Policy Issues: *Policies for the Developed Economy. Policies for the Underdeveloped Economy.*

16. Inflation   263

Introduction. The Source of Inflation: *The Keynesian, Excess Demand, or Inflationary Gap Approach. The Quantity Theory Approach.* Mechanisms of Inflation: *Demand-Pull. Cost-Push. Sector-Shift Inflation.* Inflation versus Unemployment: The Critical Trade-Off: *A Look at the Phillips Curve. An Alternative View of the Phillips Relationship.* Policy Issues: *Empirical Evidence on the Effect of Inflation. The Implied Policies.*

17. Recent Developments in Macroeconomic Theory   286

Critique of the Basic Model. Disequilibrium Approaches: *Market-Clearing Friction. Job Acceptance Friction. The Equilibrating Process.* Radical Economics: *Growth of Radicalism. The Nature of Radical Economics.*

Index   301

part one

THE NATURE AND MEASUREMENT OF AGGREGATE ECONOMIC ACTIVITY

1

Introduction

PURPOSE OF MACROECONOMIC ANALYSIS

"The time has come for a new economic policy for the United States. Its targets are unemployment, inflation, and international speculation."[1] With these words President Nixon, in 1971, outlined another attack on some very old macroeconomic problems. Unemployment in particular has been troubling policy makers for many decades. It was unemployment that was of major concern to John Maynard Keynes when he constructed the theory which has become the core of macroeconomics since the 1930s.[2]

To a great extent developments in modern macroeconomics have taken place in response to specific problems that have risen from time to time. The *General Theory* might have been written years later, and perhaps might have been written by someone other than Keynes, had not the world faced an immense depression in the 1930s. The Employment Act of 1946 continues to provide a stimulus to research in macroeconomic model building and empirical methods. If the government is to follow the act's mandate and engage in vigorous policies to insure the health of the whole economy, it is imperative that policy advisors know how the economy works, how to forecast problems be-

---

[1] Address before the nation by Richard M. Nixon, August 15, 1971. Reproduced in Roger Leroy Miller and Raburn M. Williams, *The New Economics of Richard Nixon: Freezes, Floats and Fiscal Policy* (San Francisco: Canfield Press, 1972), pp. 70–76.

[2] See John Maynard Keynes, *The General Theory of Employment, Interest, and Money* (New York: Harcourt, Brace and World, Inc., 1936), pp. 372–84.

fore they arise, and be able to evaluate the effects of policy. Consequently, considerable direct and indirect government support has been provided to research in macroeconomics.

The 1960s can be cited as evidence of the success of some government policies, but also as evidence of the failure of other government policies. The federal tax cut of 1964, accompanied by expansionary monetary policies, seemed to produce the desired and predicted result, namely, rapid growth in the U.S. economy and a lowering of unemployment. However, the tax surcharge of 1968 did not appear to retard the economy as conventional macroeconomic theory had predicted. Similarly, restrictive monetary policies of 1969–1970 did not quickly produce the effect on the rate of inflation that many economists had previously predicted. Such events as these stimulate a more careful assessment of macroeconomic theory on two levels. At one level, the theories themselves are modified to take account of effects not previously considered important. On another level, new empirical research is encouraged to determine quantitatively the effect of various policies on the economy.[3]

Unfortunately, while there may be general agreement on the goals of policy, there is considerable disagreement over the relative importance of each goal and the means by which the policy makers should attempt to reach the goals. By tradition and, in some cases, by specification in the Employment Act of 1946, the widely accepted goals of policy include full employment, a rapid rate of economic growth (rising per capita income at full employment), low rates of inflation, and balance of payments equilibrium. Unfortunately the vigorous pursuit of any one goal may create impediments to the attainment of the other goals. In other words, there may be a trade-off between having your cake and eating it. It may not be possible, for example, to vigorously pursue full employment without running into more rapid rates of inflation. It may not be possible to pursue rapid economic growth without incurring higher levels of environmental pollution. It may not be possible to pursue a rapid rate of economic growth without incurring disequilibrium in our international balance of payments. When a conflict does arise, the choice is inevitably subjective, reflecting the preferences of the policy makers.

---

[3] As an example of the former, see Robert Eisner, "Fiscal and Monetary Policy Reconsidered," *American Economic Review,* Vol. 59 (December 1969), pp. 897–905. As an example of the latter, see the reference to the works of Jordan and Anderson and others in Chapter 7.

Thus the policy makers, in attempting to maximize the "general welfare," must choose among competing objectives because society lacks the resources or the means to simultaneously satisfy all objectives. A household must choose among competing goods because its budget constraint prevents it from consuming as much of each good as it desires. Similarly the policy maker cannot, for example, maximize economic growth by producing the required amount of capital goods and, at the same time, provide the maximum amount of consumer goods to the populace because the total resources available to society are not unlimited. The constraint means that difficult choices must be made. If economic analysis has a role, it is in identifying the areas of conflict and determining the effects of alternative policy measures.

The evaluation of alternative policy measures is, however, not such a simple task. Consider a simple question: Which policy will produce a more powerful impact upon the economy—fiscal policy or monetary policy? A perusal of many textbooks written in the 1950s and the 1960s might lead one to answer, "Fiscal policy, of course." But this position has been challenged in the late 1960s and early 1970s by a resurgence of "monetarism."[4]

The fiscalist versus monetarist controversy is not the only controversy over policy method. The economics profession has been confronted by a radical challenge. The challenge is radical because traditional economists, in conducting their analyses and disagreeing with each other, have done so under the assumption of given institutions and given behavior patterns. However, the new challengers are unwilling to accept those assumptions. The basis of their policy recommendations is to change institutions and behavior patterns and thereby deal with problems of unemployment and inflation.[5]

Macroeconomic theory is therefore in a state of flux, and it is likely to continue in that state for years to come. However, an understanding of the present state of knowledge is essential if one is to be able to

---

[4] The major issues that divide the "fiscalists" and the "monetarists" are analyzed by David I. Fand, "Some Issues in Monetary Economics," *Banca Nazionale del Lavoro Quarterly Review,* Vol. 22 (September 1969), pp. 215–47.

[5] David Mermelstein, ed., *Economics: Mainstream Readings and Radical Critiques,* (New York: Random House, 1970) contains an excellent collection of articles challenging the methods and assumptions of traditional analysis. John G. Gurly, "Have Fiscal and Monetary Policies Failed?" *American Economic Review,* Vol. 63, No. 2 (May 1972) pp. 19–23 even argues that the "generally accepted" goals have not been pursued by the policy makers. Rather, he argues, fiscal and monetary policies have aimed primarily at the maintenance of business profits.

comprehend both the criticisms of received theory and the developments in theory that will take place in the years ahead. The core of this book, therefore, covers traditional material. Nevertheless, some major challenges—including the radical challenge—will be discussed in the final chapter.

OVERVIEW OF THE ECONOMY

It may be helpful to view the economy as a system containing only a few major interrelated parts, rather than as a microscopic collection of individual households and firms. This is not to say that one cannot analyze the economy with a model composed of the behavioral relationships of individual firms and households. Such an approach would be very cumbersome. Nevertheless, we shall assume that the behavior of each sector is reflective of the behavior of the individuals making up that sector. In fact, macroeconomics should be distinguished from microeconomics only by the extent to which units are aggregated. For example, in microeconomics we deal with individual firms or, by aggregating a little, with individual industries. In macroeconomics we carry the aggregation still further, grouping all industries into a single *business sector*. Industry behavior is deduced from firm behavior in microeconomic analysis. To be consistent, business sector behavior in macroeconomic analysis should also be ultimately deduced from the behavior of individual firms.

However, aggregation does tend to break down the partial equilibrium analysis employed in microeconomics. One may analyze the behavior of an individual firm under perfect competition, while assuming that the firm's actions do not affect the price of the product it produces. The same assumption cannot be made of the behavior of the business sector and the general level of prices. We will see that the behavior of the business sector in part determines, and is determined by, the general price level.

Sector Classification

The sector breakdown of modern macroeconomics is quite different from that of classical macroeconomics. David Ricardo, for example, viewed the economy as consisting of workers, capitalists, and landlords. The classification primarily reflected the method by which income was received. In like manner, Karl Marx broke the economy down into two principal groups—workers and capitalists. A person belonged to the worker class or to the capitalist class depending upon whether his income was derived from wages or from profits.

A modern economy, such as that of the United States, does not lend itself easily to that kind of classification. Most individuals derive their income from more than one source. Many workers, for example, are indirect recipients of profits. The pension funds to which the workers contribute are usually used to buy the stocks of corporations as well as bonds, both public and private. To the extent that a worker's future source of income is augmented by the dividends received through his pension plan, he is a recipient of profits. Landlords also cannot be classified as a separate group, for many landlords work for wages to supplement their rental income. Hence classification by source of income is, at best, inconvenient, and at worst it confuses the behavior patterns of the recipients of various types of income. Is there any reason to suppose that I spend my salary differently than I spend the interest I receive from my savings account or the dividends I receive from the stocks I hold?

Modern macroeconomics, therefore, divides the economy into somewhat different subgroups. One group or sector supplies all of the factors of production, accrues or earns all of the national income, and buys consumer goods. We call this the *household sector*. Another sector, already introduced, transforms the factors of production into goods and buys capital goods. Although the business sector buys capital goods, the ultimate ownership of such goods resides with the household sector. Hence, payment for capital goods services accrues to the household sector. To these two sectors, we add the *government sector* which includes all federal, state, and local units. The government sector, presumably reflecting the preferences of society as a whole, transfers income from one sector to another sector or transfers income among individuals in the same sector. For example, it taxes both the business and household sectors in order to make Social Security payments to the household sector. In addition, the government sector mobilizes resources in order to purchase those goods and services for the whole society that cannot conveniently be purchased by individuals within the society. Highways and battleships are examples.

Finally a fourth sector completes the picture. Most societies engage in trade with other societies. The other or nondomestic societies we refer to as the *foreign sector* or the *rest-of-the-world* sector.

Sector Interrelationships

In Figure 1–1 the four sectors are shown together with the flows of spending, income, and taxes among them. Note that each sector receives income and makes expenditures. The net income of the house-

FIGURE 1–1
Circular Flow of Income and Expenditure

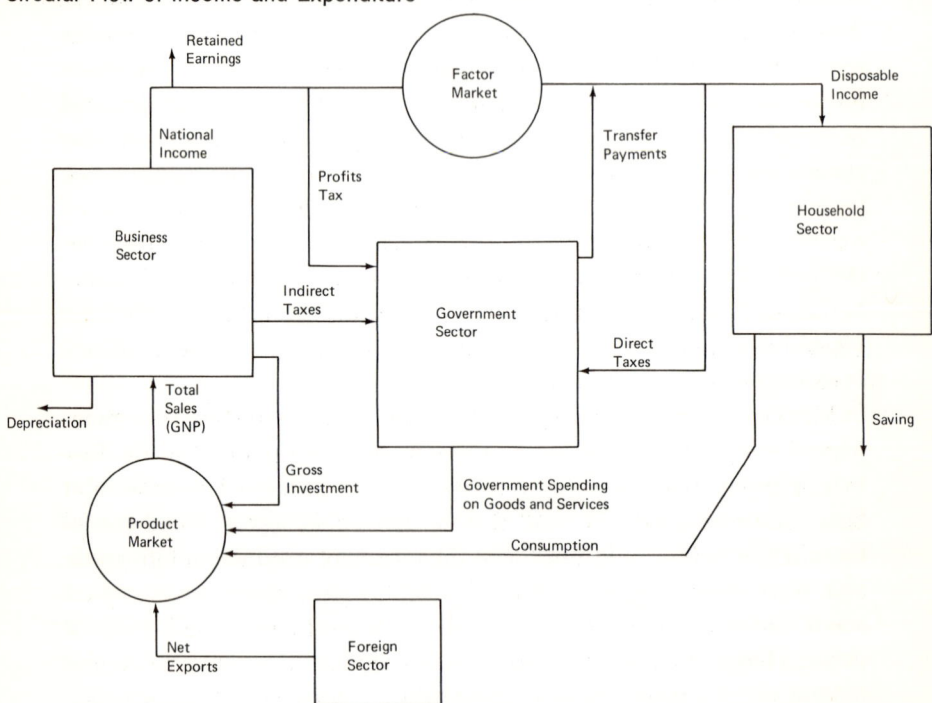

hold sector, which we call *disposable income,* is used for either *consumption* or *saving.* Consumption consists of expenditures on currently produced consumer goods and services. Saving is the residual (disposable income less consumption) which is usually used to increase the household's stock of financial assets such as money, time deposit balances, government bonds, etc.

The income (sales less factor costs, taxes, and dividends) of the business sector consists of an allowance to replace worn-out capital equipment (depreciation) plus the retained earnings (undistributed profits) of corporations. The business sector in turn buys capital equipment, the services of which are used in the productive process. The purchase of such capital equipment we call *gross investment*.

The government sector receives income in the form of taxes which are collected from both the business and household sectors. The budget expenditures of the government sector consist of purchases of goods and services and transfer payments. The transfer payments are made primarily to the household sector in the form of welfare payments, Social Security payments, unemployment insurance payments, etc. Analytically, transfer payments are additions to household disposable income, and taxes are subtractions from disposable income. Thus transfer payments can be treated as negative taxes (or taxes can be treated as negative transfers). For simplicity, later we will assume away the existence of transfer payments. This has the same effect as netting transfers against taxes.

The foreign sector receives income by exporting goods to our economy, and it makes expenditures by buying goods from us.

The exchanges among the sectors are made in the markets which are also shown in Figure 1–1. In the *factor market,* wages and salaries, rent, interest, and profits are paid by the business sector to the household sector in return for the services of the *factors of production* such as *raw materials, labor, and capital.* In the *product market,* the business sector sells the goods and services it has produced in return for the dollars spent by all four sectors. The markets are the same as those employed in microeconomics. We have simply taken all the individual markets for goods and services and aggregated those into a single product market. In the following chapters, we will identify the determinants of demand and the determinants of supply for that market as well as for the other markets.

Some idea of the relative magnitudes of the various flows (for the 1973 U.S. economy) in Figure 1–1 can be gained by reference to Table 1–1. Note that as far as expenditures in the product market are concerned, consumption spending by the household sector is the largest. Net exports, on the other hand, is relatively minor. On the income side, the household sector receives the vast bulk of its income from wages and salaries.

Figure 1–2 shows the relative changes in expenditures since 1929. The share of the government sector has increased, while the share of the private sector has decreased, most of the change occurring prior to 1954. This does not mean that the household sector is consuming less than it did years ago relative to total expenditures in the product

TABLE 1–1
Gross National Product by Income and Expenditure, 1973 (billions of dollars)

Income	Amount	Percent	Expenditure	Amount	Percent
Wages, salaries, supplements......	$ 785.3	61.0	Consumption.......	$ 805.0	62.5
Professional and farm income..........	84.3	6.5	Gross private investment. Government spending on goods and services†...	201.5 277.2	15.6 21.5
Rent	25.1	1.9	Net exports:		
Corporate income.....	109.2	8.5	Exports..... $101.3		
Interest...........	50.4	3.9	Imports .... −96.7	4.6	0.4
Depreciation........	109.6	8.5			
Indirect business taxes* .	122.0	9.5			
Statistical error	2.3	0.2			
Gross national product	$1,288.2	100.0	Gross national product	$1,288.2	100.0

* Includes business transfer payments (+) and subsidies less current surplus of government enterprises (−)
† These are expenditures onc urrent output in the product market. Government transfer payments amounted to $112.5 billion.
Source: *Economic Report of the President, 1974.*

FIGURE 1–2
Relative Shares of Gross National Product

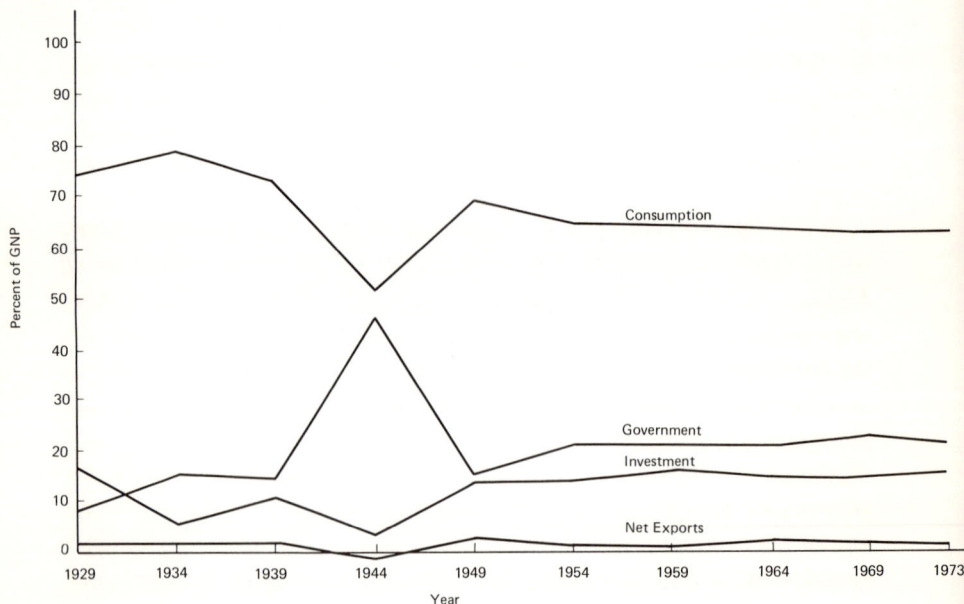

Source: Shares computed from data contained in the *Economic Report of the President, 1974.*

market. Rather, the types of goods that the household sector consumes have shifted away from conventional consumer goods to what are called *public goods,* such as schools, public parks, public roads, and so on.

A Simplified Framework

Figure 1–1 highlights the major flows for the U.S. economy. Still more detail can be obtained by further disaggregation. We might, for example, divide the government sector into its federal, state, and local components. However, the core of modern macroeconomic theory can still be introduced with the use of a more simple, rather than a more detailed, framework. The simplification can be accomplished by making the following assumptions, some of which can be relaxed later:

1. There are no transfer payments. All government expenditures are for goods and services.
2. There are no taxes on corporate profits or indirect business taxes. All taxes are direct taxes levied against the personal income of the household sector.
3. There are no retained earnings. All corporate profits are paid to the household sector.
4. There is no foreign sector.
5. The current depreciation allowance is equal to the amount necessary to replace worn-out capital. This will enable us to work with net national product and net investment by subtracting depreciation from GNP and gross investment.

While these assumptions will enable us to deal with the basic thrust of macroeconomic theory, we need greater detail for empirical work. Figure 1–1 will provide the context for a discussion of the basic data sources—namely, the national income and flow of funds accounts—in the next chapter.

The simplified framework will be the basis for the construction of a basic macroeconomic *model* which will be used throughout most of the book. An economic model is a set of statements (verbal, algebraic, or graphical) that explains something about the economic environment (in this book, how such things as aggregate output and employment are determined). Generally the *structure* of a model contains three kinds of statements (or *structural equations*):

1. *Behavioral statements* are statements about the way in which economic units respond to various stimuli. For example, a statement may be made about the way in which consumers respond to changes in income.
2. *Definitions* or *identities* are statements about the economic environment or institutions that are true under all conditions. For example, we will define household disposable income to be the difference between net national product and taxes (in the context of the simplified framework).
3. *Equilibrium conditions* define the state of the model when it is at rest—when there is no further tendency for the variables in the model to change. Equilibrium conditions hold only under certain circumstances. They should not be confused with identities.

Elements such as income, consumption, taxes, etc. are known as *variables*. Two types of variables should be distinguished: *Endogenous* variables are variables which the model itself determines; *exogenous* variables are determined by forces outside of the influence of the model. We shall return to this distinction in Chapter 6 when we analyze the complete model.

The three types of statements are often combined to obtain a solution for a selected endogenous variable. The statement that results from this makes the selected endogenous variable a function of the exogenous variables and the parameters of the model. Such a statement, derived from the structure, is often called a *reduced form* equation. The reduced-form statements and the behavioral statements provide the model builder with hypotheses about the real world that are testable. That is, data about the real world can be gathered and examined to see whether they are consistent with the implications contained in the behavioral and reduced-form statements or equations.

Some hypotheses in the model may not be testable, at least not directly. For example, behavioral statements about the household sector may be based upon the assumption that consumers attempt to maximize utility or satisfaction. This assumption is not testable, but the implications of the assumption, contained in behavioral and reduced-form statements, usually are testable.

We will be making use of these concepts as we construct the basic model used in this book. For the development of the basic model or theory, our initial framework will be that shown in Figure 1–3. Note several basic relationships. Each expenditure item reflects, we shall assume, the *intentions* of the sector from which it originates

FIGURE 1-3
Simplified Circular Flow of Income and Expenditure

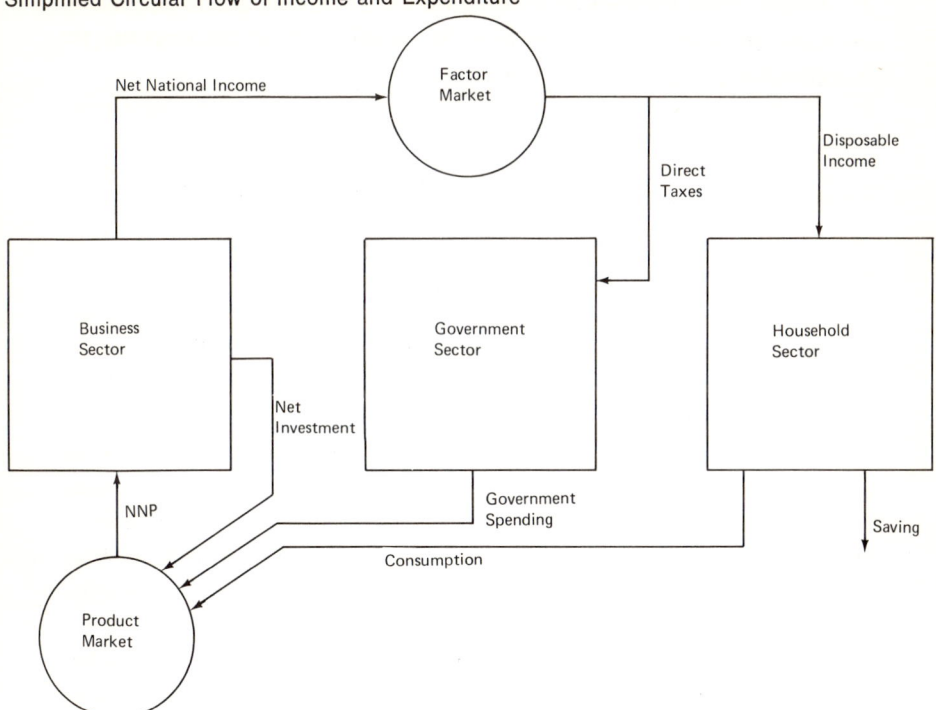

rather than the amounts actually expended. The product market is in *equilibrium* when these *planned* or *intended* expenditures on goods and services (*aggregate demand*) for investment (I), consumption (C), and government use (G) are equal in total to the intended output (intended aggregate supply—Y, for short) of the business sector. That is, when

$$Y = C + I + G \qquad (1\text{--}1)$$

This equilibrium condition, together with two definitions, yields another basic relationship. Note that the disposable income (Y_D) of the household sector is the difference between net national product (Y) and personal taxes (T).

$$Y_D \equiv Y - T \qquad (1\text{--}2)$$

Further, the household sector allocates its income between consumption (C) and saving (S).

$$Y_D \equiv C + S \qquad (1\text{--}3)$$

These two definitions or identities[6] can be combined with the product market equilibrium condition, equation (1–1), to yield an alternative equilibrium condition. If we rearrange equation (1–2) and substitute in place of Y in equation (1–1) we have:

$$Y_D + T = C + I + G$$

Substituting equation (1–3) in place of Y_D and rearranging:

$$C + S + T = C + I + G$$
$$S = I + (G - T) \qquad (1\text{–}4)$$

The last equation is formally equivalent to equilibrium in the product market. Thus we can also say that the product market is in equilibrium if the saving of the household sector is equal to the net investment of the business sector plus the government deficit $(G > T)$ or surplus $(T > G)$.

A third market, the *money market,* is not shown in Figures 1–1 and 1–3 but is important in the analysis to follow. Households and business firms *hold* money *balances* for a number of reasons. We will deal with these in Chapter 4 and again in Chapter 11. Money, as conventionally defined in the United States, consists of currency and coin in circulation outside banks plus demand deposit (principally checking account) balances. Although the money market is not part of the circular flow of income and expenditure, it does exert an influence on that flow.

We should note here that the product market is a *flow* market in which quantities are exchanged *per unit of time.* For example, household expenditure on automobiles is expressed in terms of x number of automobiles purchased per year (or per month or week, etc.). The money market is a *stock* market in which the quantity of money held is expressed *as of a point in time.* For example, the stock of money held as of December 1973 was $270.4 billion.

Flows accompany changes in stocks. For example, suppose 2 million automobiles were produced in 1973 and none of the existing automobiles was destroyed. Then the stock of automobiles as of December 31, 1973 was 2 million more than it was on December 31, 1972. Individuals can increase their stocks of money balances by adding the flow of saving to them. Similarly, they can reduce their stocks

---

[6] We use the sign ≡ to denote an identity or definition which is true under all conditions.

of money balances by generating a flow of spending or lending with the undesired balances.

INSTITUTIONAL AND BEHAVIORAL ASSUMPTIONS

While the above flow diagrams tell us something about the organization of the economy, they don't tell us anything about the behavior of the individual sectors of the economy. We will be interested in answering such questions as, "What factors determine the level of intended consumption by the household sector? How do those factors, working through changes in consumption, affect the total level of economic activity? What role does the business sector play? How is intended spending on investment goods determined?" Before we can answer, or attempt to answer, these questions, we must make some assumptions about the institutional and behavioral framework within which the economy operates.

We will assume that the economy described by our model is a private property economy. That is, the means of production and goods and services are, or can be, owned privately. We assume that individuals and business firms can exercise relatively free choice in the disposition of goods and factors of production. In short, we assume that members of the household sector can buy the kinds of goods that they choose to buy without hindrance and that the business sector can combine factors of production in any way it chooses without interference.

We assume that firms in the business sector are in business to make profits. Carrying this assumption one step further, we shall assume that given factor and product prices, firms buy such quantities of factors of production and produce such quantities of finished goods so as to make the maximum profits. We assume that members of the household sector allocate their incomes between consumption and saving so as to maximize utility—that is, they consume and save (buy present and future goods) in such a way as to maximize the amount of satisfaction received from such goods. We also assume that the amount of factors of production offered by the household sector, in particular the amount of labor offered for sale, is part of the utility-maximizing decision.

These assumptions may seem abstract, but the intent is to derive basic principles. Theories are not constructed to describe everything that goes on in the economy, but to pinpoint the major forces that make the economy operate. Toward that end we abstract from the maze of detail and make a few crucial, but simple, assumptions. We shall, in the process, resort to such tools as equations and graphs to facilitate the analysis. Lest one fall into the common trap of thinking that such symbols cannot adequately represent human behavior, remember that we use symbols in a musical score to represent some of the deepest of human emotions.

There is, however, a dual nature to theorizing in economics. Economics is, after all, an empirical science. The variables with which it is concerned are often capable of measurement. It seems apparent that theorizing in economics should involve both the process of deduction and induction. Economic models may be constructed or deduced from a set of assumptions, but then, in turn, the implications of those models should be tested by recourse to the appropriate real world data and, if need be, the assumptions of the model revised and the model reconstructed. It is in this spirit that we will consider some of the evidence that exists on the various theories that have developed over the last 40 years of macroeconomic model building. One further point deserves mention: Because of its necessarily abstract nature, no theory completely describes the reality of its domain. Moreover, few, if any, theories contain implications all of which conform exactly to real world events. That does not destroy the theory's usefulness, if it provides substantial insight into the functioning of the world it seeks to explain. Failure of an implication to conform with reality may only mean that the theory needs revision rather than rejection. The theories presented in this book evolved through just such a process of revision.

PLAN OF THE BOOK

Most of the macroeconomic theory with which we will be concerned in this book is *static* theory which compares equilibrium points in order to make statements about the effect on the economy of a particular stimulus such as a change in government spending on goods and services. However, all comparative statics analyses of this type do imply some underlying *dynamic* structure which describes the process by which the economy moves from one equilibrium position to another. We shall describe a dynamic process in Chapter 6, although we shall do so in an informal sense. Chapter 15 will deal more formally with dynamics.

We complete this first part with a discussion, in the next chapter, of the measurement of the various flows and stocks in the model. Figure 1–1 forms the framework for that discussion. In Part II the basic model will be developed for a closed economy based upon the context described by Figure 1–3. The model is a simplified view of the current status of macroeconomic theory and is useful in enabling us to pinpoint some of the problems that economists have faced in working with macroeconomic models. It will also enable us to acquire a feel for the manipulation of policy tools to accomplish the various goals discussed earlier. In Part III we will survey more recent developments that have taken place in the theory of the household sector, business sector, the labor market, money demand, and money supply. In connection with these discussions, the results of various empirical studies will also be discussed. Some of the later developments have implications for stabilization policy, and hence in Chapter 13 we will take a second look at stabilization policy and introduce some issues not previously discussed.

SUMMARY NOTES

1. Modern macroeconomic analysis divides the economy into four sectors: the household, business, government, and foreign sectors.
2. The household sector supplies the services of factors of production to the business sector which converts the factor services into final goods and services.
3. Wages, interest, rent, and profits accrue to the household sector in return for the factor services it supplies. After taxes are deducted, the household sector allocates the remaining disposable income to consumption and saving.
4. The business sector pays for the factor services and taxes out of total sales (gross national product). The balance, consisting of undistributed profits and depreciation allowances, is used to purchase capital equipment.
5. The government sector makes purchases of public goods such as roads and schools and makes transfer payments to the household and business sectors. The funds are obtained primarily through taxes.
6. Goods and services are exported to, and imported from, the foreign sector.
7. Aggregate demand in the product market consists of the sum of expenditures by the household sector (consumption), business sec-

tor (investment), government sector (government spending on goods and services), and foreign sector (net exports).

DISCUSSION QUESTIONS

1. Suppose we did live in the classical world of David Ricardo with clearly identifiable workers, capitalists, and landlords. Try to construct a flow chart similar to Figure 1–3 to identify the relationships among those groups.

2. The utility or satisfaction-maximizing assumption has often been questioned. List some alternative motives for human behavior. What do you suppose is meant by the phrase, "getting the most for your dollar" or "getting your dollar's worth"?

3. The profit-maximizing assumption has also been questioned. Suppose you owned a business. What would motivate your behavior? If you owned the only grocery store in town would your motives be different from the case in which you owned only one of a great many stores in town?

2

Measurement

NATIONAL INCOME ACCOUNTING[1]

WITHOUT a system of national income accounting much of macroeconomic theory would be of intellectual interest only. Policy makers, basing their decisions on the predictions of economic theory, would be unable to evaluate the impact of their policies upon the economy. Economists would be unable to subject various theories to empirical verification. Fortunately, most of the concepts with which economists deal are capable of measurement. It is not surprising, therefore, that the development of national income accounting began over three centuries ago, even before the advent of classical economic theory. As early as 1655, Sir William Petty, acknowledged to be the father of national income accounting, estimated that England's national income was 40 million pounds.

It wasn't until the late 18th and 19th centuries that major advances were made. Scattered work finally culminated in a uniform system of accounts agreed upon by the United States, Canada, and the United Kingdom in 1944. The conventions adopted by these countries

---

[1] The discussion in this chapter is designed to acquaint the student with the types of macroeconomic data that are available. Consequently we shall not deal in depth with the philosophy and methodology behind social accounting. The interested student might peruse John W. Kendrick, *Economic Accounts and Their Uses* (New York: McGraw-Hill Book Co., 1972); and Sam Rosen, *National Income and other Social Accounts* (New York: Holt, Rinehart and Winston, Inc., 1972).

formed the basis of the first National Income Supplement to the Survey of Current Business which was issued in 1947.[2]

The framework of modern national income accounting is provided by economic theory. Categories such as "personal consumption expenditures" and "gross private domestic investment" reflect concepts of macroeconomic theory. The framework shown in Figure 1-1 in Chapter 1 will form the basis of our discussion here. The figure indicates two methods by which national income may be compiled. Gross national product is the sum of all expenditures in the product market. Alternatively, on the income side, it is the sum of all factor payments made, plus indirect business taxes and depreciation. Table 2-1 shows gross national product for 1973 computed both from income side and the expenditure side.[3]

Income

Conceptually, on the income side, the payments to the factors of production should be reflected in profits, wages and salaries, rent, and interest. Note, however, that only *corporate* profits are shown. Profits of unincorporated enterprises are not shown because the profits of such enterprises are taxed as ordinary personal income. The adjusted gross income shown on the tax return includes a return to the labor of the owners of the enterprise (wages or salary) as well as a profit (or loss). However, no separate statement of wages or salary is made because the owners normally finance their personal expenditures by simply making withdrawals from the firm's income rather than by paying themselves a salary. Any attempt by the national income accountant to separate the income of unincorporated enterprises into salaries and wages would be arbitrary. Consequently business, professional, and farm incomes are stated separately from both wages and salaries (of corporations and the government) and from corporate profits.

The two major categories on the income side that are not payments

---

[2] Estimates of national income and its components, as well as other important economic variables, may now be found in many sources, of which the *Survey of Current Business* (especially the July issue) is only one. National income, monetary, and flow-of-funds data may also be found in the *Federal Reserve Bulletin* (issued monthly). A handy source for the student is the *Economic Report of the President* (issued annually). Data for other countries may be found in the *United Nations Statistical Yearbook*.

[3] The only difference between Table 2-1 and Table 1-1 in Chapter 1 is the extent of the detail.

TABLE 2–1
Gross National Product, 1973 (by type of income and type of expenditure)

		Billions
Income:		
Employee compensation		$ 785.3
Wages and salaries	$691.5	
Supplements	93.9	
Business and professional income		57.5
Unincorporated enterprise income	60.0	
Inventory valuation adjustment	−2.5	
Farm income		26.8
Rental income of persons		25.1
Corporate income		109.2
Gross corporate profits	126.5	
Inventory valuation adjustment	−17.3	
Net interest		50.4
Capital consumption allowance		109.6
Government enterprise subsidies minus current surplus (subtract)		(0.7)
Indirect business taxes		117.8
Business transfer payments		4.9
Statistical discrepancy		2.3
Gross national product		$1,288.2
Expenditure:		
Personal consumption expenditure		$ 805.0
Gross private domestic investment		201.5
Nonresidential	$136.0	
Residential	58.0	
Change in inventories	7.4	
Net exports of goods and services		4.6
Exports	101.3	
Imports	96.7	
Government purchases of goods and services		277.2
Federal	106.9	
State and local	170.3	
Gross national product		$1,288.2

Source: *Economic Report of the President, 1974.*

to the factors of production are "indirect business taxes" and "capital consumption allowance," which primarily includes depreciation. While not factor payments, both of these are costs incurred in the production of GNP and are therefore included in its computation.

Gross national product is only one of five measures of aggregate income. Conceptually, *net national product* is the sum of all goods and services produced in the economy in a given year less the amount of goods and services that is worn out or used up in current production. Statistically, this is obtained by subtracting capital consumption allowance from GNP. We hasten to add that capital consumption allowance is by no means an accurate representation of the amount of capital actually used up in production. Depreciation allowances are influenced more by tax laws than the estimated life span of capital equipment. We shall have more to say about depreciation later.

Net national income at factor cost (or simply *national income*) should reflect the total payments to the *factors of production* that were used in producing *net national product*. This may be obtained by adding all the factor payments on the income side of Table 2–1. Alternatively, it is net national product less all those items that are not payments to the factors of production. The chief item in this category is "indirect business taxes." The figures, extracted from Table 2–1, are shown below:

	Billions
Wages, salaries and supplements	$ 785.3
Unincorporated enterprise income	84.3
Rental income of persons	25.1
Interest	50.4
Corporate income	109.2
National income	$1,054.3

Alternatively:

		Billions
Net national product		$1,178.6
Less:		
Indirect business taxes	$117.8	
Business transfer payments	4.9	
Statistical discrepancy	2.3	
Plus:		
Government subsidies, less surplus		0.7
National income		$1,054.3

Indirect business taxes include property taxes, sales taxes, license fees, excise taxes, and franchise fees which are not levied directly upon income but which are a cost of doing business. Some of these may be passed on to the consumer through higher prices. In any case, all must be paid out of total sales (GNP).

The interest figure in national income represents interest paid, by the business sector only, for the services of capital. Interest paid by the government and by consumers is not considered a payment for factor (capital) services. It is therefore excluded from national income (and NNP and GNP) and is instead treated as a transfer payment.

However, since transfer payments are received by the household sector, government and consumer interest are included in personal income as we shall see below.

Personal income is designed to measure the current income of persons of which factor payments constitute only a part. Specifically, it would exclude from national income those factor payments that accrue to persons but are not received by them. It adds to national income those payments that are made to persons but are not in exchange for current productive services (that is, transfer payments). The figures for 1973 are shown below:

		Billions
National income.		$1,054.3
Less:		
Corporate income taxes	$56.2	
Undistributed profits.	42.4	
Social Security payments	92.1	
Inventory valuation adj.	−17.3	
Plus:		
Business transfer payments		4.9
Government transfer payments		112.8
Net interest on government debt		14.6
Interest paid by consumers		22.5
Personal income		$1,035.7

Of the total of gross corporate profits, normally only about 25 percent is actually received by persons; the remainder is either retained by the firm or paid to the government sector through the corporate income tax. Thus we subtract these items from national income which includes gross corporate profits. In like manner, Social Security contributions, which are payments to labor, are not actually received but are instead transmitted to the government. We add to this payments to persons which are not made for current productive services. These include transfer payments by the government sector (welfare, unemployment insurance, and interest on the government debt are examples) and transfer payments by the business sector, such as pension payments. Transfers made by the household sector—that is, transfers made from person to person such as gifts—cancel out.

The last measure is personal income after taxes or *disposable personal income*. This measure presumably reflects spendable income after obligations to the government are paid. In 1973 personal tax and nontax payments amounted to $152.9 billion. Subtracting this from personal income leaves us with disposable income of $882.6 billion. This was distributed by the household sector between personal outlays ($828.7 billion) and saving ($53.8 billion).

Expenditure

On the expenditure side the categories established generally conform to the sector classification introduced in Chapter 1. The household sector makes consumption expenditures consisting of expenditures on durable and nondurable goods, and services. Durable goods include such items as automobiles and furniture; nondurable goods include food and clothing; services include rent and transportation. It should be noted that consumption includes payment for housing *services* as measured by rent (actual or imputed) and not the purchase price of a new house. Expenditure on new housing is included in "gross private domestic investment." Given the long-term nature of housing, it is not reasonable to treat a new house as being entirely "consumed" in the period in which it is purchased.

Gross private domestic investment includes expenditures on new buildings and durable equipment by the business sector, as well as on new residential housing. Increases (decreases) in business inventories are treated as investment (disinvestment) in inventories and are included in "gross investment." These categories are further split into farm and nonfarm components.

One might well ask whether consumer durables should be treated in the same fashion as residential housing. After all, isn't it also unreasonable to assume that new automobiles, for example, are entirely consumed in the year in which they are purchased? As a matter of fact some economists argue that certain expenditures by the household sector should be classified as investment. However, valuation of durable goods services presents problems that have kept the Commerce Department from doing so.

Government expenditures on goods and services include only those expenditures made in the product market and excludes transfer payments. Federal, state, and local expenditures are included. Many items purchased by the government sector, such as buildings, are capital goods. However, these are treated in a fashion analogous to consumer goods and are not counted as investment. Thus, a billion dollars spent on highways is treated as a current expenditure. If treated as investment some annual value would have to be imputed to the service provided by the highways, a rather difficult task.

All three sectors purchase goods and services in foreign product markets, and these purchases are included in the three categories of expenditure discussed above. Since the U.S. GNP attempts to measure total spending in the U.S. product market, these imports must be deducted. In addition, expenditures by foreigners in the U.S. product market must be included in the U.S. GNP. The procedure is to net total imports against total exports and add the difference to the other categories of expenditure.

Conceptual Problems

1. While the national income accountant may attempt to measure the total value of output of goods and services in the economy, difficulties of measurement and definition prevent him from doing so to his complete satisfaction. Gross national product primarily measures the value of *marketed* goods and services and therefore understates the actual output of goods and services to the extent that some goods and services produced are not marketed. The weekend handyman, for example, who refinishes his basement is producing a product. However, this product is not sold and consequently is not included in GNP. If all housewives suddenly became domestic servants and were paid for their labors, GNP would rise sharply. All the food grown in back yard gardens which is not sold in the marketplace provides satisfaction to the consumers of that food but, nevertheless, is not counted in GNP.

Some attempt is made to correct for the more glaring omissions by imputing values to some of the goods and services that have not been sold in the marketplace. For example, imputed values are assigned to the rent of owner-occupied housing, to food and fuel produced on farms and consumed by the farmer instead of being sold, to food furnished to government and military employees, to clothing issued to military personnel, and so on. While such imputation may not accurately reflect the market value of those products and services, they make GNP a more accurate measure of the total value of goods and services produced than if they were excluded.

2. On the other hand, some market transactions are not counted in GNP because they do not reflect a contribution to the current output of goods and services. Capital gains and losses, to cite one example, reflect changes in the market value of existing assets and not the production of new assets. The market value of housing may change because of changes in existing market forces, but because that change

in the value of housing is not due to new production, such change is excluded from GNP.

Illegal goods and services, even though marketed and part of current production, are excluded in calculating gross national product. This exclusion is arbitrary and reflects society's value judgments as contained in existing laws more so than difficulties with accounting or economic concepts. Marijuana and the services of prostitution, for example, are generally considered by current law to be harmful and on that basis are not counted in computing GNP. Should the value system of society change and those products and services become legal, then GNP would immediately increase. Since value systems differ from country to country, an activity which may be legal in one country and therefore be included in its GNP may be illegal in another and therefore be excluded from its GNP. This complicates any comparative analysis of countries.

Transfer payments constitute another source of income to individuals which is excluded from gross national product because such income does not constitute a payment for current services in the production process. Interest paid on the government debt increases the personal income of the household sector; but because there is no corresponding current flow of produced output, the interest payment is treated as a transfer and is not counted in GNP. Prizes given by the business sector to the household sector in contests are not payments for the services of factors of production in the current period and are therefore excluded from GNP.

All market transactions which involve the transfer of existing assets rather than newly produced assets are not counted in GNP, although if repairs, improvements, or modifications are made to an asset before its transfer, the value of such improvements or modification is included in GNP.

3. In order to avoid double counting, only final product is included in GNP. If we included, for example, the value of steel sold by steel companies to the automobile industry and, in addition, the value of the automobiles sold by the automobile industry to consumers, we would be counting the value of the steel twice. It would be counted first as output of the steel industry and secondly, as part of the value of the finished automobile. Consequently, we count only the value of the finished product which includes the value of all the intermediate products.

The major exception to this rule is depreciation. Depreciation is the largest component of capital consumption allowance, and as such it is part of GNP. However, the cost of a final product includes an allowance for depreciation which is an intermediate product. In other words, the total output of capital equipment (gross investment) is part of the total output of goods and services in the economy. Yet, part of that capital equipment, as measured by the depreciation allowance, is used up in the process of producing all the other goods and services. Consequently, that part is counted both as final product and as intermediate product in GNP, although not in NNP. The problem is compounded by the fact that depreciation allowances, as measured in the accounts of the business firms, probably do not measure the actual wear and tear of capital equipment. The various accounting methods of straight-line or accelerated depreciation are designed more to take advantage of existing tax laws than they are designed to measure the actual consumption of capital equipment.

One further problem exists with depreciation. All of the items in GNP are valued at current prices. However, depreciation is valued at original cost rather than replacement cost which might reflect current prices. In a period of rising (falling) prices, this procedure would understate (overstate) the capital consumption allowance.

4. In our simplified model we assume that all output or product originates in the business sector. In the real world, some output does originate in the household and government sectors. The household sector actually includes some nonbusiness organizations such as churches and schools that do produce a product or service. Since the output is not marketed, market prices cannot be used in the valuation of such output. Consequently it is assumed that the value is equal to the wage and salary cost of producing the service.

The same approach applies to the valuation of government services. In addition to wages and salaries, imputed values are attached to the food and clothing issued to military personnel. One might suppose that government output should be measured by the payment made for it, namely taxes. But since taxes tend to be involuntary, we must first ask if people would have voluntarily paid that amount if the services had been offered to them by private firms in the product market. For many government services that question probably cannot be answered.

The combined output originating in these two sectors currently amounts to about 15 percent of GNP.

5. We might mention one other problem here which is likely to

take on greater importance in the future. The total output of industry includes products that yield utility to the consumer and other products that yield disutility to the consumer. The former are included in GNP; the latter are ignored. The latter would include all those waste or pollution products that are part of the productive process. These externalities impose costs upon society which are not currently reflected in GNP as long as no one is employed to dispose of such waste.

GNP, to the extent that it is used as a measure of welfare for the population, overstates such welfare because the joint products that include waste and other elements that pollute the environment tend to reduce satisfaction and utility. It might be appropriate, therefore, to monetize the value of removing these wastes and subtract that from GNP in order to arrive at a more accurate representation of the welfare of society. It may, of course, be argued that GNP is not designed to be a measure of welfare and should not be so used. The fact is, however, that many economists and politicians do use GNP as an index of the progress of societal well-being. In any case, rather than subtract the costs of removing pollution, as the cleaning up of pollution becomes mandatory, we are likely to do just the opposite. Increased factor services will be required to handle waste products of the industrial process. On the income side, this means that factor payments and hence national income and hence GNP will rise if idle resources are drawn upon. On the product side, the cost of cleaning up pollution will be reflected in higher prices, thus implying a higher GNP. In any event, the handling of pollution presents severe conceptual difficulties for the national income accountant if GNP is to be used as a measure of society's welfare.

Not only are there difficulties in accounting for gross national product for a single country, but there are also additional difficulties in comparing the performance of one country to another by using such measures as GNP. The difficulties we noted above are not uniformly severe for each country. For example, consider the exclusion of non-marketed products and services. In an underdeveloped country, a considerable portion of the food is produced by households for their own use. Any measure of agricultural production that includes only those products brought to the marketplace will severely understate the total agricultural production in the country. Consequently, it is necessary in such a case to rely more on imputations than on market flows. Unfortunately, the more extensively imputations are used, the greater the potential error.

Aside from these difficulties, GNP measured at current prices is not a very useful measure in comparing different countries. The welfare of individuals in a country is more accurately reflected by GNP per capita. However, even this measure has its difficulties as long as GNP is measured in current prices. If the nation's GNP per capita has risen by 10 percent, but the rate of inflation in the country is, say, 11 percent, then the population is becoming worse off rather than better off. Hence, real GNP in constant dollars per capita is a better measurement than GNP in current dollars per capita. The basic model developed in the following chapters will make a distinction between changes in real output and changes in the price level in order to distinguish real from nominal changes.

With all these difficulties, the various aggregates in the national income accounts are still useful for purposes of evaluating policy, for testing theories, and for making projections about the future. However, any use of the accounts should be tempered by an awareness of the difficulties involved in their construction.

THE FLOW-OF-FUNDS ACCOUNTS

The first attempt at accounting for the flow of funds was accomplished by Morris Copeland in 1952.[4] U.S. government involvement began in 1948 with work done under the sponsorship of the Federal Reserve System. The Federal Reserve's efforts subsequently led to the regular publication of quarterly figures in the *Federal Reserve Bulletin.*[5]

Essentially, the flow-of-funds accounts attempt to show the flows of money and credit from one economic unit to another and reflect the way in which the units finance their operations over time. In other words, the accounts show the changes that take place both in financial and real assets, in net worth, and in liabilities for each economic unit or sector for a given time period.

The accounts show transactions involving both current output (and income) and existing assets. In that sense they differ from the national

---

[4] Morris A. Copeland, *A Study of Moneyflows in the U.S.* (New York: National Bureau of Economic Research, 1952).

[5] Data from 1945 as well as descriptions of the most current conventions used in the accounts may be found in *Flow of Funds Accounts, 1945–1968* (Washington, D.C.: Board of Governors of the Federal Reserve System, March 1970). A highly readable discussion is found in Lawrence S. Ritter, *The Flow of Funds Accounts: A Framework for Financial Analysis* (New York: New York University, 1968).

income accounts which reflect current output only. Moreover, the flow-of-funds accounts give detailed attention to the purely financial transactions rather than to income. The national income accounts take the receipts (current income) of each sector and show how those receipts are distributed among current account purchases (consumption), capital account purchases (investment), and saving. The flow-of-funds accounts start with gross saving and show how this is distributed (along with current borrowing) among purchases on capital account and the acquisition of financial assets.

In tabulating the transactions, nine sectors or economic units are used—four of which are financial sectors. Each sector account shows the sources and uses of funds for that sector and the various categories in which the transactions take place.

Sources of funds for a given unit reflect changes in the unit's net worth (saving) and changes in the unit's liabilities (borrowing). Uses of funds are reflected in changes in real assets, changes in nonmoney financial assets (lending), and changes in money holdings.

Table 2-2 is a reproduction of the flow-of-funds matrix for the U.S. economy as constructed by the Federal Reserve System. Note that unlike the national income accounts, the business sector is divided into financial and nonfinancial components. More importantly, the two systems of accounts also differ in their definition of gross saving and gross investment. Unlike the national income accounts, gross investment in the flow-of-funds accounts includes expenditures by the household sector for consumer durables.

In addition, changes in financial assets and liabilities are netted and included in the gross investment figure. Thus, gross investment is the sum of gross real investment and net financial investment. Gross saving and gross investment for each sector are consequently equal in the flow-of-funds account, whereas current saving and current investment for each sector in the national income accounts need not be equal. Indeed in the national income accounts, the household sector is usually a surplus sector since its current saving exceeds its current investment while the business sector is usually a deficit sector because its current investment exceeds its current saving.

To illustrate the differences, suppose in a given year the gross saving of the household sector was $150 billion and the sector purchased $100 billion of consumer durables and $50 billion of government bonds. The flow-of-funds accounts would show gross saving equal to $150 billion and gross investment equal to $150 billion (consisting

TABLE 2-2
Summary of Flow-of-Funds Accounts for Second Quarter 1971 (seasonally adjusted annual rates; in billions of dollars)

	Sector	\multicolumn{8}{c}{Private domestic nonfinancial sectors}	\multicolumn{10}{c}{Financial sectors}					
		\multicolumn{2}{c}{Households}	\multicolumn{2}{c}{Business}	\multicolumn{2}{c}{State and local govts.}	\multicolumn{2}{c}{Total}	\multicolumn{2}{c}{U.S. Govt.}	\multicolumn{2}{c}{Total}	\multicolumn{2}{c}{Sponsored credit agencies}	\multicolumn{2}{c}{Monetary auth.}	\multicolumn{2}{c}{Coml.[1] banks}	\multicolumn{2}{c}{Pvt. nonbank finance}	\multicolumn{2}{c}{Rest of the world}	\multicolumn{2}{c}{All sectors}	Discrepancy	Natl. savings and investment	
Transaction category		U	S	U	S	U	S	U	S	U	S	U	S	U	S	U	S	U	S	U	S	U	S	U	S	U		
1	Gross saving		187.3		94.0		−7.3		274.1		−26.7		6.1		.1		*		3.5		2.5		3.7		257.2	3.9	253.5	1
2	Capital consumption		94.7		83.4				178.1				2.6				*		1.0		1.5				180.7		180.7	2
3	Net saving (1−2)		92.7		10.6		−7.3		96.0		−26.7		3.5		.1		*		2.4		1.0		3.7		76.5	4.0	72.9	3
4	Gross investment (5+10)	194.2		82.0		−13.6		262.6		−30.7		9.2		.1		*		4.4		4.6		12.3		253.3			240.9	4
5	Private capital expenditures	131.4		120.0				251.4				1.8						.8		1.0				253.2			253.2	5
6	Consumer durables	100.8						100.8																100.8			100.8	6
7	Residential construction	24.9		14.8				39.7																39.7			39.7	7
8	Plant and equipment	5.8		99.5				105.3				1.8						.8		1.0				107.0			107.0	8
9	Inventory change			5.7				5.7																5.7			5.7	9
10	Net financial investment (11−12)	62.8		−38.1		−13.6		11.1		−30.7		7.4		.1		*		3.7		3.7		12.3		.1		−12.3	10
11	Financial uses	106.6	43.8	21.9	59.9	3.3	17.0	131.8	120.7	20.8	51.5	131.4	123.9	−5.6	.1	.7	.7	62.0	58.4	74.2	70.5	23.2	10.9	307.2	307.1		10.9	11
12	Financial sources													−5.7		.7										−.1	23.2	12
13	Gold, SDR's, and official fgn. exchange									−2.1		−1.3				−1.3						2.6	−.7		−.7	−.7		13
14	Treasury currency and SDR ctfs									.6		.7				.7									.7	−.1		14
15	Demand deposits and currency	15.6		4.9		−2.3		18.2		−.3		38.0		−.1		5.5		32.4		.1		−.2		33.7	38.0	3.3		15
16	Private domestic											−.3				6.2		15.1		−.1				17.9	21.2			16
17	U.S. Government							15.9				16.2				−.5		17.7						15.9	16.9	1.0		17
18	Foreign											−.2				−.1		*		−.1		−.2			−.2			18
19	Time and savings accounts	67.8		−1.5		2.4		68.7		.1		1.8		.3				30.0		1.8		2.6		73.3				19
20	At commercial banks	26.0						26.9						.3				30.0		1.5				30.0				20
21	At savings institutions	41.8						41.8				1.5								43.3				43.3				21
22	Life insurance reserves	4.9						4.9				4.8								4.9				4.9				22
23	Pension fund reserves	23.5						23.5				19.5								19.5				23.5				23
24	Interbank items									4.0		−4.6				−.6	−3.8	−1.0	−.8		−.2	−4.6		−4.6	−4.6			24
25	Corporate shares	−3.1			16.4			−3.1	16.4			19.5				−.3				19.5		.5		16.4				25
26	Credit market instruments	1.8	39.0	6.5	49.7	3.0	16.5	11.2	105.2	4.4	47.7	112.0	−.3	.7	1.9	.2	60.6	.2	55.1	1.5	30.8	5.9	158.5	158.5			26
27	U.S. Government securities	−4.5		6.0		.3		1.8		*		17.9		.7	2.7	2.2		15.6		2.8		28.8		48.5	48.5			27
28	State and local obligations	−1.4		−.7		16.3		14.0				17.9						13.4		.6				16.3	16.3			28
29	Corporate and foreign bonds	7.8		3.4		2.5		10.3	22.1			16.0					.4	1.5		14.5	2.5	−.2	1.1	26.0	26.0			29
30	Home mortgages	−1.0	22.7		22.0		*		24.7		−.1	29.4		5.7				7.0		17.0	3.8			28.4	28.4			30
31	Other mortgages	.9	1.4		18.9			.9	20.4	.4		19.1		1.4				3.4		14.3				20.0	20.0			31
32	Consumer credit	9.0	2.5	2.5				11.5	2.5			6.5						4.1		2.2				9.0	9.0			32
33	Bank loans n.e.c	4.7	5.9					4.7	5.9			3.5		.3				15.1		−10.2		2.3	2.3	15.1	15.1			33
34	Other loans	−5.5	−.9			−.2		−5.7	−.9	4.0		−6.0	−9.9	−9.8		−.3		−.6		3.5			2.5	−.2	−5.2			34
35	Security credit	−1.2	3.8			−1.2		−1.2	3.8			1.8	−3.5					−1.8		2.6	−3.5	−.4	−.1	−.3	−.3			35
36	To brokers and dealers									−2.0	−3.5								−.2	−3.5	−.4		−.3				36
37	To others	−1.2	3.8					−1.2	3.8			3.8						1.0		2.8				3.8	3.8			37
38	Taxes payable	.6			5.8	.2		.8	5.8	−5.4	−5.4	.4				.1			*	.4		−.9		6.0	5.3	−.7		38
39	Trade credit				−6.5				−6.5	3.3	−3.3		−1.3											−3.5	−5.7	−2.3		39
40	Equity in noncorporate business	−5.8	.3	−5.8				−15.8	−5.8	−.1		1.3	−.3	.3		−.9		6.2	−3.5	−5.1	8.7	−11.7	4.4	4.8	−5.8	−.7		40
41	Miscellaneous claims	3.2		12.0	.3			15.2	.3		−.1		−2.1	−.4						−2.1				3.9	3.4	−1.4		41
42	Sector discrepancies (1−4)	−6.9		12.1		6.3		11.5		4.1		−3.1				*		−1.0		−2.1		−8.6		3.9			12.7	42

[1] Commercial banks and unconsolidated affiliates.

Source: *Federal Reserve Bulletin*, October 1971, A-72.

32   Macroeconomic Theory

of $100 billion private capital expenditures and $50 billion net financial investment.) The national income accounts, on the other hand, count consumer durable purchases as consumption, not investment; and they do not show financial investment as investment. Therefore for the household sector, current saving would be $50 billion and there would be no current investment.[6]

OTHER INDICATORS

The national income and flow-of-funds accounts are systems for the measurement of income, expenditure, and the sources and uses of funds. Other indicators are available for the evaluation of economic performance. These include indices of prices and employment as well as financial indicators such as interest rates, credit, and the money supply. Table 2–3 lists four measures pertinent to the analysis in the chapters to follow.

TABLE 2–3
Selected U.S. Economic Indicators 1960–1973

Year	Price*	Unemployment† (percent)	Interest Rate‡ (percent)	Money Supply§ ($ billions)
1960	103.3	5.5	3.85	$144.2
1961	104.6	6.7	2.97	148.7
1962	105.8	5.5	3.26	150.9
1963	107.2	5.7	3.55	156.5
1964	108.8	5.2	3.97	163.7
1965	110.9	4.5	4.38	171.3
1966	113.8	3.8	5.55	175.4
1967	117.6	3.8	5.10	186.9
1968	122.3	3.6	5.90	201.5
1969	128.2	3.5	7.83	208.6
1970	135.2	4.9	7.72	221.2
1971	141.6	5.9	5.11	235.2
1972	146.1	5.6	4.69	255.7
1973	153.9	4.9	8.15	270.4

* Implicit price deflator for GNP (1958 = 100).
† Unemployment as a percent of civilian labor force.
‡ Prime commercial paper rate, 4–6 month.
§ End of year, seasonally adjusted.
Source: *Economic Report of the President, 1974.*

The Implicit Price Deflator is a comprehensive index of final goods and services prices compiled by the Department of Commerce. Other price indices include the Consumer Price Index and the Wholesale

---
[6] The format and definitions employed in the accounts make the sector discrepancies in Table 2–2 statistical, rather than conceptual, discrepancies.

Price Index, both compiled by the Bureau of Labor Statistics. Aside from annual figures, the latter two indices are available monthly while the Implicit Price Deflator is only available quarterly. All three indices are highly correlated and, for the long run, provide about the same information as to price trends in the economy. The Wholesale Price Index is the most sensitive or volatile in the short run.

The Unemployment Rate is an important indicator showing how close the economy has come to its announced goal of "full employment." The Unemployment Rate is the percent of the civilian labor force that is "ready, willing, and able" to go to work, but that is nevertheless unemployed. The Bureau of Labor Statistics compiles the data on a monthly basis using household survey techniques.

The money supply listed in Table 2–3 is the conventional money supply which consists of the nonbank public's holdings of currency and demand deposits. The Federal Reserve System compiles this series on a variable that plays an important role in the macro economy. The interest rate in the table is only one of many interest rates in the economy. In the following chapters we shall refer to "the" interest rate, even though, in reality, many do exist. Our theoretical simplification is not too unreasonable, however, because most market interest rates tend to be highly correlated, rising and falling together.

There are many more indicators of economic performance. Those reviewed in this chapter are those which are important for relating the essentials of macroeconomic analysis to the real world.

SUMMARY NOTES

1. National income accounting, with a history of over 300 years, attempts to account for the current flows of income and output.
2. Gross national product is the value of the total current production of goods and services in the product market. GNP less an allowance for capital replacement is net national product.
3. Household personal income consists of payments to the household sector for factor services (wages, interest, rent, and profits net of corporate profits tax and undistributed profits) plus transfer payments, interest on the government debt, and consumer interest payments less Social Security contributions. Disposable income is personal income less direct taxes.
4. GNP is intended to measure the *market* value of *currently* produced *final* goods and services. Illegal goods and services, although

marketed, are not included. Imputed values are assigned to some nonmarketed goods and services such as the service of owner occupied housing.
5. The flow-of-funds accounts attempt to show how economic units finance their transactions. The transactions included are those in financial assets and both current and existing real assets.
6. Unlike the four sectors of the national income accounts, the flow-of-funds accounts employ nine sectors of which four are financial sectors. The accounts show the sources (saving plus borrowing) and uses (spending plus lending plus changes in money holdings) of funds for each sector.

DISCUSSION QUESTIONS

1. It has been claimed that the share of national income going to wages and salaries and the share going to corporate profits varies systematically with the business cycle. Test this by computing and comparing the shares for "high" employment years (less than 4.5 percent unemployment) with those for "low" employment years (greater than 5.5 per cent unemployment).

2. Compute the shares of GNP going to consumption and investment for high- and low-employment years. What conclusions do you draw? Can you advance any explanations for your observations?

3. The services produced by housewives, but not included in GNP, may be substantial. Estimate the number of housewives in the United States by dividing the total population by the average number of persons per family (about 3.5). Estimate the value of output per housewife by estimating what you think you would have to pay for all the services of a housewife for one year. Now compute the total value of housewife output (number of housewives × output value per housewife). If we added this to GNP, by what percentage would GNP increase?

4. The text assumes that we can use a single interest rate to represent all interest rates because interest rates tend to be correlated over time. Test this by gathering data on several interest rates and plotting them, against time, for the last 15 or 20 years. What do you think of our assumption?

part two

MACROECONOMIC ANALYSIS OF A CLOSED ECONOMY

3

The Basic Model: Aggregate Demand

IN THIS CHAPTER we begin to introduce formally the basic model suggested by the framework in Figure 1–3 of Chapter 1. This chapter concentrates on the components of aggregate demand in the product market while ignoring the influence of the money market. The money market will be introduced in the next chapter, and the determinants of aggregate supply will be discussed and integrated into the model in Chapter 5.

The following discussion focuses on the determinants of intended (sometimes called *ex ante*) spending in the product market as distinguished from realized (sometimes called *ex post*) spending. As we shall see later in the chapter, equilibrium and disequilibrium can be defined in terms of the coincidence or divergence of intended and realized spending.

THE COMPONENTS OF AGGREGATE DEMAND

In this model of a closed economy, total or aggregate demand consists of three components: consumption of the household sector, investment spending of the business sector, and government spending on goods and services. All variables will be expressed in real terms unless otherwise noted.

Consumption

The modern theory of the consumption function owes its origins to Keynes and the *General Theory*. Keynes theorized that current real consumption expenditures were a function of current real disposable income. Furthermore, the relationship was hypothesized to be a direct relationship: Increases (decreases) in income brought forth increases (decreases) in consumption. Of special importance was the hypothesis that the change in consumption induced by a change in income was less than the change in income. In other words, a one-dollar increase in income would lead to an increase in consumption by something less than a dollar and vice versa.

This hypothesis about the behavior of the household sector does not really depart from the microeconomic theory of consumer behavior for individual households. Given the relative prices of goods and given that most goods are normal[1] goods, it follows that individual households would increase their expenditures on goods as their income rises. At the aggregate level we take relative prices of commodities as given. The overall price level may change, but the relationship of one commodity price to another we assume remains the same. Hence, changes in income will lead to overall changes in expenditures on consumer goods. The choice that the household sector faces is not how to allocate expenditures among different goods but how to allocate expenditures between present consumption and future consumption. Since there is positive utility to consuming goods in the future, the household sector allocates some of its disposable income toward the consumption of future goods. That is, it saves part of its present income and consumes the rest. Therefore, an increase in current disposable income will lead to an increase in both saving and consumption. Since the sum of the changes in consumption and saving must equal the change in disposable income, it follows that the change in consumption will be less than the change in disposable income. For simplicity we may write the consumption function in the following linear form:[2]

$$C = C_o + bY_D$$

or

$$C = C_o + b(Y - T)$$

where C is consumption, Y_D is disposable income and T is taxes.

Since total saving and total consumption must equal total disposable income, we can obtain a saving function from the consumption function by subtracting the consumption function from disposable income.

---

[1] A normal good has a nonnegative income elasticity of demand.

[2] Where feasible, we shall use linear relationships. This will simplify algebraic manipulations. All parameters (for example, C_o, and b) are positive numbers in this and all subsequent equations.

3 / The Basic Model: Aggregate Demand

Using the above consumption function we therefore derive the following saving function:

$$Y_D - S = C_o + bY_D$$
$$S = -C_o + (1 - b)Y_D$$

or

$$S = -C_o + (1 - b)(Y - T)$$

where S is saving.

In Figure 3–1, hypothetical consumption and saving functions are plotted. The slope of the consumption function (b), which is the

FIGURE 3-1
Consumption and Saving Functions

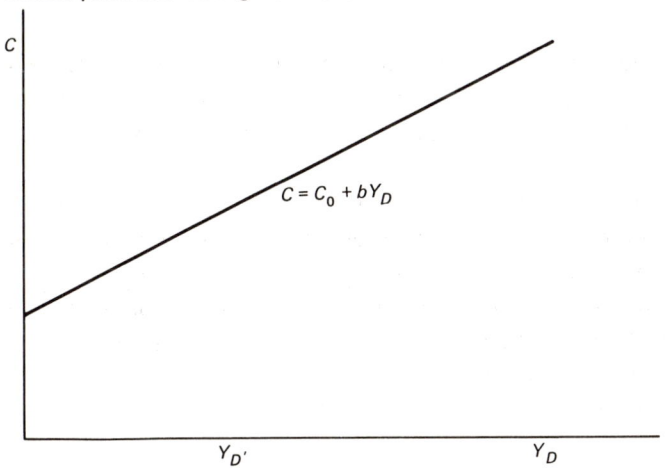

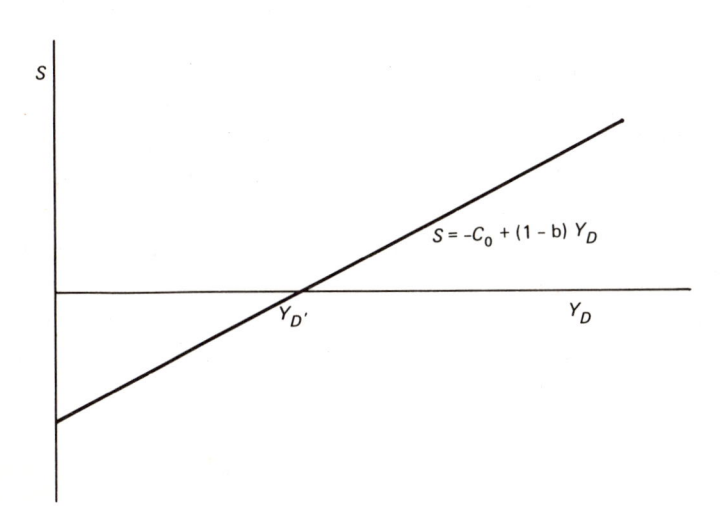

change in consumption for a given change in disposable income, is usually called the *marginal propensity to consume* (MPC).

For all practical purposes, the economy will be operating in the range of disposable income that is consistent with positive saving of the household sector.[3] In terms of Figure 3–1, the economy will usually be at levels of disposable income greater than Y_D'. This means that the aggregate household sector (but not necessarily every individual) will be financing its current consumption expenditures completely out of current disposable income. The sector will also be generating positive saving.

Investment

The purpose of spending on capital goods by the business sector is to generate a stream of profits which extends into the future. Assuming that firms in the business sector desire to maximize profits, we can identify those factors that will induce the business to change its investment spending. One approach or theory which we shall use in this chapter compares the rate of return that might be obtained by purchasing additional capital equipment with the market interest rate—that is, the rate of return that could be obtained by instead lending the funds to others or, alternatively, the rate of interest that must be paid to obtain the funds. One method of obtaining the rate of return on new capital goods makes use of the concept of present value.

A new capital good is designed to produce goods or services for some time into the future. That is, for each year of its expected life the machine or factory is expected to produce a certain number of units of a good which will be sold at some expected price. To obtain the profit for each year, we subtract from the total expected sales the total expected costs (other than the interest costs of financing the project). The result is a stream of expected profits for each year over the expected life of the piece of capital equipment. Now we simply cannot add each year's expected profit to get a figure for the total expected profits that the machine will yield, because a dollar today is not the same as a dollar a year from now. Given some market rate of interest, a dollar today will be worth a dollar plus the interest

---

[3] The only period in modern times when this was not true in the United States was for the years 1932–1933.

earnings one year from now. If the rate of interest, for example, is 5 percent, a dollar today is worth $1.05 one year from now. More generally, the value of a certain sum one year from now is given by the following formula:

$$P_1 = P_0(1 + i)$$

Where P_0 is the amount (the principal) at the beginning of the year, P_1 is the amount at the end of the year and i is the rate of interest. At the end of two years the principal is equal to:

$$P_2 = P_1(1 + i)$$
$$= P_0(1 + i)(1 + i)$$
$$= P_0(1 + i)^2$$

Rearranging the above equation, we can find the *present value* of a payment made two years from now given the rate of interest:

$$P_0 = \frac{P_2}{(1 + i)^2}$$

Suppose we have a stream of payments extending n years into the future. The present value of the stream of payments will be the sum of individual payments each discounted back to the present.

$$P_0 = \frac{P_1}{(1 + i)} + \frac{P_2}{(1 + i)^2} + \frac{P_3}{(1 + i)^3} \cdots + \frac{P_n}{(1 + i)^n}$$

We can use the above formula in a slightly different fashion. Suppose each payment made in the future is a net profit on some investment. Suppose instead of P_0 we insert the present cost of purchasing the machinery that will yield that stream of profits on into the future. We might then ask the question "What value of i will make the stream of future profits equal to the present cost of the piece of machinery?" That value for i we might call the rate of return on the investment or, as Keynes called it, the *marginal efficiency of capital*.[4]

Each kind of capital equipment or each piece of machinery will

---

[4] We are assuming that a single, positive rate of return can be found. However, the shape of the income stream may yield multiple rates. William H. Jean, "On Multiple Rates of Return." *Journal of Finance,* Vol. 23 (March 1968), pp. 187–91 has shown that multiple positive rates are possible if negative payments occur in the middle of the income stream. These would occur, for example, if remodeling costs exceeded the income from the piece of capital equipment.

have a different marginal efficiency depending upon such factors as its expected life, the expected quantities of goods it will produce, the expected selling price of the goods it will produce, and the expected cost of operation. If a firm has a number of production options, a number of possible investment opportunities will be open to it. It can calculate a marginal efficiency for each project and then rank them in order from the highest to the lowest. As a hypothetical example, suppose we consider a firm with five investment opportunities. In Table 3–1, the opportunities are ranked according to their marginal efficiencies, and the dollar cost of each project is also listed. Suppose the market rate of interest is 5 percent, and assume that there are no restrictions on the amount that the firm can borrow at 5 percent. Given that the firm wishes to maximize profits, it will be to its advantage to borrow sufficient funds to engage in projects A, B, and C—all of which yield a rate of return or have a marginal efficiency greater than the cost of borrowing, namely 5 percent. Were the market rate of interest lower, the amount of borrowing and spending on investment projects would be greater; and if the market rate of interest were higher, the amount of spending on investment projects would be less. If the rate of interest fell to 4.5 percent, project D would also be feasible.

The schedule shown in Table 3–1 is a hypothetical investment demand schedule for an individual firm. If firms in general in the busi-

TABLE 3–1
Hypothetical Investment Projects for an Individual Firm

Project	Cost	Rate of Return (percent)
A.	$100,000	9.0
B.	85,000	7.5
C.	120,000	6.3
D.	105,000	4.8
E.	75,000	4.0

ness sector act on the same principle, we can construct an investment demand schedule for the entire business sector. Such a schedule is shown in Figure 3–2. Given that new investment projects arise each year and given their marginal efficiencies, it follows that the annual rate of spending on capital equipment will vary inversely with the

FIGURE 3-2
Investment Demand Schedule

$$I = I_0 - ai$$

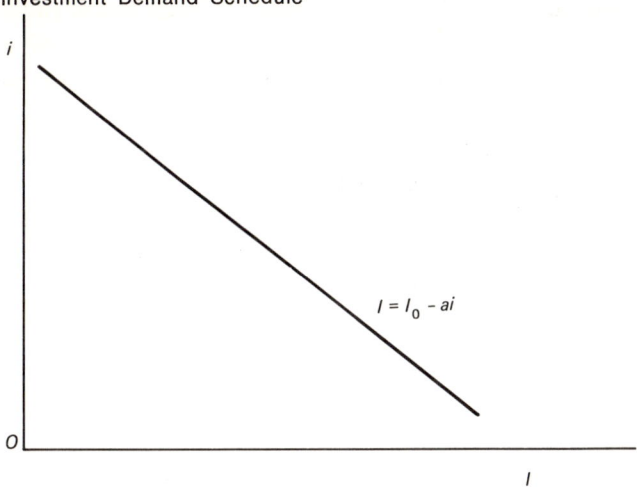

rate of interest. Algebraically we shall write the investment function as follows:

$$I = I_0 - ai,$$

where I is investment.

Within the context of our basic model, all of the expenditures on investment goods must be financed by borrowing because, by the assumptions made in Chapter 1, the business sector has zero net saving. The ultimate source of funds is the saving of the household sector.

Government Expenditures on Goods and Services

We presume that the government purchases goods and services for reasons that do not include the maximization of utility or the maximization of profits. Instead such spending is done to accomplish certain social objectives with respect to education, national defense, and so on. In short, we treat government spending as being determined by forces (political?) outside the model.

The government may finance its spending through one or more of three sources. It may obtain funds by increasing taxes, it may borrow along with the business sector, or it may finance increased expenditures through creation of new money in cooperation with the central bank. For analytical purposes, we treat each method of financing, as well as the expenditures themselves, as independent actions. The decision to change the level of government spending we assume will be independent of the decision to finance by one method or another. For example, the government may increase its expenditures without changing taxes, without changing the money supply, but by increasing its rate of borrowing. Alternatively, the government may finance an increase in its expenditures by increasing taxes, with no change in the money supply and no change in its rate of borrowing.

Total demand in the product market consists of the sum of expenditures by the business, household, and government sectors. In Figure 3–3, total demand (measured on the vertical axis) is shown as a func-

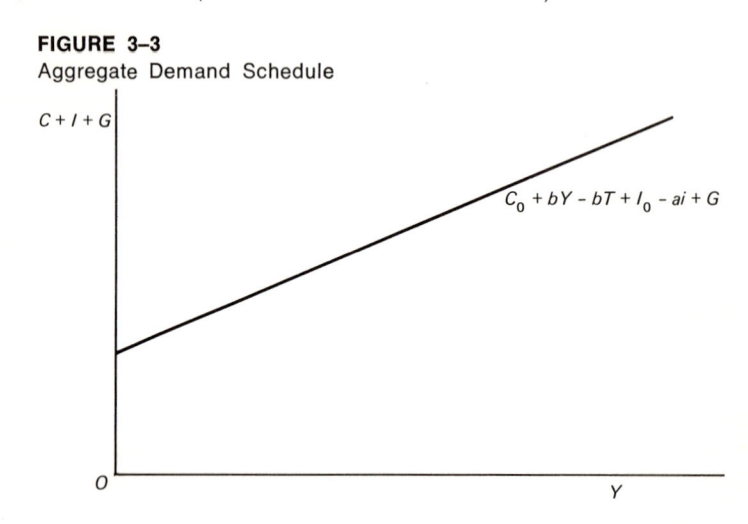

FIGURE 3–3
Aggregate Demand Schedule

$C + I + G$

$C_0 + bY - bT + I_0 - ai + G$

Y

tion of net national product (measured on the horizontal axis). The curve slopes upward because as net national product increases, the disposable income of the household sector increases and the consumption component of total demand increases. Disposable income is also affected by the level of taxes. Changes in the level of taxes would be translated into shifts in the total demand schedule. For example, if we increased the level of taxes, given the value of Y, disposable income would fall and consumption would fall, shifting the total demand curve downward.

Similarly, an increase (decrease) in the rate of interest would reduce (increase) investment spending by the business sector and thereby shift the total demand curve downward (upward). Finally, an increase (decrease) in government expenditures would increase (decrease) total demand, shifting the schedule upward (downward).

A SIMPLE MODEL OF INCOME DETERMINATION

The components of aggregate demand can be combined to produce a model of real income determination as long as two crucial assumptions are made. First, we assume that changes in aggregate demand and changes in the equilibrium level of real income do not produce changes in the interest rate. Under this assumption, investment is fixed in the model. Second, we assume that firms will alter their production plans in the face of changes in aggregate demand without any change in the price level. In other words, aggregate output or supply is perfectly elastic with respect to the price level (as long as there are resources left to be employed). The latter assumption means that, for this simple model, all changes in income, consumption, etc. are real changes. The price level is constant as long as there is unemployment.

Equilibrium occurs when aggregate supply (Y) is equal to aggregate demand ($C + I + G$). Figure 3–4 reproduces the aggregate demand schedule shown in Figure 3–3. Also plotted in Figure 3–4 is a line showing the locus of points for which aggregate demand

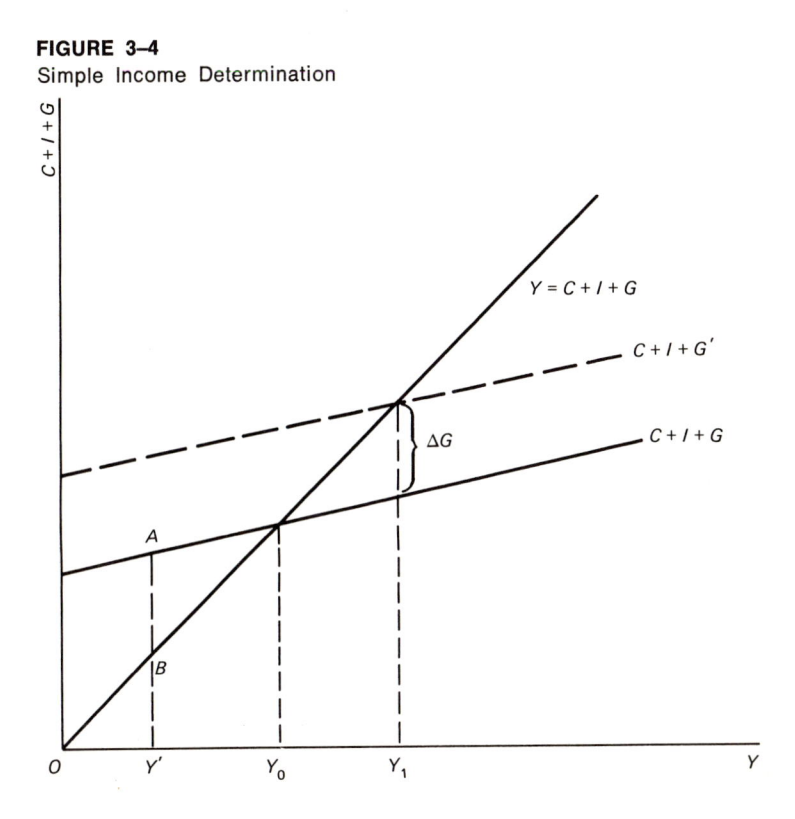

FIGURE 3–4
Simple Income Determination

46 *Macroeconomic Theory*

and aggregate supply are equal (the equilibrium condition). This is the line drawn at a 45° angle through the origin.

There is one equilibrium point, at Y_0. To see that this is an equilibrium point, consider some income level less than Y_0, say, Y'. At this income level, aggregate demand (measured vertically, $Y'A$) is greater than aggregate supply (OY' or $Y'B$). Thus the three sectors, in total, will be purchasing all of current output *plus* some of the existing stock of inventories. Producers, seeing their inventories fall, will expand output without, by assumption, any increase in the price level. Put another way, *intended* investment will be greater, at Y', than *realized* investment (which includes the unplanned reduction in inventories). Producers can correct for this by increasing production, thus adding to inventories at a faster rate, sufficient to make the unplanned change in inventories zero. This moves us to Y_0 at which point all of current output, no more and no less, is purchased. The reverse of all this occurs if the initial income is greater than Y_0.

The equilibrium level of Y can be obtained algebraically by equating aggregate demand and supply and solving for Y.

$$\begin{aligned} Y &= C + I + G \\ &= C_0 + bY - bT + I_0 - ai + G \\ (1-b)Y &= C_0 - bT + I_0 - ai + G \\ Y &= \frac{1}{(1-b)}(C_0 + I_0 - bT - ai + G) \end{aligned} \qquad (3\text{--}1)$$

Should one of the components on the right side change, the equilibrium level of income will change. Suppose that G changes holding C_0, I_0, T, and i constant. We then have

$$\Delta Y = \frac{1}{(1-b)} \cdot \Delta G$$

where $\Delta C_0 = \Delta I_0 = \Delta T = \Delta i = 0$. The coefficient $1/(1-b)$ is often called the *autonomous spending multiplier* because it relates autonomous changes in spending (by any sector) to the change in equilibrium income under the assumptions made earlier about the interest rate and the price level. Note that as long as $0 < b < 1$ the multiplier is greater than 1. Thus, an autonomous change in spending leads to a multiple change in income.

This effect can also be seen with the aid of Figure 3–4. Suppose, through an increase in government expenditures, aggregate demand shifts upward from $C + I + G$ to $C + I + G'$. The equilibrium level of income rises to Y_1 as a result. Visual inspection will indicate that the change in income from Y_0 to Y_1 is greater than the vertical shift in aggregate demand (ΔG).

A multiplier can also be derived for a change in taxes which, from equation (3-1), is $-b/(1-b)$. This multiplier is opposite in sign and numerically smaller than the multiplier for G (and C_0 and I_0). It is opposite in sign because increases (decreases) in T lead to decreases (increases) in consumption. It is smaller because consumption changes by only a fraction (b) of the change in taxes.

This simple model is useful in illustrating the importance of changes in aggregate demand in determining macroeconomic equilibrium. However, the model is unrealistic in two respects. Both the interest rate and the price level play no role in the determination of the equilibrium level of Y. Thus the model ignores the effects of financial changes in the economy. We will deal with this issue in the next chapter by incorporating the money market into the model. Price level determination will be treated in Chapter 5.

SUMMARY NOTES

1. Consumption expenditures by the household sector are assumed to be a function of disposable income. The marginal propensity to consume (change in consumption/change in disposable income) is assumed to be positive and less than one.
2. Assuming that firms seek to maximize profits, investment spending varies inversely with the market rate of interest.
3. Consumption, investment, and income are *endogenous* variables determined by the system. Government expenditures and taxes are assumed to be *exogenous* variables determined by noneconomic forces.
4. Assuming that the interest rate and the price level are constant, changes in government spending induce a multiple change in income. The change in income with respect to the change in government spending is called the autonomous spending multiplier and takes the general form: 1/(1-marginal propensity to consume).

DISCUSSION QUESTIONS

1. Use the simple model of income determination to analyze the effect of changes in the interest rate (holding government expenditures and

taxes constant) on equilibrium output (Y). For example, with an increase in the interest rate, what happens to aggregate demand ($C + I + G$) and to output?

2. The parameter letters (C_0, a, b, etc.) in the consumption and investment equations represent numerical values. For example, the consumption function may be written, $C = 50 + 0.75Y_D$. If so, what is consumption if $Y = 500$ and $T = 75$? What is consumption if T increases by 25 (Y constant); if Y decreases by 25 (T constant)?

3. Suppose the investment function is $I = 100 - 5i$, where i is stated in percentage terms (4.5 percent, 7.3 percent, etc.). What is investment if the interest rate is 5 percent? 10 percent?

4. Using equation (3–1) in the chapter and the parameter values in question 2 and 3, find the equilibrium value of Y if $i = 6.0$ percent, $G = 100$, and $T = 100$. What is the change in Y if G increases to 125? What is the change in Y if *both* G and T increase to 125?

4

The Basic Model: The Money Market

THE INTRODUCTION of the money market in this chapter will permit us to drop one of the restrictive assumptions made previously. The addition of the money market enables the expanded basic model to determine the interest rate as well as income. In the following section we discuss the determinants of the demand for money balances to hold, for whatever reason, as of a point in time. It is important to distinguish this from the demand for *credit,* which is the demand for a *flow* of dollars per unit of time. Credit flows may be used to change the stock of money balances, but in the basic model developed here we will concentrate on the demand for (and supply of) money balances. (See Appendix A of Chapter 5 for a further discussion of the relationship between the money market and the credit or loanable funds market.)

THE DEMAND FOR MONEY

For purposes of the basic model, the stock of money is the stock of all those assets in the economy that act as exchange media, where a medium of exchange is an asset that is readily or generally accepted in exchange for any good or service. For the U.S. economy this consists of two assets: coins and currency in circulation outside banks and checking account balances or demand deposits. Not only do these two assets act as exchange media, but they also act as stores of value.

Wealth can be held in the form of money as well as in the form of real estate, TV sets, etc.

Since money is the economy's medium of exchange, we assume in the first instance that people demand money for the purpose of carrying out transactions. We assume that the volume of transactions in the economy is a function of the economy's level of income. That is, as income rises (falls) more (fewer) transactions are carried out. The demand for money, the exchange medium, to carry out these transactions will therefore be a direct (or positive) function of the level of income.

Since money also serves as a store of value, presumably people will hold some money balances in excess of what they plan to use to carry out transactions. Now money is not the only store of value. Horses, houses, etc. are also stores of value to the extent that they can be exchanged for other goods. However, money is unique in that it is the most liquid store of value. It is liquid because money can be exchanged for any good, and any good can be exchanged for money. This is not true of any other asset. There is, however, a disadvantage to holding money as a store of value. The disadvantage is that money earns no interest. It would be just as convenient to hold interest-earning financial assets as a store of value as it is to hold checking account balances. Those interest-earning assets provide some income, whereas money does not. However, those other interest-earning assets are not as liquid as money. The higher liquidity of money is a benefit in holding money as a store of value, but the lost interest earnings represent a cost. Presumably individuals would hold money balances as a store of value up to a point where the marginal value of the liquidity service of money is just offset by the marginal cost of interest earnings lost. Should the interest rate increase, then individuals would shift away from money toward a greater proportion of interest-earning assets. If the interest rate falls, then the liquidity service becomes relatively more valuable, and people would increase their money holdings.

In addition, it may also be possible to economize on the quantity of money held to carry out transactions. If the interest rate rises, individuals will try to economize on their transactions balances—that is, use them more effectively. If the interest rate falls, then the incentive to economize on transactions balances is diminished. There is less marginal benefit relative to the marginal cost of reducing those transactions balances, and thus people would hold a larger stock of transactions balances.

We assume that individuals are aware of the effect of price level changes. Changes in the price level alter the real value (the purchasing power) of money balances. It is therefore the real value of money balances that is adjusted in response to changes in real income and the rate of interest.

Summarizing, the demand for real money balances varies directly with the level of income and inversely with the rate of interest. A

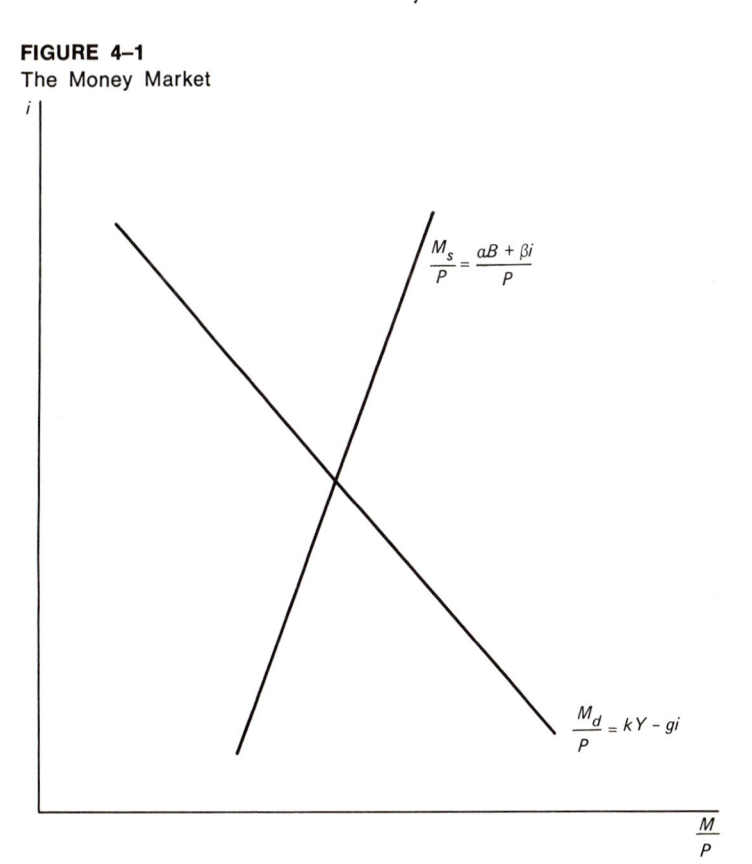

FIGURE 4–1
The Money Market

$$\frac{M_s}{P} = \frac{\alpha B + \beta i}{P}$$

$$\frac{M_d}{P} = kY - gi$$

demand function for money is found in Figure 4–1. We shall also use the following algebraic representation:

$$\frac{M_d}{P} = kY - gi,$$

where M_d is *nominal* money demand and P is the price level. M_d/P is therefore *real* money demand.

THE SUPPLY OF MONEY

By the *money supply* we mean a function that relates the quantity of money supplied to its determinants in the same way that the term *money demand* referred to the function discussed in the previous section. We will sometimes refer to the *money stock* which is the equilibrium quantity of money (supplied and demanded)—that is, the intersection of the demand and supply functions.

As we shall see in greater detail in Chapter 12, the supply mechanism of money depends to a large extent on the structure of the central and commercial banking system in the country. Our discussion is therefore confined to the U.S. context. Briefly, the U.S. banking system consists of a group of profit-making privately owned commercial banks and the Federal Reserve System, which acts as a central bank for the U.S. economy. Expansion and contraction of the money supply takes place principally through expansion and contraction of demand deposit liabilities of commercial banks. Commercial banks are required to maintain reserves behind their demand deposits, but these reserves are only a fraction of the total stock of demand deposits. In 1971, for example, commercial banks under control of the Federal Reserve System were required to hold about $0.17 in reserves behind every dollar of demand deposits. Banks may hold more reserves than are required, but they cannot hold less without incurring fines levied by the Federal Reserve. Typically, private banks do hold some excess reserves. However, there is a cost to holding excess reserves since the two forms in which reserves are kept do not earn interest. Reserves may be held in the form of cash in the vault or in the form of deposits with the Federal Reserve. In the U.S. economy about 80 percent of these reserves are held in the form of deposits with the Federal Reserve System. The private bank earns no interest on either one of these forms of reserves. If the bank is in business to make profits and if excess reserves provide no benefits, presumably it will try to keep zero excess reserves. However, excess reserves do provide a cushion, or liquidity benefit, against unexpected withdrawals that might reduce the bank's reserves below the amount required. This cushion involves a cost—foregone interest earnings. In fact, the higher the interest rate the greater the earnings foregone by holding excess reserves and, thus, the lower banks will prefer to keep their excess reserves. If the interest rate falls, the interest earnings foregone also fall, and the banks will be willing to hold a larger stock of excess reserves.

Consider a situation in which the interest rate increases and as a consequence banks desire to reduce their excess reserves. They will attempt to reduce those reserves by purchasing other assets which earn interest. Suppose, for example, the banks increase their loans to the general public. The loans are made, in the final analysis, by expanding the loan assets and deposit liabilities of the banks. The public receives an increase in its loan liabilities and an increase in its deposit assets. The increase in the deposit assets of the public is an increase in the money supply. Thus, if profit-maximizing banks change their desired level of excess reserves inversely with changes in the interest rate, the money supply will then vary directly with the interest rate.[1]

In addition to the action by private banks, the money supply can be changed through central bank action. The Federal Reserve has three general tools for accomplishing changes in the money supply. The total stock of reserves in the banking system, and therefore the stock of excess reserves in the banking system, can be changed if the Federal Reserve buys U.S. government securities from or sells securities to the banking system or to the household or business sectors. In the first case, the bank reserves are changed directly because the Federal Reserve pays for the securities by increasing the reserve account of banks or is paid for the securities by reducing the reserve account of banks. In the second case, the public will take the proceeds of the sale of government securities and deposit those in the banking system, thus increasing the reserves of the banking system; or it will pay for the securities by drawing checks against its demand deposits, thus lowering the reserves of the banking system.

In addition, the Federal Reserve can encourage banks to change their reserves by borrowing from the Federal Reserve. The banks must pay interest to the Fed when they borrow, and borrowing can be encouraged or discouraged by lowering or raising the interest rate which the banks will pay. Finally, the percentage of deposits that banks must hold in reserve (the required reserve ratio) may be changed by the Federal Reserve. Given the total level of reserves, an increase in the required reserve ratio decreases excess reserves and limits the banks' lending capacity and, therefore, its money supply creation. A decrease in the required reserve ratio, given the total amount of reserves, increases excess reserves, thereby increasing the potential for loan, deposit, and money supply expansion. Figure 4–1 shows a prototype money supply equation. The variable B shown in the equation represents a policy variable under the control of the Fed-

---

[1] Other sources of the interest sensitivity of the money supply are discussed in Chapter 12.

eral Reserve. For now we will simply refer to it as the *monetary base*. The supply equation is expressed in real terms by deflating by the price level. We will develop a more specific function reflective of the institutional arrangements in the United States in Chapter 12.

We assume that discrepancies between the amount of money demanded and the amount of money supplied are resolved by the purchase or sale of securities (such as bonds). If the amount of money supplied exceeds the amount of money demanded, money holders will attempt to rid themselves of the excess by purchasing securities. This raises security prices and lowers the yield or interest rate. The reverse occurs if money demand exceeds money supply.

THE MONEY MARKET AND AGGREGATE DEMAND

Consider the intersectoral linkages developed in this and the previous chapter. Changes or shifts in aggregate demand alter the equilibrium level of income; changes in income shift the money demand schedule which leads to interest rate changes; changes in the interest rate affect investment which is one component of aggregate demand. The chain of causation is a circle. Events in the product market influence the money market, but events in the money market in turn affect the product market. In short, income in the product market and the interest rate in the money market are determined jointly or simultaneously.

In order to arrive at a solution we will make use of a tool called the "Hicks-Hansen" diagram.[2] We take the many equations of the two markets and condense them into two equations that can easily be manipulated on a single graph or diagram. First consider the money market which consists of the money demand and supply equations plus an equilibrium condition.

$$M_d/P = kY - gi$$
$$M_s/P = (\alpha B + \beta i)/P$$
$$M_d/P = M_s/P$$

We have three equations in four unknowns, M_d/P, M_s/P, Y, and i. The price level is fixed by the assumption made in Chapter 3. If we substitute the demand and supply equations into the equilibrium con-

---

[2] John R. Hicks, "Mr. Keynes and the 'Classics': A Suggested Interpretation," *Econometrica*, Vol. 5 (April 1937), pp. 147–59; and Alvin H. Hansen, *A Guide to Keynes* (New York: McGraw-Hill Book Co., Inc., 1953).

dition we can obtain a single equation in two unknowns, Y and i.

$$kY - gi = (\alpha B + \beta i)/P$$
$$Y = \alpha B/kP + (\beta/PK + g/k)i \qquad (4\text{--}1)$$

Equation (4–1) is known as a *reduced form* equation, in this case for the money market. This equation, also known as the *LM schedule*, provides us with combinations of income and the interest rate that are consistent with equilibrium in the money market, *given the monetary base and the price level*. The schedule can also be derived graphically. In Figure 4–2A the money market is portrayed with three de-

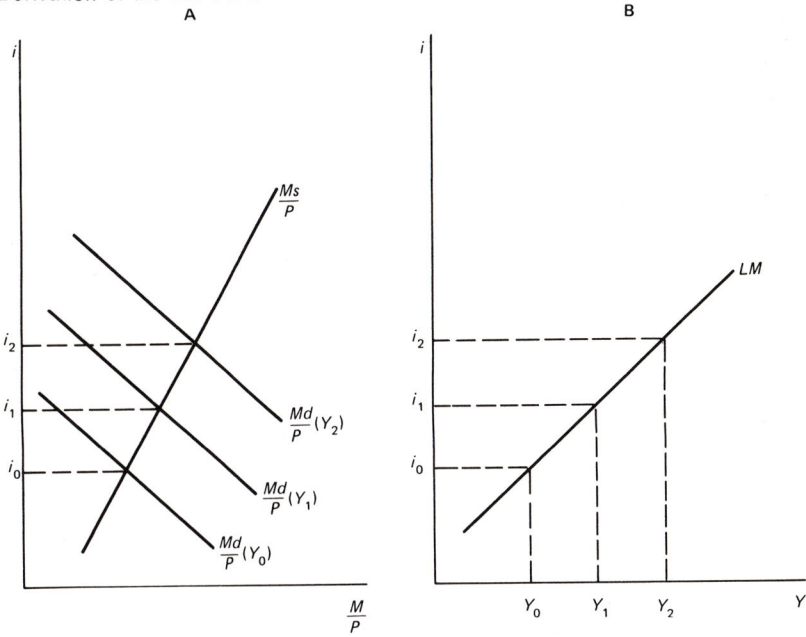

FIGURE 4–2
Derivation of the LM Curve

mand curves, one for each of three different income levels (where $Y_0 < Y_1 < Y_2$). The corresponding equilibrium interest rates are i_0, i_1, and i_2. In Figure 4–2B those interest rates are plotted on the vertical axis, and the corresponding income levels are plotted on the horizontal axis. The locus of interest rate-income combinations is the LM curve.

Along the LM curve the relationship between income and the interest rate is direct—the LM curve is upward sloping. This is confirmed by noting that the coefficient in front of the interest rate in equation (4–1) is a positive number.

The same approach may be used to derive a reduced form equation for the product market. Figure 4–3A is similar to Figure 3–4, except that three aggregate demand (AD) schedules are drawn, one for each of three different interest rates, where $i_0 < i_1 < i_2$. Remember that as the interest rate *falls*, aggregate demand *increases* (shifts upward) because investment increases. The corresponding equilibrium income levels are $Y_2 > Y_1 > Y_0$. The locus of these points is known as the *IS schedule* and is plotted in Figure 4–3B. Since, in the product market, lower interest rates are associated with higher equilibrium income levels, the IS schedule is downward sloping.

The algebraic form of the IS schedule has already been derived in Chapter 3. The equation, reproduced below, provides us with combinations of interest rate and income that are consistent with equilibrium in the product market.

$$Y = \frac{1}{(1-b)} (C_0 + I_0 - bT - ai + G) \qquad (4\text{--}2)$$

Taxes, government expenditures, and the parameters C_0 and I_0 are held constant along the IS curve. Inspection of equation (4–2) indicates that the coefficient of the interest rate is negative, confirming that the IS curve in Figure 4–3B is indeed downward sloping. Like the LM schedule, the IS schedule is a single equation in two unknowns, Y and i. Both curves are plotted in Figure 4–4.

The simultaneous solution occurs when an interest rate and income combination is selected that is consistent with equilibrium in both markets. The only point that lies on both curves is (i_0, Y_0). Suppose, instead, that the interest rate is i' and income is Y'. That point is consistent with product market equilibrium but not with money market equilibrium because it lies on the IS curve only. At Y' the interest rate would have to be i'' for equilibrium to prevail in the money market. Thus, i' is too low for equilibrium in the money market, resulting in excess demand for money balances (note in Figure 4–1 that money demand exceeds money supply when i is below equilibrium).

The excess money demand forces the interest rate to rise, and this depresses investment and aggregate demand. The falling aggregate demand causes producers to cut back on output (by assumption with no change in prices). With the interest rate rising and income falling, the economy moves from point (i', Y') toward (i_0, Y_0). Once equilib-

FIGURE 4-3
Derivation of the IS Curve

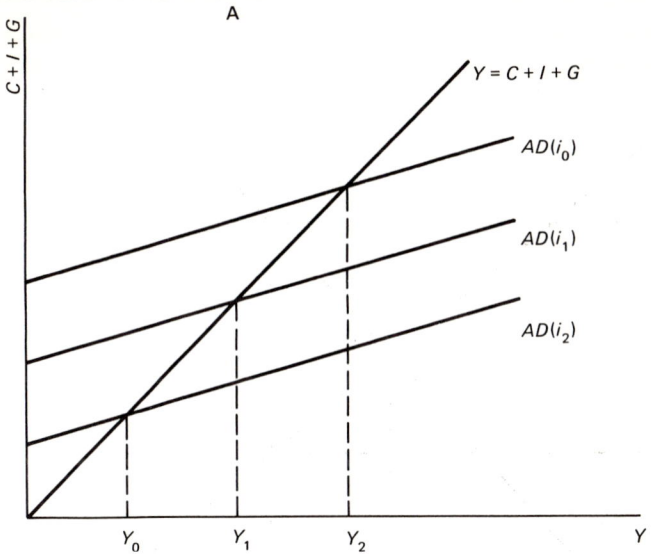

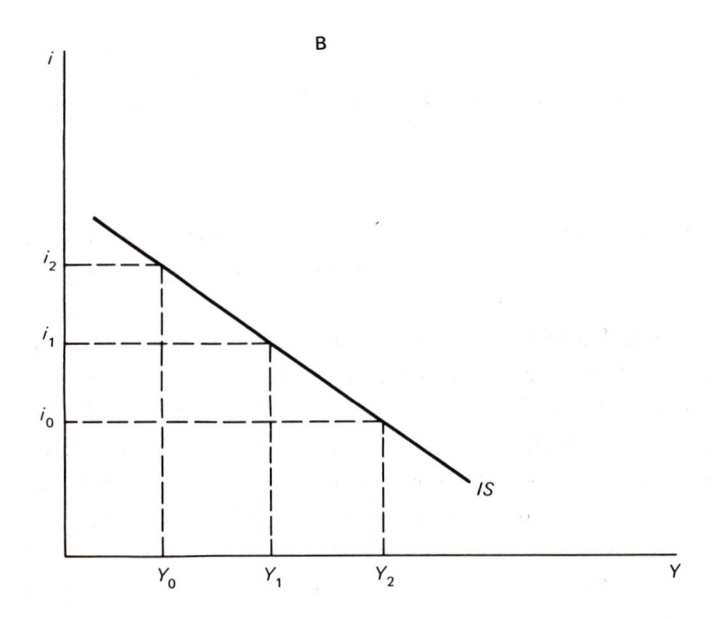

FIGURE 4–4
The IS-LM Model

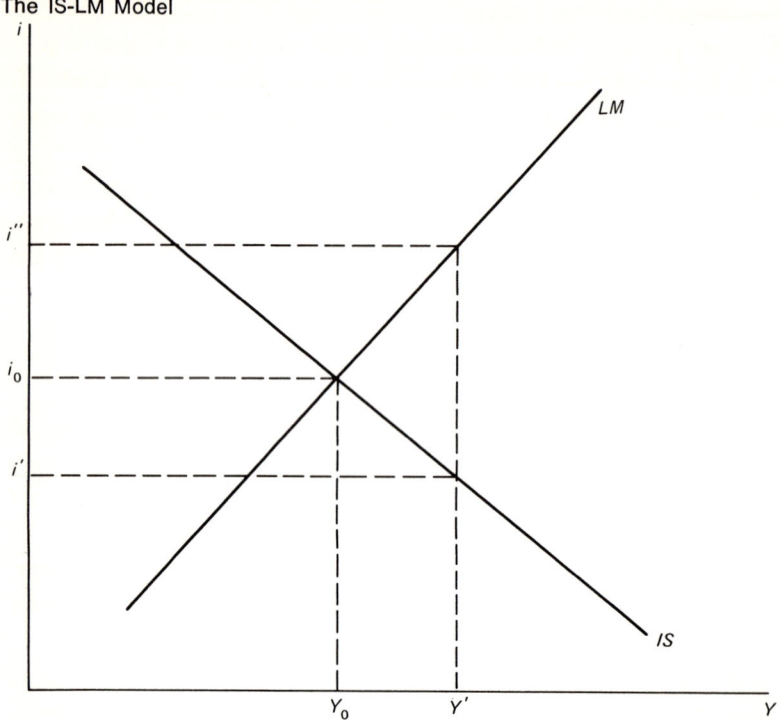

rium has been restored in both markets, pressure for change ceases. Similar experiments may be conducted with other disequilibrium points.

The IS-LM model is a widely used model of income determination. It has the advantage of including the influence of the money market on aggregate demand as well as the feedback from the product market to the money market. Both the interest rate and income are determined by the model. As it stands, however, it has a deficiency that can easily be rectified. Aggregate supply was assumed to be perfectly price elastic, so that changes in aggregate demand were immediately translated into equal changes in real income (output) with no change in the price level.

This assumption is inconsistent with the microeconomic foundations upon which macroeconomics should be built. In microeconomics we conclude that increases (decreases) in output in the short run are subject to rising (falling) marginal costs. Thus firms under perfect competition will expand (contract) output when price increases (decreases).

Another problem with the constant price assumption is that it prevents us from using the IS-LM framework to analyze a policy trade-off of major concern—that between unemployment and the price level. These problems will be dealt with in the next chapter by incorporating an aggregate supply function into the model. The supply function will be built with the tools employed in microeconomics. Thus completing the basic model, we will be in a position to analyze changes or shifts in the functions of the model in Chapter 6.

SUMMARY NOTES

1. Money serves as a medium of exchange and as the most liquid store of value. Assuming that the volume of transactions, for which money is needed, varies directly with real income, the demand for money will vary directly with real income.
2. The opportunity cost of holding money is represented by the interest rate. The demand for money varies inversely with the interest rate.
3. The demand for nominal money balances is assumed to be proportional to the price level. Therefore the demand for real money balances depends on real income and the interest rate.
4. Assuming that banks manage their assets (reserves and loans) so as to maximize profits subject to the constraint imposed by the need for liquidity, the supply of money will vary directly with the interest rate. The money supply also varies directly with the monetary base which is under the control of the central bank (Federal Reserve System).
5. The money market can be integrated with the product market to form a model that determines equilibrium real income and the interest rate. The model is known as the Hicks-Hansen or IS-LM model.
6. The IS curve shows interest rate and income combinations that are consistent with equilibrium in the product market. The LM curve shows interest rate and income combinations that are consistent with equilibrium in the money market.
7. Simultaneous solution of the IS and LM curves yields the equilibrium interest rate and income combination, given that the price level is constant.

DISCUSSION QUESTIONS

1. Consider the IS-LM diagram below:

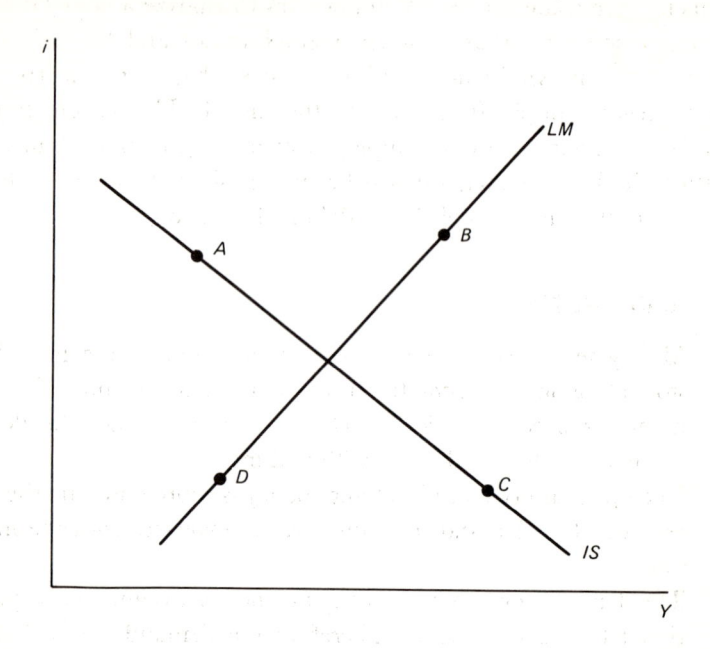

   For each of the points shown (A, B, C, D), indicate which market is in equilibrium and which is in disequilibrium. For the market in disequilibrium, deduce whether the market condition is one of excess demand or excess supply.

2. Using Figure 4–2 derive an LM curve. Now draw a new money supply curve which reflects an increase in the monetary base and derive a new LM curve. In which direction (right or left) has the increase in the monetary base shifted the LM curve?

3. Using Figure 4–3 derive an IS curve. Now draw a new set of AD curves which reflect an increase in government expenditures and derive a new IS curve. In which direction (right or left) has the increase in government expenditures shifted the IS curve? Repeat the procedure for an increase in taxes.

4. With the information gained from questions 2 and 3, deduce the changes in the equilibrium values of i and Y for changes in B, G, and T.

5

The Basic Model: Aggregate Supply

THE INCLUSION of the aggregate supply function adds a third equation or curve to the basic model. The three functions, IS, LM, and aggregate supply, will determine the interest rate, real income, and the price level. The values of the underlying variables, such as consumption, investment, and money demand and supply, can be determined by substituting the equilibrium values of i, Y, and P into the consumption, investment, money demand, and money supply functions. Thus we will be able to analyze changes in all the variables of the model by starting with the IS, LM, and aggregate supply curves. The procedure will be discussed in the next chapter. In this chapter we will derive and integrate the aggregate supply function.

AGGREGATE SUPPLY

In constructing the (short run) aggregate supply function, we will assume given technology and a fixed stock of capital. The only factor of production which may be altered in the short run in our model is the quantity of labor employed by the business sector. The relationship between the amount of labor employed and total output (net national product) is given by the aggregate production function shown in Figure 5–1. Note that as the quantity of labor employed increases, total output increases, but at a diminishing rate. The production function, therefore, is subject to the principle of diminishing marginal product. As more of the variable factor of production (labor) is added to the fixed factor of production (capital), output expands, but at a diminishing rate. The marginal product of labor, which is the slope of the production function, is also shown in Figure 5–1.

According to the theory of the firm, a firm (under perfect competition) will be maximizing profits when it hires labor up to the point

FIGURE 5–1
Production Function and Marginal Product of Labor Schedule

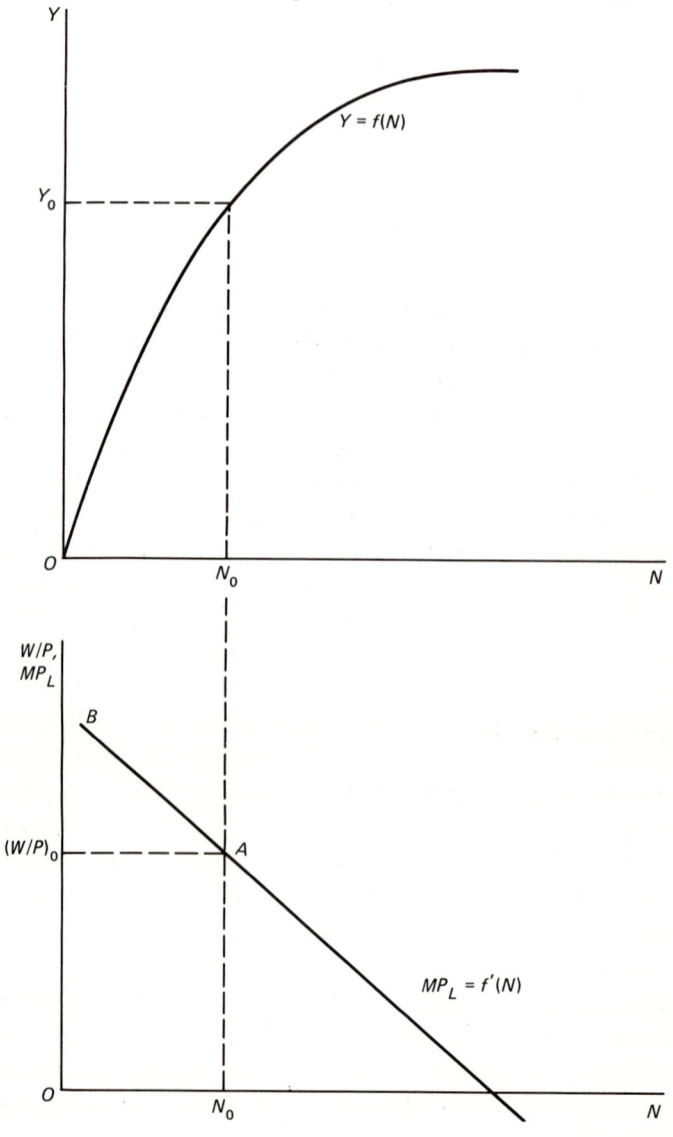

at which the marginal product of labor and the real wage rate are equal. If, for example, the real wage rate is given by $(W/P)_0$, then the profit maximizing amount of labor hired would be N_0 and that amount of labor would produce output Y_0. Total output is also measured by the area under the marginal product curve up to N_0. The distribution of total output between the two factors of production—labor and capital—can be determined from the lower graph. The share going to labor, the total wage bill, is given by the rectangle $O(W/P)_0AN_0$. The share going to capital is the triangle $(W/P)_0BA$.

Aggregate supply then will vary inversely with the nominal wage rate (W) and directly with the price level (P). If the nominal wage rate should fall, given the price level, the real wage rate will also fall, and this will induce profit-maximizing producers to hire more labor and hence produce more output. Should the price level fall, given the nominal wage rate, then the real wage rate will rise, and this will lead producers to hire less labor and produce less output.

Since the production function is nonlinear, we cannot express the aggregate supply function in linear form as we did with the elements of aggregate demand. To keep things manageable, we shall simply express aggregate supply as a function of the real wage rate. It will be sufficient to remember that aggregate supply varies directly with the price level and inversely with the nominal wage rate.

THE LABOR MARKET

The demand for labor schedule follows from our discussion of the aggregate supply of goods. Given the marginal product of labor schedule, the quantity of labor demanded depends upon the real wage rate, given that producers wish to maximize profits by equating the marginal product of labor with the real wage rate. In short, the demand for labor schedule is, in fact, the marginal product curve of labor.

On the labor supply side, we assume that workers allocate their time between work and leisure so as to maximize utility. Leisure can be considered a good, and the income derived from working is also a good. The individual cannot obtain as much as he wants of both these goods since his working day is constrained to 24 hours. Of course, he will need time to sleep and eat, so the actual available working day is less than that. In any case, his time resources are finite and must be allocated between the earning of income and leisure so as to maximize satisfaction. Should the wage rate increase, then each working hour becomes more valuable relative to each hour of leisure. Alternatively, we might say that the opportunity cost of leisure has increased. It follows that the worker will allocate more of his day to work and less to leisure. In short, the number of hours offered for work increases (decreases) as the wage rate increases (decreases).

One point should be made in passing: Other influences on labor supply may offset the effect of substitution between labor income and leisure. A possibility exists that the supply curve could be vertical or even downward sloping. However, the following discussion will not be significantly affected by a vertical supply curve (or even a downward sloping curve) as long as the supply curve is steeper than the demand curve. We will return to this in Chapter 10.

We assume that workers are aware of changes in the purchasing power of their earnings. The number of hours offered for work varies only to the extent that the real value of the wage rate varies. For example, should the nominal wage rate double and the price level double, we assume that there will be no increase in the number of hours offered for work. The labor supply schedule derived from this discussion is shown in Figure 5–2. On the vertical axis we measure the real wage rate. On the horizontal axis, the number of units of labor (usually measured in man-hours) offered is shown. Such things as the size of the population and tastes are held constant along the supply schedule.

We have also drawn in Figure 5–2 the labor demand schedule previously shown in Figure 5–1.

Equilibrium occurs in the labor market shown at wage rate $(W/P)_0$. At this real wage rate the quantity of labor supplied and the quantity of labor demanded are equal to N_0. Since the amount of labor offered for sale is equal to the amount of labor purchased, there is no involuntary unemployment in the labor market. To introduce the concept of unemployment in our model we will make a very simple assumption. Let us say that in the short run at least, the nominal wage rate is rigid. In other words, although the price level of goods may change in the short run, the nominal wage rate does not. A number of reasons have been set forth to justify this assumption. We might, for instance, assume that contracts are generally renegotiated annually and that our short period is less than a year so that nominal wage adjustments cannot take place within the time span of our analysis. Alternatively, we might argue that the existence of large-scale labor unions in some parts of the labor market introduces

FIGURE 5-2
The Labor Market

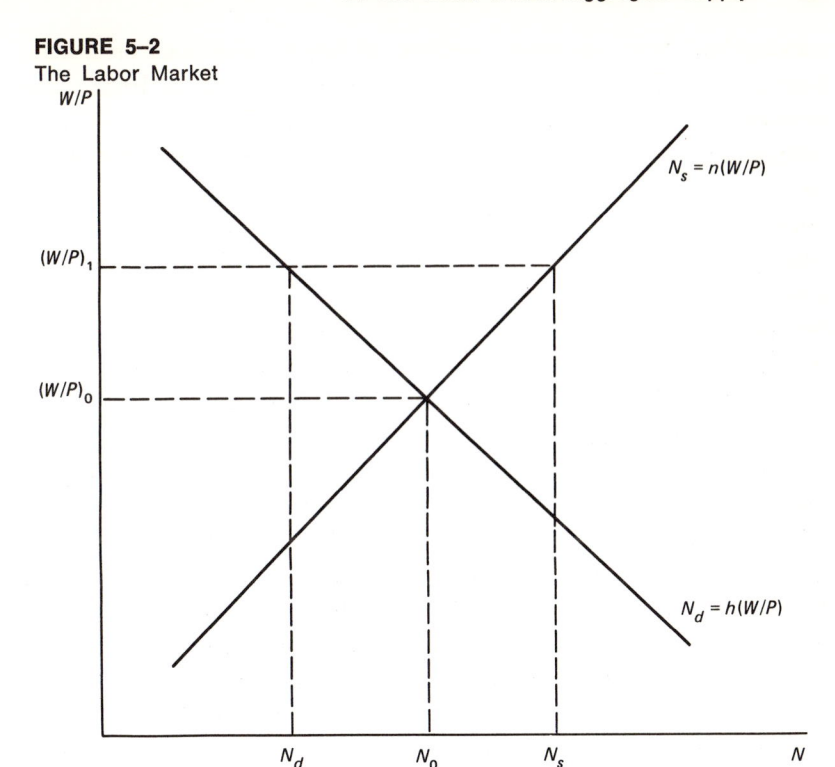

rigidity into the nominal wage rate because, in the presence of excess supply, labor unions would be more willing to accept some unemployment than to accept cuts in the nominal wage rate. Furthermore, as long as the economy is at less than full employment, there is no upward pressure on the nominal wage rate. In any case, the assumption is quite common in Keynesian type models.[1]

It should be stressed that the rigid wage assumption is a short-run

---

[1] The rigidity assumption is ascribed to Keynes by Alvin H. Hansen, *A Guide to Keynes* (New York: McGraw-Hill Book Co., Inc., 1953), p. 23. Other writers have made use of the assumption in models similar to ours. Examples include Franco Modigliani, "Liquidity Preference and the Theory of Interest and Money," *Econometrica*, Vol. 12 (January 1944), pp. 45–88; and Warren L. Smith, "A Graphical Exposition of the Complete Keynesian System," *Southern Economic Journal*, Vol. 23 (October 1956), pp. 115–25. More recently some writers have argued that the assumption is a misrepresentation of Keynes in that it detracts from the essentially dynamic character of his analysis and forces it into a neoclassical mold. See Axel Leijonhufvud, *On Keynesian Economics and the Economics of Keynes* (New York: Oxford University Press, 1968), pp. 81–102. We will return to this in Chapter 17. See also the discussion of money illusion in Chapter 10.

assumption which has been advanced by previous writers as a possible explanation for the labor market's failure to clear. In addition, it attempts to provide an explanation for the different rates of change of nominal wage rates and the price level. For example, during the impressive expansion phase of the 1960s, nominal compensation per man-hour (adjusted for changes in output per man-hour) rose at an average annual rate of about 1 percent (1962–1966). The price level during the same period rose 1.5 percent, on average, per year. Thus the real wage rate fell an average of 0.5 percent per year. In a sense, the rigid wage assumption is an abstraction made to reflect the fact that prices and wages don't change at the same rate.

On the other hand, the present model (and those upon which it is based) implies that employment and the real wage rate vary inversely. At times this is consistent with reality, but too often it is not. This has become an important, recent criticism of Keynesian macro models, to which we will return in Chapter 17. For now it is well to recall the warning made in Chapter 1 that a theory need not explain all of reality in order to be a useful framework for discussion.

Suppose then that the nominal wage rate is fixed at $\overline{W}$ and the price level of goods is such that the real wage rate is indicated by $(\overline{W}/P)_1$. At that level the amount of labor demanded is N_D, and the amount of labor supply is N_S. Since producers will not hire more than they actually demand, the amount of labor employed is N_D. The excess labor supply or the amount of unemployed labor is the difference between N_S and N_D.[2] Given a fixed nominal wage rate, no automatic adjustment takes place in the labor market to restore equilibrium. In fact, equilibrium can only be restored if the price level changes and thereby changes the real wage rate. In the case illustrated, it would take an increase in the price level sufficient to lower the real wage rate to $(W/P)_0$ to restore full employment.

As long as we have unemployment in the model, the feasible range of operation for the employers of labor is the range of the labor demand schedule above the labor supply schedule. Variations in the price level will induce producers to move along that portion of the labor demand schedule changing the amount of labor employed and therefore changing the amount of output produced. Within that range, then, output varies directly with the price level. Employment also varies directly with the price level, and unemployment varies inversely

---

[2] Frictional unemployment due to a mismatch between jobs and skills, labor immobility, etc. is not part of this model. See the discussion in Chapter 7.

with the price level. This can be summarized by noting that labor demand and, in fact, employed can be written as:

$$N = h(\overline{W}/P) \tag{5-1}$$

The production function is:

$$Y = f(N) \tag{5-2}$$

Substituting (5–1) into (5–2) we obtain the following expression for aggregate supply (AS):

$$Y = f[h(\overline{W}/P)]$$

or more conveniently:

$$Y = f(\overline{W}/P) \tag{5-3}$$

THE COMPLETE BASIC MODEL

The basic model now contains an IS schedule, an LM schedule, and an aggregate supply (AS) schedule. All three schedules are shown in Figure 5–3. The rate of interest does not enter into the AS schedule, and the curve is therefore plotted as a vertical line. We will no longer assume that the price level is fixed, and therefore adjustments in the model will take place through changes in the interest rate, income, and the price level. Maximum feasible output, or full employment output, is shown as Y_f on the graph.

The AS schedule indicates the current level of output, given $\overline{W}$ and P, under the assumption that producers are attempting to maximize profits. The IS schedule can now be interpreted as showing, for different interest rates, the level of output necessary for aggregate demand and aggregate supply to be equal. The LM schedule shows, for different interest rates, what level of income (output) is necessary for equilibrium in the money market. Equilibrium in the product and money markets occurs when, at a given interest rate, current output is equal to that necessary for equilibrium in both the product market and the money market. This occurs at i_0 and Y_0 in Figure 5–3 or, in other words, where the three curves intersect.

If the curves do not intersect at the same point, adjustments will take place through interest rate, price, and income changes to restore equilibrium. For example, consider the situation depicted in Figure 5–4. Given the position of the AS curve, current output is Y_0. Suppose the interest rate is i_0. At this interest rate, output would have to be

FIGURE 5–3
Equilibrium in the Basic Model

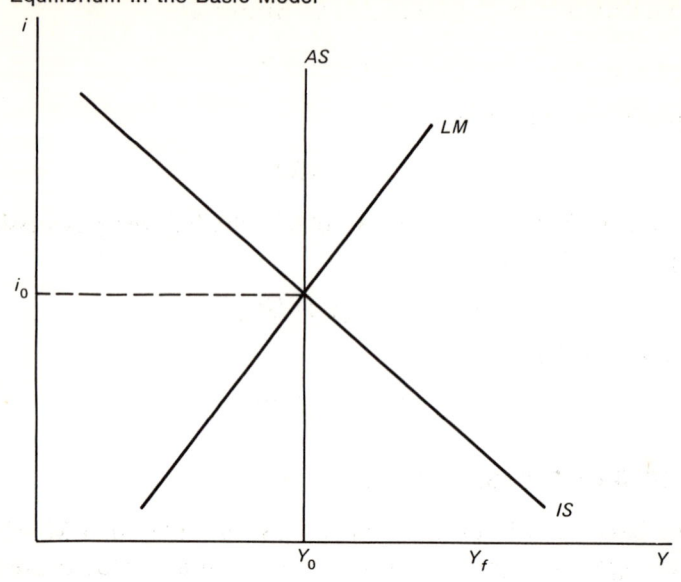

FIGURE 5–4
Disequilibrium in the Basic Model

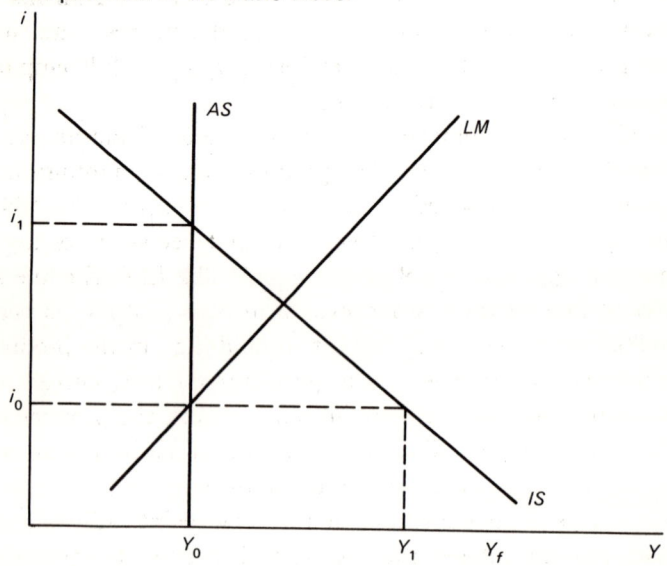

Y_1 for equilibrium to prevail in the product market. Viewed from another perspective, at income Y_0 the interest rate would have to rise to i_1 to restore equilibrium in the product market. Thus the product market is in disequilibrium, and this condition will lead to price and output changes which will eventually restore equilibrium. These changes will be analyzed in detail in the next chapter.

We will also be able to deduce the changes that take place in the interest rate, income, and the price level, given, for example, some policy change that affects the level of government spending, taxes, or the monetary base. Reference back to the detailed parts of the model will enable us to deduce what effect such policy changes produce on the level of unemployment, consumption, investment, money demand, and money supply. We now turn to the next chapter to see exactly how this is done.

SUMMARY NOTES

1. The aggregate production function relates output to the quantity of labor employed, given the stock of capital.
2. Assuming that producers wish to maximize profits, they will hire the amount of labor that is consistent with equality between the real wage rate and labor's marginal product. Given that the marginal product varies inversely with the quantity of labor employed, the demand for labor varies inversely with the real wage rate. Therefore aggregate supply varies inversely with the real wage rate.
3. The supply of labor is assumed to vary directly with the real wage rate. Unemployment (excess supply of labor) is introduced by assuming rigidity in the nominal wage rate which prevents the labor market from clearing.
4. Integration of the aggregate supply function into the IS-LM model permits the model to determine the price level as well as the interest rate and income.

DISCUSSION QUESTIONS

1. Some economic models (linear programming and input-output models) make use of linear production functions. In that case, the function $Y = f(N)$ in Figure 5-1 would be a straight line through the origin. Recalling that the marginal product of labor is the slope

of the production function, what effect would a linear production function have on our labor market where (a) the nominal wage rate is flexible and (b) the nominal wage rate is rigid?

2. Suppose you were working at a full-time, nonunion job, and one day your employer said that he was going to cut your wage rate by 20 percent. Would you accept the cut (after a fight, of course) or would you quit and look for another job? Why? Assume in your answer that you cannot effectively look for another job while working.

3. If, in the preceding question, you chose to quit and it took two months to find a job at the acceptable pay level, would you say that you had been unemployed for two months? If so, would you classify your unemployment as voluntary or involuntary?

6

Operation of the Model

THE basic outlines of our macroeconomic model were developed in Chapters 3–5. It is now time to explore the operating characteristics of that model. The basic reduced form equations developed are listed below.

$$\text{IS curve: } Y = \frac{1}{1-b}(C_0 + I_0 + G - bT - ai)$$

$$\text{LM curve: } Y = \frac{\alpha}{k}\frac{B}{P} + \left(\frac{\beta}{Pk} + \frac{g}{k}\right)i$$

$$\text{AS curve: } Y = f(\bar{W}/P)$$

Remember that the IS curve tells us what the level of aggregate demand would be for given values of government spending, taxes, and the rate of interest (and the parameters such as b, C_0, and I_0) if aggregate demand and aggregate supply were in equilibrium. The LM curve indicates those combinations of interest rates and income that would prevail if the money market were in equilibrium, given the monetary base and the price level (and parameters such as k and g). The aggregate supply (AS) curve tells us what the current level of output is, given the nominal wage rate and price level. All variables are expressed in real terms except B and $\bar{W}$.

The three equations form a system in three unknowns. The unknowns (the variables that the system determines) are income, the price level, and the rate of interest. These are normally called *endogenous* variables. The system also contains variables that influence the endogenous variables but are not, in turn, influenced by the endogenous variables. These we call *exogenous* variables. In our basic model the exogenous variables are the level of government spending on goods and services, the level of taxes, the monetary base, and the assumed rigid nominal wage rate. Changes in the *exogenous* variables will induce changes in the *endogenous* variables, but not vice versa. Changes in the exogenous variables are often called *autonomous* changes. We shall be interested in finding out what change takes place in the endogenous variables in response to autonomous changes in the exogenous variables. Before we do that, however, it will be helpful if we determine how each equation changes (or shifts) in response to a change in the exogenous variables in that equation.

AUTONOMOUS CHANGES

In Figure 6–1 we have derived a shift in the IS schedule due to an increase in government spending. Figure 6–1A shows aggregate demand for two values of the interest rate before [$AD(i_0)$ and $AD(i_1)$] and after [$AD'(i_0)$ and $AD'(i_1)$] the increase in government spending, where $i_0 < i_1$. The equilibrium interest rate-income combinations are (i_0,Y_1) and (i_1,Y_0) before the government spending increase and (i_0,Y_1') and (i_1,Y_0') after. By projecting these points down to Figure 6–1B, we can obtain the IS curve before (IS) and after (IS') the increase in government spending. The horizontal distance between the curves is $1/(1-b)$ times the change in G. This is confirmed by noting that the coefficient on G in the IS equation is $1/(1-b)$. Since the coefficient is positive an increase (decrease) in G shifts the IS curve to the right (left), consistent with the results shown in Figure 6–1.

The opposite shift occurs when taxes increase. Figure 6–2 shows the IS curve before and after an increase in the level of taxes, holding government expenditures constant. In this case, the IS curve shifts to the left when taxes increase. The reason for this can be seen by examining the equation for the IS curve. The coefficient on the tax variable is negative. It is negative because a tax increase reduces disposable income and therefore reduces the consumption component of aggregate demand. An increase in taxes, all other things held constant, will decrease the equilibrium level of aggregate demand by $-b/(1-b)$ times the change in the tax level.

The LM curve shifts in response to changes in the monetary base.

FIGURE 6-1
Shift in the IS Schedule Due to an Increase in Government Spending

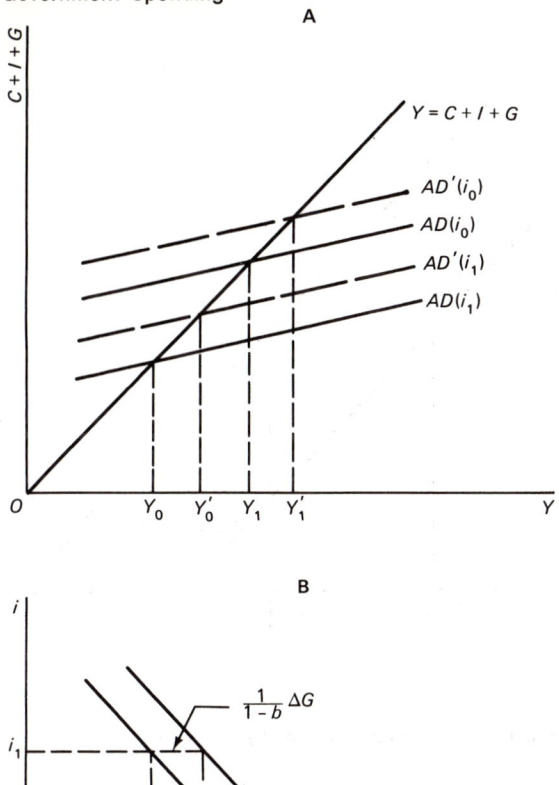

Figure 6–3 illustrates a shift in the LM schedule due to an increase in the monetary base. In Figure 6–3A, two money demand curves are drawn $[M_D/P(Y_0)$ and $M_D/P(Y_1)]$ for two levels of income, where $Y_0 < Y_1$. The money supply curve before the increase in the monetary base is M_s/P, and the money supply curve after the increase is M'_s/P.

74   Macroeconomic Theory

FIGURE 6–2
Shift in the IS Schedule Due to an Increase in Taxes

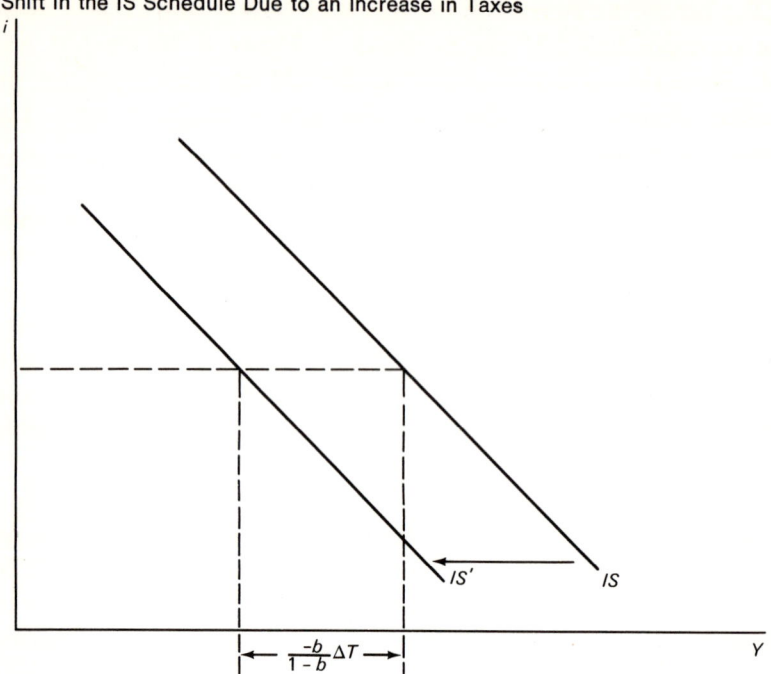

$\frac{-b}{1-b}\Delta T$

FIGURE 6–3
Shift in the LM Curve Due to an Increase in the Monetary Base

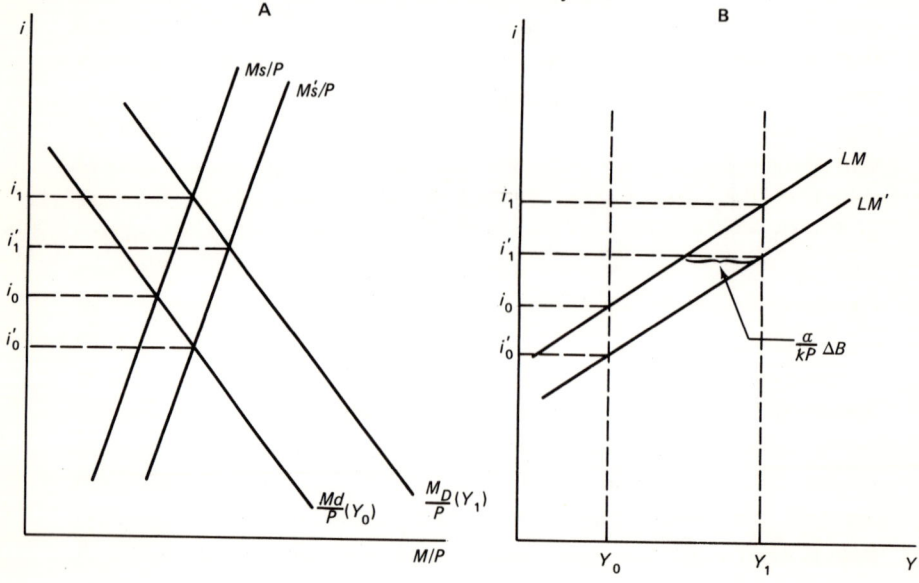

A

Ms/P, Ms'/P, $\frac{Md}{P}(Y_0)$, $\frac{M_D}{P}(Y_1)$, M/P

B

$\frac{\alpha}{kP}\Delta B$, LM, LM', Y_0, Y_1

The equilibrium interest rate-income combinations are (i_0, Y_0) and (i_1, Y_1) before the increase in the base and (i_0', Y_0) and (i_1', Y_1) after. The corresponding LM curves drawn in Figure 6–3B are LM and LM'. Since the coefficient on B/P in the LM equation is positive, an increase (decrease) in B shifts the LM curve to the right (left). The magnitude of the shift is equal to α/kP times the change in B as is shown in Figure 6–3B.

Finally, autonomous changes in the nominal wage rate will shift the aggregate supply schedule. An increase in the nominal wage rate relative to the price level increases the real wage rate, thus inducing profit-maximizing producers to reduce the amount of labor employed. Given the stock of capital[1], a reduction in the amount of labor employed will result in a reduction in output. Hence, in response to the increase in the nominal wage rate, the aggregate supply schedule moves to the left.

Changes in one of the endogenous variables will also shift certain of the schedules. The IS schedule in our basic model contains no endogenous variables other than income and the rate of interest. The IS schedule will therefore only *shift* in response to changes in the exogenous variables, while changes in i and Y will result in movements along the schedule. Changes in some variables are represented by shifts simply because we are representing an equation with more than two variables on a two-dimensional diagram. Changes in i and Y are shown by movements along the two dimensions, while changes in the other variables are translated into shifts. However, both the LM equation and the AS equation contain the price level as a variable. A change in the price level will shift the LM curve and the aggregate supply curve just as autonomous changes in the exogenous variables shift those schedules. In particular, an increase in the price level will shift the LM curve to the left for the same reason that a decrease in B shifts the LM curve to the left. The real value of the monetary base (B/P) decreases when either B decreases or P increases. Holding the interest rate and all other parameters constant, a lower level of income is required to clear the money market.

The change in the price level also alters the slope of the LM curve. Specifically, the slope of the LM curve is the following:

$$\Delta i / \Delta Y = \frac{1}{(\beta/Pk + g/k)}$$

---

[1] The rate of utilization is also a given. Capital, like labor, need not be fully employed. Indeed, it usually is not.

76   Macroeconomic Theory

An increase in the price level reduces the value of β/Pk, thereby reducing the value of the denominator in the above fraction and increasing the value of the fraction. Thus, an increase in the price level increases the slope of the LM curve (making it steeper) and also shifts the LM curve to the left. Of importance in the economic analysis, however, is the price induced shift in the schedule. The price induced twist in the schedule is due to the particular form of the money supply function we have used. Consequently in all of the following analysis we shall concentrate only on the shift in the schedule.

In the case of the aggregate supply schedule, an increase in the price level reduces the real value of the wage rate. Producers find it profitable to hire more labor. With a given stock of capital and more labor employed, aggregate supply will increase. The various shifts are summarized in Table 6–1.

TABLE 6–1
Summary of Schedule Shifts

Increase in	Curve	Direction	Magnitude of Shift
G	IS	right	$[1/(1-b)]\Delta G$
T	IS	left	$[-b/(1-b)]\Delta T$
B	LM	right	$[\alpha/kP]\Delta B$
P	LM	left	$-(\alpha B/kP^2 + \beta i/P^2)\Delta P$*
P	AS	right	†
W	AS	left	†

* Approximate for other than extremely small changes in P.
† Unspecified without an explicit form for the AS schedule.

Thus far, we have only analyzed the effect of a change in an exogenous variable on the equation in which that exogenous variable appears. However, a change in any one of the exogenous variables will affect all of the equations of the model. This is because a change that affects, say, the IS schedule will induce changes in the endogenous variables, which in turn will produce an effect upon the LM schedule and the AS schedule (a shift or movement along). The effects can easily be traced out once we determine what the adjustment mechanisms are in each market.

ADJUSTMENT MECHANISMS

Consider first an example from microeconomics. The quantity demanded of any product is generally assumed to be in part dependent on the price of that product. The quantity supplied is also assumed to be dependent in part on the price of the product. For example, a price increase leads to a reduction in the quantity demanded and an increase in the quantity supplied, all other things being equal. A price decrease leads to the opposite conclusion. We usually assume that when a market is in disequilibrium, the price of the product changes to restore equilibrium. If the quantity demanded exceeds the quantity supplied, we expect the price to rise; and if the quantity supplied exceeds the quantity demanded, we expect the price to fall. The price level is the adjustment mechanism in that market. We usually summarize this by saying that the rate of change in the price is a function of the difference between the quantity demanded and the quantity supplied. For short: $dP/dt = f(Q_D - Q_S)$.

Our approach is no different in macroeconomics. We are concerned with three major markets: the product market, the money market, and the labor market. For the product market we assume that when aggregate demand exceeds aggregate supply the general price level rises, and vice versa. But wait—the model with which we are dealing is usually characterized by unemployment. Is it reasonable to assume that the price level will rise in response to an increase in aggregate demand when resources are unemployed? To answer that question, consider the period of greatest unemployment in U.S. history. From 1933 to 1939 the unemployment rate declined from an incredible 25 percent to a still unacceptable 17 percent. Output increased by 48 percent over the period. Did the price level rise? It did, by over 10 percent. Thus the assumption is realistic even when unemployment is massive. (See the Appendix to Chapter 10 for a discussion of the elasticity of output with respect to changes in the price level.)

In the case of the money market, we assume that when the quantity of money demanded exceeds the quantity of money supplied, the interest rate will rise, and vice versa.

The assumptions under which we constructed our basic model allow for no adjustment mechanism in the labor market, however. We assumed in Chapter 5 that the nominal wage rate was fixed in the short run by contract or for institutional reasons. Hence the nominal wage rate in the short run cannot respond to excess demand or excess supply in the labor market. Had we assumed that the nominal wage rate served as an adjustment mechanism, then we could not analyze the problem of unemployment (at least in the context of this type of static model). With a flexible wage rate, the labor market would tend towards equilibrium, which we define as full employment. In the long run, nominal wages may be flexible and there may still be unemployment. This may occur if the supply of labor is increasing rapidly and the nominal wage rate adjusts only slowly, for example. We will discuss other sources of unemployment in Chapters 16 and 17.

We should note here that the above discussion *does not* mean that the commodity market *alone* determines the price level or that the money market alone determines the interest rate. A disturbance that ultimately alters the values of *all* the endogenous variables could originate anywhere in the model. The adjustment mechanisms simply specify which variables are likely to change *first,* given a disturbance in a particular market. Thus a shift in aggregate demand will first affect the price level and will ultimately affect the interest rate, output, etc.

We can now illustrate how the full model responds to an autonomous change in one of the exogenous variables. Although we shall discuss the changes as a sequence of events, it should be recognized that in a static model, such as ours, all changes are taking place *simultaneously,* and the sequence description is for exposition purposes only. In particular, nothing should be deduced from our discussion about the relative speeds of adjustment in the different markets. First consider an increase in government spending on goods and services without a change in taxes. At the initial (equilibrium) level of income, aggregate demand has therefore increased relative to aggregate supply, and, as a result, prices are bid up. A rise in the price level by lowering the real wage rate induces producers to expand output by hiring more labor. The increased output and consequent sales yield an increased disposable income to the household sector (given the level of taxes). Increased household disposable income leads to increased consumption and further increases in aggregate demand.

However, the process does not continue indefinitely because counteracting forces are also set in motion. The increase in real income (output) leads to an increase in real money demand. The rising price level reduces the real value of the monetary base and shifts the money supply function to the left. Hence, excess money demand develops which forces up interest rates. The rising interest rate "chokes off" private investment spending. Further, because the marginal propensity to consume is less than unity, each successive increment in household income leads to a successively smaller induced increment in consumption and aggregate demand. The rise in consumption therefore "tapers off." The whole process can be summarized by the use of the

IS-LM-AS diagram. At the initial equilibrium, we start at the point of intersection of the three curves in Figure 6–4. The government was assumed to increase its annual rate of spending on goods and services without a change in taxes. (Where the funds come from if

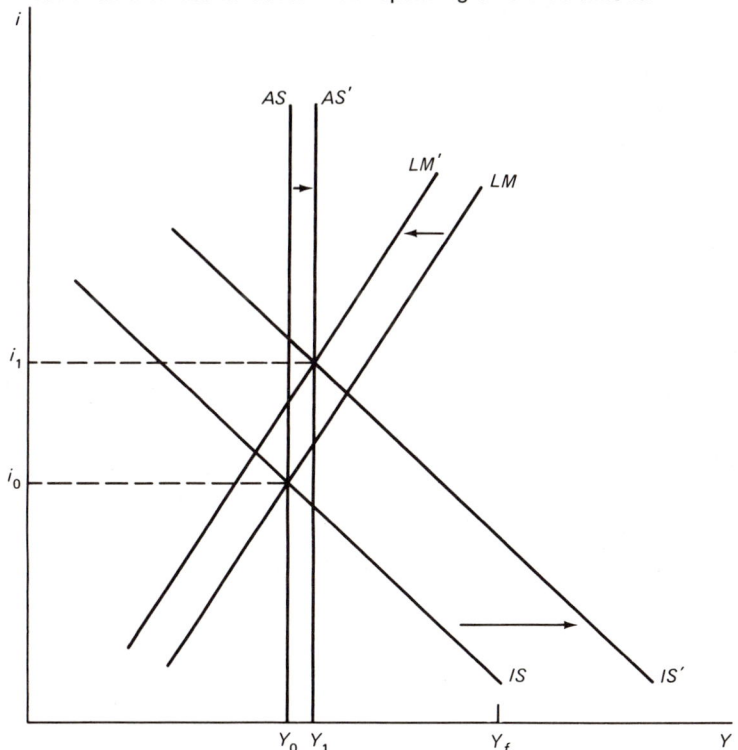

FIGURE 6–4
Effect of an Increase in Government Spending on the Full Model

taxes are not increased is discussed in the next section.) This shifts the IS schedule to IS′. At the initial equilibrium level of income, aggregate demand now exceeds aggregate supply by the amount of the increase in government spending. The price level therefore tends to rise. The rising price level produces an impact on both the LM and AS schedules. Specifically, the LM schedule shifts to the left as the real monetary base is reduced by the rising price level. The rising price level also has the effect of reducing the real wage rate, leading profit-maximizing producers to hire more labor and expand output, shifting the AS schedule to the right.

With the real money supply function decreasing relative to real money demand, the interest rate tends to rise. The price level, interest rate, and income continue to rise until equilibrium is restored in both markets. The new equilibrium occurs at the intersection of the IS′ curve, the LM′ curve, and the AS′ curve. Given the structure described by the model, the increase in government spending results in an increase in the level of income (from Y_0 to Y_1), an increase in the rate of interest (from i_0 to i_1), and a fall in unemployment. The final change in income is less than the horizontal distance between IS and IS′. The autonomous spending multiplier of the complete basic model is therefore less than that of the simple model discussed in Chapter 3 by virtue of the "feedback" through price and interest rate changes. Further, regardless of the increase in aggregate demand, the new output level cannot exceed the full employment level, Y_f.

Next consider a shift in the money supply function. Suppose the Federal Reserve purchases government securities from member banks and pays for the securities by crediting the reserve accounts of those banks. This increases the nominal monetary base and shifts the LM curve to LM′ in Figure 6–5 as banks increase their loans and deposits. The excess of real money supply over real money demand now results in a fall in the rate of interest. Money holders attempt to reduce their money balances by using the excess funds to purchase interest-earning assets such as bonds (that is, to lend the funds). The resulting increase in the demand for bonds forces bond prices upward and their market yields downward. The fall in the rate of interest in turn increases aggregate demand by increasing private investment spending. The increase in aggregate demand over the current level of aggregate supply results in a rising price level. The rising price level shifts the aggregate supply curve towards the right and shifts the LM schedule back to the left away from LM′. At the new equilibrium, indicated by the intersection of the IS schedule, the LM″ schedule, and the AS′ schedule, prices are higher than before. Income is higher than before, and the rate of interest is lower than before. Similar experiments can be conducted with changes in, say, the level of taxes. We shall do so when discussing stabilization policies in the next chapter.

FINANCING AUTONOMOUS SPENDING

It should be pointed out at this stage that the ability of changes in autonomous spending, such as government spending, to change

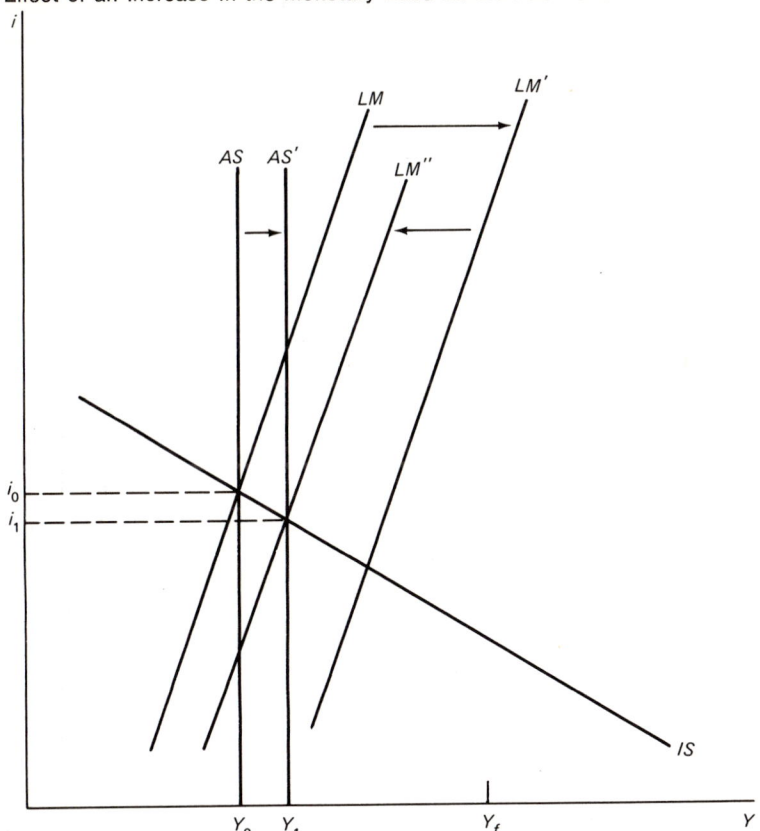

FIGURE 6–5
Effect of an Increase in the Monetary Base on the Full Model

the level of income is dependent upon the fact that financing is available for such spending. Consider the case of an increase in government spending with no change in the level of taxes and no change in the monetary base. To finance the excess of spending over taxes, the government must borrow from the private sector. This means that the government will be obtaining funds that might otherwise be used for private spending by business firms. Whether or not the resulting decrease in private spending will offset the increase in government spending is a question that can be answered by considering the sources of funds.

In our model, the excess of government spending over taxes plus any private borrowing is financed by the current flow of private saving *in equilibrium*. Should that equilibrium be disturbed by, for example, an increase in government spending—and therefore an increase in government borrowing—the current flow of private saving will be inadequate. In other words, initially, there will be an excess of private plus government borrowing over the current flow of private saving.[2] This excess borrowing will not be resolved until income rises and generates a higher flow of saving. The initial discrepancy is made up by a decrease in the stock of idle money balances held by the public.

Remember that when we discussed the money market in Chapter 5 we saw that not all of the money balances held by the public were used to finance current transactions. A portion of those balances was held as an asset because money provides a service that we ordinarily refer to as liquidity. The amount held as an asset varied inversely with the opportunity cost of holding money as an asset—namely, the rate of interest. The holders of such idle balances could be induced to give up some of those idle balances and instead lend them out either to the government sector or to the business sector, if a higher rate of interest than the current market rate of interest were offered. This is exactly what happens in our model. The government intends to increase its spending over its tax receipts and is therefore forced to borrow. By increasing the supply of bonds, the market rate of interest is forced up, disturbing the equilibrium in the money market. Individuals holding idle balances are therefore induced to release or give up some of those idle balances and instead convert them into bonds. Thus, the government deficit is financed without fully bidding away funds destined for private spending. There is a net increase in aggregate demand which ultimately drives the economy to a higher equilibrium level of income. At that higher equilibrium level of income, the flow of private saving will be great enough to finance private borrowing plus the higher level of government borrowing.

The importance of the financing question is not minor, for it forms the basis of much of the disagreement between those who prefer, on the one hand, the use of monetary policy and those who prefer, on the other hand, the use of fiscal policy. The extremes can be illustrated with the tools used and discussed in this chapter.

Suppose, for example, that individuals and business firms did not desire to hold money as an asset but only desired to hold money for

---

[2] We defer to a later chapter the case in which saving increases, at the expense of consumption, in response to an increase in the rate of interest. The financing problem also applies in this case because funds must be found to keep the fall in consumption from completely offsetting the increase in government spending.

the purpose of carrying out transactions. This can be illustrated by making the demand for money depend only upon the level of income.[3] The coefficient of the interest rate in our money demand equation would be equal to zero. Also, suppose that banks did not desire to change their excess reserves in response to changes in the interest rate. The effect of these conditions on the shape of the LM curve is to make the curve vertical, as shown in Figure 6–6A. In equilibrium

FIGURE 6–6A
Effect of an Increase in Government Spending When Both Money Supply and Demand Are Interest Inelastic

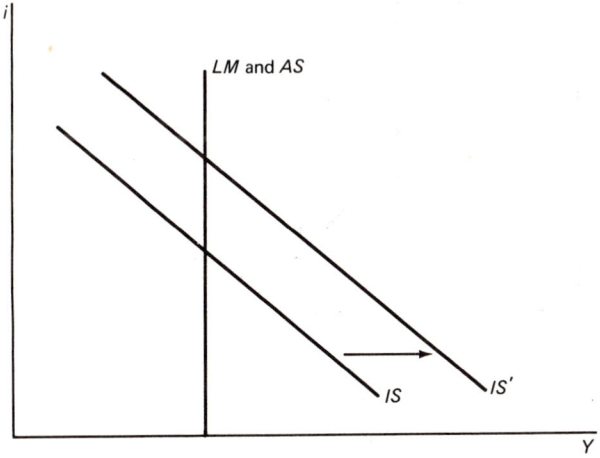

the aggregate supply curve would be coincident with the LM curve. The IS curve is also shown in the figure.

Consider an increase in the level of government spending with no change in taxes which shifts the IS curve to IS'. With no idle balances available, the government would only be able to finance the increased spending by bidding funds away from the private sector. This would occur by a rising rate of interest. As the government attempted to borrow, the rate of interest would be forced up, choking off private investment spending. Since there would be no idle balances forthcoming, the rate of interest would continue to rise until private investment spending fell by the amount of the increase in government spending. With changes in investment and government spending exactly off-

---

[3] Actually, the transactions demand for money may also depend on the rate of interest, as we shall see in Chapter 11.

setting each other, there would be no increase in the level of aggregate demand—hence, no change in the price level and no further induced changes in the LM curve or the aggregate supply curve.

The opposite situation is shown in Figure 6–6B. Here we assume

FIGURE 6–6B
Effect of an Increase in Government Spending When Either Money Supply or Demand Are Interest Elastic

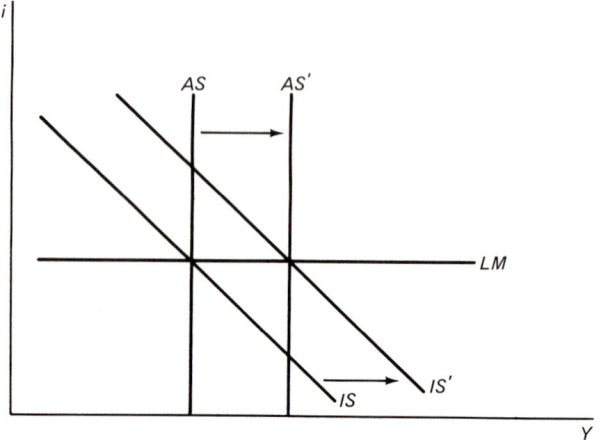

that there is a virtually unlimited supply of idle balances. Holders of those idle balances will be willing to buy any new bonds that came on the markets at the existing level of interest rates. If the government were to increase its spending relative to taxes and therefore be forced to borrow, it could obtain these idle balances with no increase in the rate of interest. If the rate of interest does not rise, then private investment spending is not choked off. Aggregate demand increases, resulting in a higher price level and a higher level of output and income.

Figure 6–6A is representative of the assumptions employed by those who argue that monetary policy is more effective than fiscal policy, and Figure 6–6B is representative of the assumptions used by those who argue that fiscal policy is more effective than monetary policy, *at least in the context of our basic model.*[4] We shall have the occasion to discuss these issues in greater detail in the next chapter. In addition,

---

[4] At least one monetarist considers the IS-LM model to be suitable for a comparison of fiscalist and monetarist views. See Milton Friedman, "A Theoretical Framework for Monetary Analysis," *Journal of Political Economy*, Vol. 78 (March/April 1970), pp. 193–238.

the empirical evidence that bears on the issues will be reviewed in Chapters 11 and 12. Finally, it should be remembered that the mechanism by which monetary policy affects the real sector in our basic model represents only one (although widely accepted) type of transmission mechanism. Specifically, we have assumed that monetary policy affects aggregate demand indirectly through changes in the interest rate which lead to changes in investment. Other mechanisms are part of the theoretical literature, and we shall discuss these in Chapter 13.

AN ALTERNATIVE VIEW: VELOCITY AND THE EQUATION OF EXCHANGE

A different, and older, view of the link between money and income is summarized in the *equation of exchange*. This equation shows the relationship between the flow of spending generated by a given stock of money and the level of money income as follows:

$$MV = PY$$

M, P, and Y have the same definitions that were used earlier, V is the *velocity of circulation*, which can be interpreted as the number of times the average dollar passes through the product market per year. MV is therefore the flow of spending supported by the given stock of money, M. This is equal to the flow of nominal income, PY.

In order to use the equation of exchange to develop a theory of nominal income determination (the "quantity theory"), the determinants of M and V must be identified. Under the assumption that M is effectively determined by the central bank (M is exogenous), the main thrust of research has been to identify the determinants of velocity.[5] These determinants are contained in the money demand function. (For this discussion we will maintain the usual quantity theory assumption that the money stock is exogenous.) The interest rate is a crucial determinant, the effect of which has been seen in the previous section. At one extreme, the interest elasticity of money demand tends toward infinity (the horizontal LM case). We discovered in that case (Figure 6–6B) that P and Y could be increased

---

[5] For example, see Milton Friedman, ed., "The Quantity Theory of Money: A Restatement," *Studies in the Quantity Theory of Money* (Chicago: University of Chicago Press, 1956).

by fiscal policy with no change in the money stock. Velocity had no upper bound.

The other extreme occurs when the interest elasticity of money demand is zero (the vertical LM case). In that case (Figure 6–6A), fiscal policy could not change P or Y as long as the money stock was held constant. Velocity was a constant. In between the extremes velocity varies directly with the interest rate.

Generally, quantity theorists argue that velocity is stable (meaning *predictable*), so that changes in the money stock can be related, in a predictable fashion, to changes in nominal income. Moreover they argue that velocity, the link between the nominal money stock and nominal income, is more stable than the autonomous spending multiplier which links nominal income with nominal autonomous expenditures.

SUMMARY NOTES

1. Increases (decreases) in government expenditures shift the IS curve to the right (left). Increases (decreases) in taxes shift the IS curve to the left (right).
2. Increases (decreases) in the monetary base shift the LM curve to the right (left). Increases (decreases) in the price level shift the LM curve to the left (right).
3. Increases (decreases) in the nominal wage rate shift the AS curve to the left (right). Increases (decreases) in the price level shift the AS curve to the right (left).
4. Consistent with microeconomic markets, the price level is assumed to increase (decrease) in response to excess demand (excess supply) in the product market. The interest rate is assumed to increase (decrease) in response to excess demand (excess supply) in the money market.
5. The existence of (idle) money balances in excess of the amount necessary to finance current transactions provides an initial source of funds to finance an autonomous increase in spending. In equilibrium, current investment spending and any government deficit is financed out of current saving.
6. In the basic model, fiscal policy attains maximum strength when the LM curve is horizontal. Monetary policy attains maximum strength when the LM curve is vertical.
7. The equation of exchange provides an alternative framework in

which the nominal stock of money is linked to nominal income through the velocity of circulation. Velocity varies inversely with money demand (directly with the rate of interest).

APPENDIX A

While the previous discussion of interest rate and income determination makes use of a product market and a money market, alternative approaches are available. One approach makes use of the market in which the current flow of lending and borrowing takes place—the *loanable funds* market. This market serves to channel the saving of the household sector to the business sector (to finance current investment spending) and the government sector (to finance the deficit). In addition, the loanable funds market provides a means by which money holders may reduce their money holdings (by lending) or increase their money holdings (by borrowing).

Inspection of the equilibrium conditions for the product, money, and loanable funds markets will show the interrelationships among them. (The labor market, which by assumption does not clear, can be ignored in this discussion. It does, however, lurk in the background.) Product market equilibrium is defined by the following:

$$Y = C + I + G \qquad (6\text{--}1)$$

This, as we discovered in Chapter 1, is formally equivalent to the following:

$$S = I + (G - T) \qquad (6\text{--}2)$$

While equation (6–2) relates a flow of lending (saving) to the borrowing of the business and government sectors, one other element needs to be added to convert (6–2) into an equilibrium condition for the loanable funds market.

The equation shows one source of funds (current saving) and two uses of funds (business borrowing to buy capital goods and government borrowing to finance the deficit). There is another source (use) of loanable funds which originates in the money market. Households and business firms hold money balances for the reasons discussed in Chapter 4. Should money holders desire a larger or a smaller stock of money balances than they currently hold, they can attempt to reduce such balances by lending the excess, or increase such balances by borrowing in the loanable funds market. In short, the attempt to *change* the stock of money held results in a *flow* of lending or borrowing (dishoarding or hoarding). That flow can be added to the other flows in the loanable funds market with the addition of another assumption. Assume that the discrepancy between money supplied and demanded is cleared in the time period defined by the other flows in the loanable funds market. If S, I, etc. are annual flows, then any discrepancy between M_S/P and M_D/P in the beginning of the year must be cleared by the end of the year. Hence the equilibrium condition in the loanable funds market is:

$$S + (M_S/P - M_D/P) = I + (G - T)$$

Now consider this equilibrium condition together with the equilibrium conditions for the other two markets.

Product market: $Y = C + I + G$
Money market: $M_S/P = M_D/P$

Suppose, for example, that the money market is in equilibrium ($M_S/P = M_D/P$). Then equilibrium in the loanable funds market only requires that $S = I + (G - T)$. But since this is equivalent to $Y = C + I + G$, we have one unnecessary or redundant condition. Two of the three equilibrium conditions would suffice.

Again suppose, for example, that the product market is in equilibrium. This means that $Y = C + I + G$ or that $S = I + (G - T)$. Equilibrium in the loanable funds market requires only that $M_S/P = M_D/P$. Once again, two of the three conditions would suffice. A little further experimentation should convince the reader that equilibrium in any two markets assures equilibrium in the third market.[6]

A macroeconomic model may be constructed in terms of any two of the three markets. The product and money markets are most widely used because the thrust of theory has been to develop hypotheses about the forces that determine the stock of money demanded and the stock of money supplied rather than about the forces that determine hoarding and dishoarding. In other words, modern macroeconomics treats hoarding and dishoarding as a residual after the decisions to demand and supply money are made.

The existence of a substantial body of data relating to the loanable funds market may lead to changes in our approach in the future.

The flow-of-funds accounts capture the transactions made in the

---

[6] The student of general equilibrium theory should recognize this as a rudimentary application of Walras' Law.

loanable funds market and certain of the transactions made in the product market.[7] For example, lending by the household sector to the business sector would be entered on line 29 (Table 2–2) under uses of funds for the household sector and on line 29 under sources of funds for the business sector. The flow of funds should therefore provide a rich source of data for testing hypotheses about each sector's behavior in the loanable funds market. Unfortunately these data have not been tapped to the extent that national income data have. Partly this is due to the newness of the flow-of-funds accounts relative to the national income accounts. More importantly, we lack a generally accepted body of theory that can draw upon the flow-of-funds accounts in the same way that Keynesian theory has drawn upon the national income accounts.

In the context of the model used in this book, changes in the loanable funds market, and thus in the financial section of the flow-of-funds account, result from changes in the saving habits of the household sector, changes in intended real investment by the business sector, changes in the government deficit (whether planned or unplanned), and changes in money demand (supply) relative to money supply (demand). One might, however, develop hypotheses about how behavioral changes *originating* in the loanable funds market affect the rest of the model. The flow-of-funds accounts then become a useful source of data to test those hypotheses.[8]

It may very well be that the renewal of interest in monetary theory during the 1960s will intensify interest in the flow-of-funds accounts and pave the way toward more integrated models of macroeconomic behavior that make use of the loanable funds market.

APPENDIX B

Tradition has dictated the presentation of the basic model in the (i,Y) plane. However, the model can also be displayed in the price-quantity (P,Y) plane, as is the case for microeconomic markets. The IS and LM curves, which determine aggregate demand, can be com-

---

[7] The product market transactions that do not show up in the flow-of-funds accounts include household expenditures on services and nondurables and government expenditures on goods and services. See also Lawrence S. Ritter, *The Flow-of-Funds Accounts: A Framework for Financial Analysis* (New York: New York University, 1968), pp. 25–31.

[8] As a starter, the interested student might examine the articles by Dusenberry, Copeland, Weiler, and O'Leary in the *Flow-of-Funds Approach to Social Accounting* (Princeton: National Bureau of Economic Research, 1962).

FIGURE 6–7
An Alternative View of the Basic Model

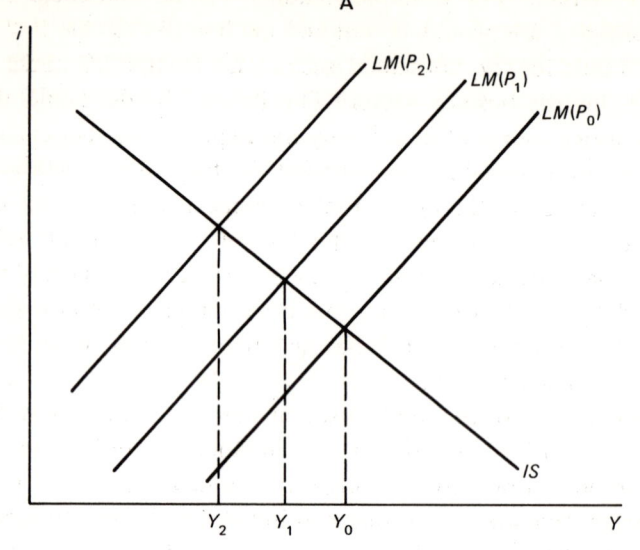

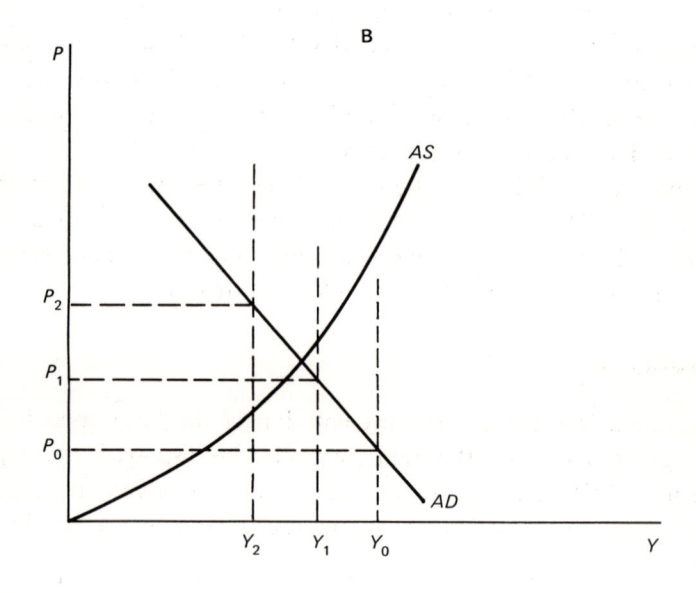

bined to yield a relationship containing P and Y as the only two endogenous variables. This is easily seen graphically. The IS and LM curves are plotted in Figure 6–7A. Three LM curves are shown corresponding to three price levels, where $P_2 > P_1 > P_0$. Intersection with the IS schedule indicates the corresponding levels of aggregate demand, $Y_2 < Y_1 < Y_0$. These (P,Y) combinations are plotted in Figure 6–7B giving us an aggregate demand schedule that varies inversely with the price level.

The aggregate supply schedule slopes upward when plotted against P. Intersection of the aggregate demand (AD) and aggregate supply (AS) curves determines the equilibrium (P,Y) combination. The equilibrium interest rate can then be found by substituting the equilibrium Y into the IS curve (or substituting the equilibrium P and Y into the LM curve) and solving for i.

While the format clearly indicates how aggregate demand and aggregate supply determine the price level, the more familiar format developed thus far will be used throughout the remainder of the book (with a brief exception in Chapter 17).

DISCUSSION QUESTIONS

1. Analyze the effect of a decrease in taxes, with no change in G or B, on the equilibrium price level, interest rate, and income.

2. Suppose the nominal wage rate is completely flexible, but the price level is fixed by government decree. At what employment level does equilibrium take place? What are the effects of an increase in the monetary base with no change in government spending or taxes?

3. Assume that the government decrees that the nominal wage rate must be fully adjusted to reflect changes in the "cost of living." In effect, employers must raise or lower the nominal wage rate by the same percentage as changes in the price level (which is assumed to be flexible in this question). What is the effect of this policy on the real wage rate? If government expenditures are increased, what changes will take place in the price level, interest rate, output, and employment?

4. Experiment with changes in government spending, taxes, and the monetary base (singly or in combination) with the object of reducing unemployment without altering the price level.

7

Stabilization Policy: A First View

WHILE THE MODEL developed in the previous chapters is relatively simple, it does provide the framework within which policy issues can be discussed. In any consideration of policy we need to define goals or objectives of policy, the tools the policy makers can directly manipulate, and the framework within which those tools operate. Our basic model provides the framework. In this chapter we shall discuss the goals of policy, the tools the policy makers can use to accomplish those goals, and some problems in selecting the appropriate policy tools.

THE GOALS OF POLICY

Unemployment

The Employment Act of 1946 specifies one of the more important goals of macroeconomic policy. Specifically, the act requires the federal government to use whatever means it has at its disposal to insure maximum employment. Now maximum employment has not been interpreted to mean zero unemployment. Most industrialized economies such as the U.S. economy will exhibit a certain degree of frictional unemployment. This arises partly because individuals are free to change jobs at will and to move from one section of the country to another. Individuals also, from time to time, change occupations. The switch from one occupation to another is not instantaneous, and for a time there may be an increase in unemployment during the adjustment period. However, this is accompanied by an increase in the number of job openings. If I quit my present job and move to California and then begin to look for a new job, I will be unemployed during the interim. However, I have also created a job vacancy (my old job). In general, an increase in frictional unemployment is accompanied by an increase in the number of job vacancies.

Possible solutions to such unemployment involve more rapid retraining of individuals, greater information so that jobs and job seekers can be matched, or, in the extreme, the state might require individuals to obtain permission before changing jobs. The last option would be unacceptable in a free society, and therefore some frictional unemployment is generally tolerated.

The unemployment with which we are concerned occurs when there is an increase in the number of persons seeking work, but no corresponding increase in the number of available jobs. Such unemployment is said to be cyclical or due to deficient demand. For example, if aggregate demand falls and producers decide to cut back on their output by reducing the number of workers hired, then, given the labor force, there will be an increase in the number unemployed. Full employment in the context of our discussions in this book will be defined to be the absence of cyclical or deficient demand unemployment.

Such unemployment is explicitly treated in our basic model. Given our assumed rigid nominal wage rate and given the state of technology and the size of the labor force, unemployment varies inversely with the level of aggregate demand. Consequently, we shall be able to observe the effects of various policy moves directly on the level of unemployment. All other things being equal, the policy goal is to reduce the level of unemployment (as defined here) as close as possible to zero.

Price Stability

Another policy goal that can be treated within our model is the goal of a stable price level. This goal, together with the previous one, provides us with our first conflict. Given the assumptions of the model, an increase in aggregate demand will, at the same time it lowers the level of unemployment, raise the price level. Hence the goal of a reduction in unemployment and the maintenance of a stable price level are in conflict with each other. In short, there exists a trade-off between these two policy goals.

Inflation and deflation (positive or negative *rates of change* in the price level) occur in this model only during disequilibrium. For example, should there be an increase in the level of aggregate demand, inflation will occur—that is, the price level will rise until a new equilibrium is established. At that new equilibrium the price level will be higher than it was before, but the rate of change in the price level will return to zero. For our purposes we define the price stability objective as a desire to prevent the price level from either rising or falling significantly.

Economic Growth

Since we are dealing with a static model, economic growth is not explicitly included. A growth model is dynamic in character and would involve growth functions for the stock of capital and for the population or the labor force. We will defer a discussion of growth and dynamics to Chapter 15. However, the present model does contain some implications for growth. In particular an increase in the rate of capital formation (increase in investment spending by the business sector net of replacement) will contribute to economic growth. Net investment is a component of aggregate demand in the model, and changes in the model that change net investment spending contain implications for economic growth. Specifically, if the equilibrium of the model changes so as to result in a low rate of investment, presumably this would retard economic growth. If changes occur in the model that increase the rate of investment spending, this would increase the rate of economic growth. Hence, even though we do not treat growth explicitly in the basic model, we can discuss the implications for growth of changes in the model.

The economic growth goal would not necessarily be the maximum rate of economic growth. Any proposal to engage in policy measures that would increase the rate of economic growth would have to consider the implications of such increased growth on, for example, environmental pollution. Furthermore, policies designed to increase growth will, of necessity, divert resources from present consumption to the construction of capital goods. A consumer-oriented society would therefore no doubt opt for a lower rate of economic growth than a society that is not so consumer oriented. In short, we should talk about an optimal rate of economic growth rather than maximum economic growth.

Balance of Payments

Another goal of economic policy that is not explicitly treated in the present model is the goal of balance of payments equilibrium. We will discuss the balance of payments and international economics in more detail in Chapter 14. For now we can briefly describe the balance of payments as consisting of the net balance of two accounts, the *current* account and the *capital* account. The balance of the current account is the difference between the value of currently produced goods and services exported from the United States and the value of currently produced goods and services imported into the United States. The current account balance is also called *net exports* or the *balance of trade*.

U.S. firms and individuals make financial investments (buy securities) and also make direct investments (buy plant and equipment) in foreign countries. Foreigners do the same in the United States. The capital account balance is the net of such foreign capital entering the United States and U.S. capital leaving the United States. The sum of the current account and capital account balances is the balance of payments.[1] Both accounts contain other elements such as U.S. government capital flows and unilateral transfers. We will abstract from these in this chapter but will return to them in Chapter 14.

Given fixed exchange rates between two countries, it is generally assumed that the exports and imports between those countries will be in large part a function of the relative prices of the two countries. For example, should the price of consumer goods rise in the United States relative to the price of consumer goods in the United Kingdom, U.S. residents will buy relatively more goods made in the United Kingdom and residents of the United Kingdom will buy relatively fewer U.S. goods. The current account balance for the United States will experience a decreased surplus or an increased deficit. By assuming that the prices of goods in foreign countries are held constant (that is, exogenous in our model) we can deduce the implications of a

---

[1] Adding the balance of payments to the IS-LM-AS framework presents no particular problems. For an analysis that does just that, see Dwayne Wrightsman, "IS, LM, and External Equilibrium," *American Economic Review*, Vol. 60 (March 1970), pp. 203-8 and Chapter 14 of this book.

changing price level in the United States for the current account balance. To illustrate, should some fiscal policy be implemented that tends to lower the domestic price level, we should expect, all other things constant, that the United States will experience increased exports and decreased imports.

The domestic level of income will also affect the current account balance by affecting imports. As income rises, consumption of both domestic and foreign goods increases. Given the level of total exports, this would decrease net exports. An increase (decrease) in domestic prices and/or income will tend to decrease (increase) net exports.

The capital account balance is assumed to respond to changes in relative interest rates between the United States and other countries. For example, should the rate of return rise in the United Kingdom relative to the United States, U.S. investors would, instead of investing in new plant and equipment domestically, invest in the United Kingdom. This may be accomplished either by buying the securities of firms in the United Kingdom or by buying plant and equipment directly in the United Kingdom. Changes in the rate of interest in our basic model thus have implications for the flow of capital in the capital account.

In short, domestic stabilization policies will produce changes in the price level, income, and in the rate of interest. We can deduce what effects those changes will have upon the current account balance and the capital account balance and consequently upon the total balance of payments, even though we do not explicitly treat the balance of payments in our basic model in this chapter. In this connection we note another possible conflict between goals. A policy that tends to lower the internal rate of interest so as to increase domestic investment and thus increase the rate of economic growth will, at the same time, discourage the inflow of capital (or encourage its outflow). This may worsen our capital account balance and therefore our balance of payments which is in conflict with the goal of equilibrium in the balance of payments.

Role of the Policy Maker

How such conflicts are resolved depends upon the weights that are attached to the various goals by the policy makers. In a democratic society, the preferences of the policy makers, being elected officials, by and large should reflect the preferences of the public. This, of course, may not always be the case. In particular, any given elected official may face conflicting signals from his constituents. In that case, his own preferences may take over in policy formation. Also, changing public attitudes may induce policy makers to change their own preferences from time to time.

As an example, rapid economic growth held almost universal appeal early in the 1960s. By the time the 1970s had arrived, growing antipathy toward economic growth was being experienced. The principal reason for such antipathy is the observed conflict between rapid economic growth and environmental quality.

In addition to these problems, certain of the policy makers are not elected by the populace and therefore their preferences may be independent of the wishes of the populace. The members of the Board of Governors of the Federal Reserve Bank are appointed by the executive branch of the government and are not elected by the population. Actions of the board may, at times, be in conflict with the desires of the population and in conflict with the goals of their elected officials. These problems notwithstanding, policy does get formulated and is implemented, and the economist can play an important role in identifying all of the implications of given policy changes.

THE TOOLS OF POLICY

Policy is generally broken down into two categories: fiscal policy and monetary policy. Fiscal policy involves changes in spending or in taxes induced by the central government. We define *pure fiscal policy* as changes in either government spending or taxes or both, with no accompanying change in the *monetary base*. This requires that changes in spending, for example, be financed by taxes or by borrowing from the private sector. If the federal government increases its spending by a certain amount, and increases the level of taxes by the same amount, this would be a pure fiscal policy operation. Alternatively, if the federal government increases its spending, does not change taxes, but borrows the entire amount of the increase in spending from the private sector, this would be a pure fiscal policy operation. A reduction in spending must be accompanied by an equal reduction in taxes or by a reduction in government borrowing for the fiscal policy to be defined as pure. If the reduction in spending results in a surplus, the surplus must be used to retire outstanding federal government debt held by the private sector.

Similarly, a change in taxes must be used to retire outstanding government debt held by the private sector, in the case of an increase in taxes, or result in an increase in such debt by borrowing from the private sector, in the case of a reduction in taxes. Alternatively, if the change in taxes is accompanied by an equal change in spending it will be a pure fiscal policy operation.

In other words, a change in taxing or spending alone will change the federal deficit, and that change must be effected through borrowing from, or the retirement of debt held by, the private sector in order that the policy be defined as a pure fiscal policy operation.

Monetary policy consists of shifts in the money supply function. Such shifts may be accomplished by changing the monetary base or by changing the money supply multiplier.[2] The operation will be a *pure monetary policy* operation if the change is unaccompanied by changes in spending or taxes of the federal government. There are three major instruments with which the Federal Reserve can accomplish this shift in the money supply function. It may change the monetary base directly by buying or selling government securities from the private sector (open market operations). The monetary base may also be changed by inducing private banks to increase their borrowings from the Federal Reserve Bank. This is accomplished by lowering the interest rate (discount rate) which the Federal Reserve charges member banks for such borrowing. Finally, the Federal Reserve may alter the ratio of required reserves to total deposits. This will change the money supply multiplier and thus shift the money supply function.

A fiscal policy operation accompanied or accommodated by a monetary policy operation will be a mixed policy. As an example let us say that the federal government increases its spending without increasing its tax revenues. It will thus run a larger deficit. If it finances this deficit by selling government securities to the Federal Reserve Bank, the policy operation will be mixed. It will be mixed because the Federal Reserve Bank's purchase of those government securities will increase the monetary base and will shift the money supply function at the same time that the increased government spending adds to aggregate demand. The resulting impact on employment, output, and prices will be the consequence of combined monetary and fiscal

---

[2] The money supply multiplier is the change in the money supply with respect to a unit change in the monetary base. We shall derive its form in Chapter 12. Given the interest rate, it is equal to the parameter α in the money supply function (see Chapter 5).

policy. Under such circumstances it would be difficult to assess which policy produced the major impact on employment and output—the increase in government spending or the rightward shift in the money supply function. In order to plan more effective policy operations it is necessary for us to be able to assess the relative impact of fiscal and monetary policy on the rest of the economy. To assess those relative impacts we need to isolate pure fiscal policy from pure monetary policy and hence the reason for the above definitions.

SOME ILLUSTRATIVE POLICY CHANGES

If we keep in mind the distinction between a pure fiscal policy and a pure monetary policy we can analyze the separate effects of each. This will enable us to select the most appropriate policy, given the particular goals that are specified. To illustrate, we will consider three cases in which certain policy objectives are stated, and then we will look to see which policy—fiscal, monetary, or mixed—will accomplish the specified objective.[3]

For the first case, assume that the policy makers wish to lower the level of unemployment and at the same time wish to raise the interest rate to improve our balance of payments situation by improving net capital flows. The model developed in the previous chapters will enable us to select the most appropriate policy. Consider first an expansive monetary policy with no change in the fiscal policy stance. Suppose that the Federal Reserve Bank expands the monetary base by purchasing government securities from the private sector. This will result in a rightward shift in the money supply function leading to a fall in the rate of interest. The fall in the rate of interest will induce the business sector to expand expenditures on capital equipment, thus raising the level of aggregate demand and consequently the price level. The rising price level induces producers to expand output by hiring more labor. The rising price level also retards the rightward shift in the money supply function. The net effect of such changes is a fall in the rate of interest, an increase in real output, a reduction in unemployment, and an increase in the price level. Such changes are illustrated in Figure 7–1A.

---

[3] For a "real world" illustration of the discussion of goals and the formulation of policy in a Keynesian context, see the Report of the Council of Economic Advisers, *Economic Report of the President* (Washington: U.S. Government Printing Office, 1963), especially "The Effects of a Tax Reduction on Output and Employment," pp. 45–51.

FIGURE 7–1A
Expansive Monetary Policy

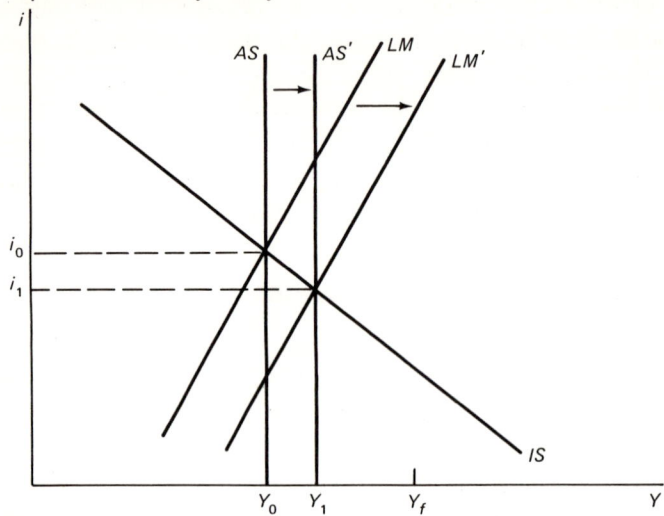

Note that while the expansive monetary policy succeeded in achieving one of the policy objectives—namely, lowering the level of unemployment—it had the opposite effect on the other policy objective. Specifically, the policy resulted in a reduction of the rate of interest, whereas it was desired to increase the rate of interest. On the other hand, consider now an expansive fiscal policy. Suppose that the federal government increases its expenditures on goods and services with no corresponding increase in its tax revenues. Under such circumstances, it will be forced to borrow from the private sector by selling Treasury bonds. At the same time, the increased spending adds to aggregate demand and creates upward pressure on the price level. Producers expand output and hire more labor in response to the rising price level. With increased income, money demand increases; but money supply decreases by virtue of the rising price level. Both effects tend to raise the interest rate. There is some retardation of aggregate demand as private investment spending falls in response to the rising interest rate.

The net effect of the changes is shown in Figure 7–1B. As a consequence of the policy, real output has expanded and unemployment has fallen, consistent with the first goal of policy.[4] The rate of interest

---

[4] In all these examples it would be well to remember that output cannot exceed the full employment level, Y_f.

FIGURE 7–1B
Expansive Fiscal Policy

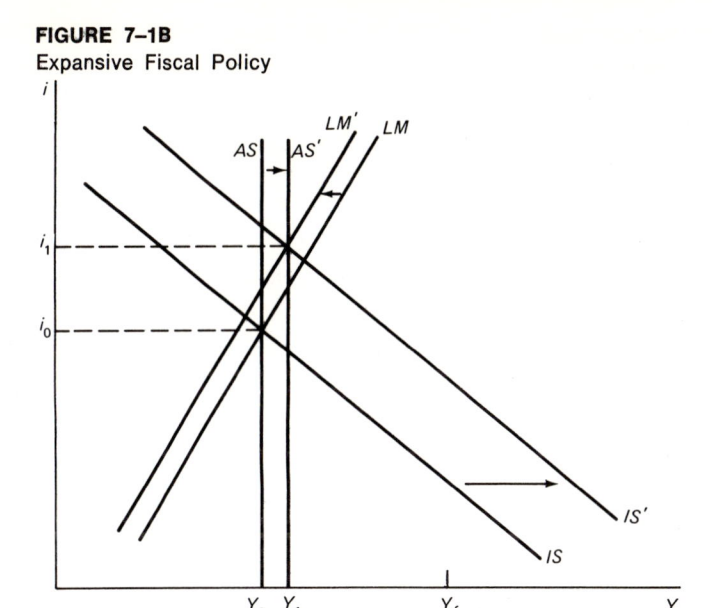

has risen, consistent with the second goal of policy. Consequently, in this circumstance, where the policy makers decided to reduce the level of unemployment and raise the rate of interest to improve our balance of payments situation, the pure fiscal policy could do what a pure monetary policy could not. One other effect requires attention: The price level and income rose under both policy changes. This would make domestic goods more expensive relative to foreign goods and increase our imports, consequently worsening our balance of trade. However in the monetary policy case, the rate of interest falls, and this also worsens the capital account. In the fiscal policy case, the capital account improves, and this offsets (to an undetermined extent) the worsened balance of trade.

As a second case, assume that the policy makers wish to lower the level of unemployment and at the same time wish to expand the rate of economic growth by inducing increases in the rate of private capital formation. The latter may be accomplished by lowering the rate of interest, and this should induce the business sector to increase its spending on investment goods. Considering the same two policies employed before the monetary policy would be the appropriate policy in this case. It was the monetary policy that resulted in a reduction in the level of unemployment and a reduction in the rate of interest, while the fiscal policy had the opposite effect on the rate of interest. Hence, given that the goals consist of a lower level of unemployment and a lower rate of interest, a pure monetary policy can do what the pure fiscal policy cannot.

For a third case, let us say that the policy makers perceive that the rate of economic growth that presently exists is appropriate and that there is equilibrium in the balance of payments. However, assume that the level of unemployment is higher than it should be. The objective, then, is to lower the level of unemployment without altering the rate of interest so as to remain neutral with respect to economic growth and the capital account component of the balance of payments. A fiscal policy by itself or a monetary policy by itself are inappropriate choices, for either policy taken alone will alter the rate of interest. However, it is possible in this case to accomplish the objective of lower unemployment with a constant rate of interest by using a mixed fiscal and monetary policy.

Note that the fiscal policy alone tended to raise the rate of interest and the expansive monetary policy alone tended to lower the rate of interest. Both policies tended to reduce the level of unemployment. Consequently, to keep the interest rate from changing we might use a combination of expansive fiscal and expansive monetary policies. In this way the objective of lower unemployment could be accomplished, yet the upward pressure on the rate of interest due to the fiscal policy would be offset by downward pressure due to the monetary policy.

The policy may be implemented by having the federal government sell the bonds needed to finance the increased spending directly to the Federal Reserve Bank rather than to the private sector. By purchasing the government securities, the Federal Reserve Bank would be expanding the monetary base, thus shifting the money supply function to the right. As income subsequently rises and money demand shifts to the right, the increased money demand will be accommodated by the increased money supply, thus keeping interest rates from rising. This situation is illustrated in Figure 7–2. The increase in government spending shifts the IS curve to the right and the increase in the monetary base shifts the LM curve to the right. Since both actions tend to raise the price level, the aggregate supply curve also moves to the right as producers expand their output.

An important qualification needs to be appended to the analysis of a mixed policy. The results shown in Figure 7–2 apply to a single period. If the government deficit continues into succeeding periods,

FIGURE 7-2
Expansive Mixed Policy

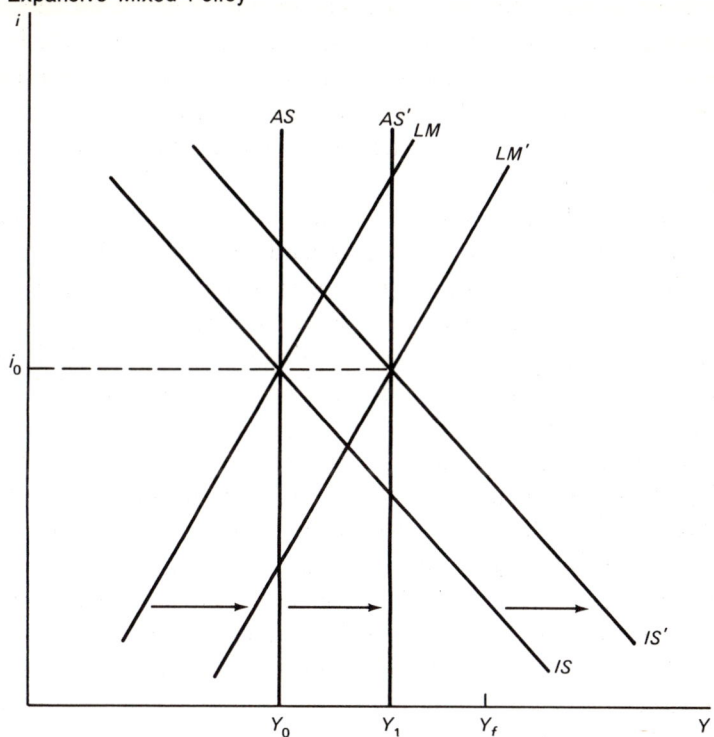

maintaining the IS schedule at *IS'*, two alternative outcomes should be noted.

First, if the Federal Reserve continues to finance the deficit, the monetary base will continue to expand, shifting the LM curve continuously to the right beyond *LM'*. That means the interest rate will subsequently fall and output will rise beyond Y_1 (but, of course, not beyond Y_f).

Second, if the deficit in periods beyond the first period is financed by borrowing from the private sector, both the IS and LM curves will remain where shown (at *IS'* and *LM'*). Thus for the results of Figure 7-2 to hold for the first and succeeding periods, the first period's government deficit must be financed by the Federal Reserve, and the deficits of succeeding periods must be financed by the private sector. This qualification needs to be kept in mind in any discussion of mixed policy.

Assuming that the policy makers know the values of the parameters of the model, and assuming that the policy moves are properly timed, there is no reason why the attack on unemployment could not take place with stable interest rates.[5] As with the other examples, the higher domestic price level and income will stimulate imports and retard exports, thus worsening the net export component of the balance of payments. The policy outlined here is really only neutral with respect to the capital account balance.

Of course, all this is easier said than done. Economists disagree over the proper means of estimating parameters. Even if they could agree, it would be difficult to get opposing political forces to agree on the timing of policy. To make matters worse, the economy is constantly being subject to random disturbances that make forecasting even more difficult. However, if conditions ever become ideal, such a policy could be implemented.

It is possible that a situation could exist in which the parameters of the model are such that one or the other policy has absolutely no effect on either income or the rate of interest. Under such circumstances, the type of policy described above would simply not work. If monetary policy, for example, were completely ineffective, then the policy maker is reduced to using only one tool, fiscal policy. Discussions involving the effectiveness of policy have become increasingly spirited in recent years, and it is appropriate here for us to consider some aspects of the controversy.

RELATIVE IMPACT OF FISCAL AND MONETARY POLICY[6]

There are really two parts to the controversy over the relative impact of fiscal and monetary policy. The first part assumes that both

---

[5] Obtaining estimates of the parameters is the task of the econometrician who will formulate the theory in mathematical terms and use a variety of statistical tools to obtain such estimates. Those students who are interested in the use of econometric models for policy formulation might consult Nancy S. Barrett, *The Theory of Macroeconomic Policy* (Englewood Cliffs, N.J.: Prentice-Hall, Inc., 1972); and Michael K. Evans, *Macroeconomic Activity* (New York: Harper & Row, Publishers, 1969).

[6] The dispute between the advocates of the two types of policy received popular attention with the publication of some research done at the Federal Reserve Bank of Saint Louis. The student may become fully embroiled in the controversy by reading the following selections: Leonall C. Anderson and Jerry L. Jordan, "Monetary and Fiscal Actions: A Test of Their Relative Importance in Economic Stabilization," *Review,* Federal Reserve Bank of Saint Louis, Vol. 50, (November 1968), pp. 11–23; Frank De Leeuw and John Kalchbrenner, "Monetary and Fiscal Actions: A Test of Their Relative Importance in Economic Stabilization—Comment," and Leonall C. Anderson and Jerry L. Jordan, "Reply," *Review,*

fiscal and monetary policy do produce an impact on such variables as the price level, output, the rate of interest, and unemployment. However, participants in this part of the discussion disagree as to the side effects of each policy, and they disagree as to which policy is most appropriate in a given set of circumstances. Some argue that a policy change ought to be neutral—that is, it should not affect the allocation of resources in the economy, but simply stimulate the economy toward a fuller use of its resources. On the other hand, others will argue that a policy should perform more than one function. Not only should the economy be moved closer to full utilization of its resources, but the mix of output should be altered, perhaps away from private goods toward public goods.

Another issue on the first side of the fiscal versus monetary controversy involves the costs of implementing policy. On this issue, some critics of fiscal policy argue that it requires a diversion of too many resources into developing large administrative structures to implement the policy. Monetary policy can be implemented with a smaller administrative apparatus. Also, there exists the issue of who is to bear the brunt of policy, especially in the case of a restrictive policy. Critics of monetary policy tend to argue that a restrictive monetary policy bears most heavily on the housing market. They argue that the demand for mortgage funds, in particular, is sensitive to changes in the rate of interest. This is especially serious in view of the fact that there is widespread agreement that the status of housing in the country could be improved.[7]

Federal Reserve Bank of Saint Louis, Vol. 51 (April 1969), pp. 6–16; Emanual Melichar, "Comments on the Saint Louis Position," *Review*, Federal Reserve Bank of Saint Louis, Vol. 51 (August 1969), pp. 9–14; and Leonall C. Anderson, "Additional Empirical Evidence on the Reverse-Causation Argument," *Review*, Federal Reserve Bank of Saint Louis, Vol. 51 (August 1969), pp. 19–23.

These studies are easier to read than the following study which appeared several years earlier: Milton Friedman and David Meiselman, "The Relative Stability of Monetary Velocity and the Investment Multiplier in the United States, 1897–1958," Commission on Money and Credit, *Stabilization Policies* (Englewood Cliffs, N.J.: Prentice-Hall, Inc., 1963), pp. 165–269. See also the challenges by Albert Ando and Franco Modigliani, "The Relative Stability of Velocity and the Investment Multiplier," and Michael DePrano and Thomas Mayer, "Tests of the Relative Importance of Autonomous Expenditures and Money," *American Economic Review*, Vol. 60 (September 1966), pp. 693–752.

[7] The housing market may not be the only sensitive market. It is often argued that small businesses, lacking bargaining power, feel the effects of a "credit crunch" before large firms do. For results supportive of this hypothesis, see Deane Carson, *The Effect of Tight Money on Small Business Financing*, Small Business Management Research Report, 1962.

In the second part of the fiscal-monetary controversy, and the one with which we will primarily be concerned, it is argued that one or the other of the two policies is completely or almost completely ineffective in altering the level of output in the economy. Underlying the debate are assumptions about the specific parameters in the model. While our model is not completely representative of the viewpoints of the monetarists, on the one hand, or the fiscalists, on the other hand, it does provide a framework within which the controversy can be analyzed. The issues revolve, in the first instance, around assumptions about the interest responsiveness of investment spending, money demand, and money supply. We saw in the last chapter that these differences could be represented by changing the slope of the IS or the LM curve or both. Specifically, a vertical LM curve indicated that monetary policy would affect the level of output in the economy, but that fiscal policy would not. A horizontal LM curve, on the other hand, made monetary policy ineffective in changing the level of output, while fiscal policy under such circumstances assumed maximum effectiveness.

The slopes of the IS and LM schedules follow from the parameters of the underlying structural equations. An expression for the slope of each curve is reproduced below.

IS slope $\quad \Delta i/\Delta Y = -(1-b)/a$
LM slope $\quad \Delta i/\Delta Y = 1/(\beta/Pk + g/k)$

Recall that a is the parameter that links changes in the rate of interest to changes in investment. The parameter g links changes in real money demand to changes in the rate of interest, and β links changes in real money supply to the rate of interest. Disagreement about the values of these three parameters is one source of controversy between the fiscalists and the monetarists.

Monetarists generally assume that both g and β are extremely small, if not zero, in value. It can be seen that if both of those parameters approach zero, the value of the slope of the LM schedule approaches infinity. That is, the LM schedule becomes close to vertical. Under this condition only monetary policy, working through *shifts* in the LM schedule, will change the level of output; fiscal policy will not. Fiscalists, on the other hand, have tended to argue that at relatively low interest rates the parameter g becomes very large, perhaps approaching infinity, so that the demand for money becomes virtually absolute.[8] Here the slope of the LM schedule approaches zero; the curve becomes horizontal. In this case, monetary policy is ineffective in changing the level of output, while fiscal policy becomes quite potent. Note that a vertical LM schedule requires that both β and g be zero, while a horizontal LM schedule requires that *either* β or g become extremely large.

In the case of the IS schedule, many fiscalists tend to argue that investment spending by the business sector is rather insensitive to interest rate changes. This would be especially true under conditions of economic recession or depression, when expectations about future profits are at a low ebb. These arguments would tend to make the parameter a extremely small. If so, the slope of the IS schedule would tend towards infinity; the IS schedule would be almost vertical. Under such circumstances, monetary policy induced shifts in the LM schedule would have little effect on the level of output because while the monetary policy change may produce a substantial impact on the rate of interest, the change in the rate of interest would have little or no effect on aggregate demand. Fiscal policy, on the other hand, becomes increasingly effective in this case. An increase in government expenditures, for example, would expand aggregate demand, increase the price level, and result in expanded output. However, the rising interest rate that accompanies the increased government spending would not retard private investment spending, and therefore the full impact of fiscal policy would be felt on aggregate demand.

On the other hand, if investment spending is very sensitive to the rate of interest, so that the parameter a becomes very large, the IS schedule becomes horizontal. An expansive fiscal policy which resulted in even a slight increase in the rate of interest would produce very large offsetting reductions in investment. The net effect on output would be negligible. An expansive monetary policy, however, would produce a large effect on the level of output because even a modest increase in the monetary base, producing a modest decrease in interest rates, would result in a substantial increase in investment spending by the business sector.

A priori arguments for or against these conditions can be advanced,

---

[8] This case is often called the "Keynesian Case" or the "liquidity trap." However, while Keynes introduced the idea as a theoretical possibility, he dismissed its practical significance. Nevertheless, his chief interpreter has suggested that the liquidity trap no doubt played a part in the depression in the 1930s. See Alvin H. Hansen, *A Guide to Keynes* (New York: McGraw-Hill Book Co., Inc., 1953), p. 132.

but in the final analysis the questions are empirical in nature. This does not mean that it is possible simply to go out and accumulate the appropriate data and measure the values of the parameters in question. The model must be specified to the satisfaction of all concerned. Our basic model has only one channel for monetary policy. Changes in monetary policy produce changes in the rate of interest which produce changes in investment, with subsequent changes in aggregate demand, output, prices, and so on. However, most monetarists would argue that this is only one possible channel of monetary policy, and many would also argue that this is the least important one. On the other hand, some fiscalists might disagree with our definition of a pure fiscal policy. They might argue that the financing of a deficit through the creation of new money is, by definition, part of a fiscal policy operation.[9]

Beside the controversy over the role of the interest rate and the nature of the transmission mechanism (the means by which money affects the economy), other issues divide the fiscalists and monetarists.[10] Generally, monetarists believe that *all* prices (including nominal wage rates) are flexible. A consequence of complete flexibility in our basic model is that the economy tends toward equilibrium at full employment. Fiscalists are more likely to assume some price or wage rigidity that prevents markets from clearing at the full-employment level. Indeed, Milton Friedman has characterized monetarists as those who assume that Y is fixed and fiscalists (or Keynesians) as those who assume P is fixed.[11]

In a monetarist world of complete price flexibility, equilibrium aggregate output and employment is determined by the system of supply and demand equations that describe the microeconomic product and factor markets. Changes in the aggregate nominal money stock affect the overall price level (as the equation of exchange, $MV = PY$, indicates when Y is fixed). Changes in government spending or taxes do not change aggregate output, but only its distribution among different kinds of goods and services.

---

[9] W. Lewis, " 'Money is Everything' Economics—A Tempest in a Teapot," *Conference Board Record,* Vol. 6 (April 1969), pp. 32–35 takes this position. The distinction receives considerable attention from David I. Fand, "Some Issues in Monetary Economics," *Banca Nazionale del Lavoro, Quarterly Review,* Vol. 32 (September 1969), pp. 215–47.

[10] See Leonall C. Andersen, "The State of the Monetarist Debate," *Review,* Federal Reserve Bank of Saint Louis, Vol. 55 (September 1973), pp. 2–8.

[11] Milton Friedman, "A Theoretical Framework for Monetary Analysis," *Journal of Political Economy,* Vol. 78 (March/April 1970), pp. 193–238.

In fact, fiscal measures do not even affect the overall price level, unless accommodated by changes in the money stock or velocity. On the other hand, monetary policy, to the extent it changes the nominal money stock, affects the price level and thus all nominal values such as nominal income and the nominal wage rate.

The behavior of households and business firms even determines the value of the *real* money stock. The best that the monetary authority can do is change the nominal money stock. If technology, the size of the labor force, preferences of households, etc. have not changed, the percent change in the price level will be equal to the percent change in the nominal money stock, and the real money stock will be unchanged.

These issues will surface again in the book, especially in Chapters 13 and 16.

SUMMARY NOTES

1. The generally recognized goals of policy include low unemployment, stable prices, acceptable growth, and balance of payments equilibrium.
2. Pure fiscal policy involves changes in government spending or taxes, with no change in the monetary base. Pure monetary policy involves changes in the monetary base, with no accompanying change in government spending or taxes.
3. In the basic model, the relative strengths of fiscal and monetary policy depend on the relative slopes of the IS and LM curves.

DISCUSSION QUESTIONS

1. Define "high employment," "reasonable price stability," "acceptable balance of payments equilibrium," and "sustainable economic growth." On a scale from 0 to 9, assign priorities to each goal (9 is the highest and 0 is the lowest). Add and rank any additional macroeconomic goals and design a set of fiscal and/or monetary policies that will accomplish your objectives.

2. With respect to question 1, are there any political leaders you know of whose programs conform closely to yours? If not, how would you, as a professional economist, go about gaining political support for your program?

3. The response of the business sector to changes in the price level is based upon the assumption that firms seek to maximize profits. Drop that assumption and substitute some alternative motive to behavior. Now analyze the effects of an increase in government spending, given your alternative assumption about firm behavior.

4. The consumption function is a key relationship in the basic model. Test its validity by obtaining annual data on real consumption and real disposable income for the last ten years. Plot the consumption-disposable income combination for each year on a graph, with consumption on the vertical axis and disposable income on the horizontal axis. Does the result conform to the theoretical consumption function? Now plot the data for the years 1941–1949. What happened?

part three

FURTHER SECTOR ANALYSIS

8

Consumption

THE ABSOLUTE INCOME HYPOTHESIS OF THE BASIC MODEL

THE consumption function used in the basic model is essentially the same as that introduced by Keynes in 1936. Specifically, current consumption was made a function of current disposable income. The hypothesis contained in this function is often referred to as the *absolute income hypothesis,* because consumption depends upon the absolute level of disposable income. The hypothesis has a basic appeal because it is simple and because it is consistent with common sense. Surely it can be argued that one's current expenditures on consumer goods are determined principally by one's current level of after tax income. However, the real test of the hypothesis is its ability to explain and predict consumption expenditures, as compared with the power of explanation and prediction of alternative hypotheses.

At first glance, the absolute income hypothesis appears to be a very powerful explanatory device. Consider the scatter diagram in Figure 8–1. Current consumption expenditures are plotted on the vertical axis, and current disposable income is plotted on the horizontal axis. The data are annual, covering the period from 1950 to 1969, and are expressed in real terms consistent with the model presented in Chapter 3. We have drawn a linear or straight-line consumption function (whose equation is $C = 4.4 + .90Y_D$) through the scatter of data points.[1] The scatter of points is fairly close to the line for the

---
[1] The student who has forgotten, or is not familiar with, statistical terminology might find it beneficial to read the appendix to this chapter.

114   Macroeconomic Theory

FIGURE 8-1
Consumption Function, 1950–1969

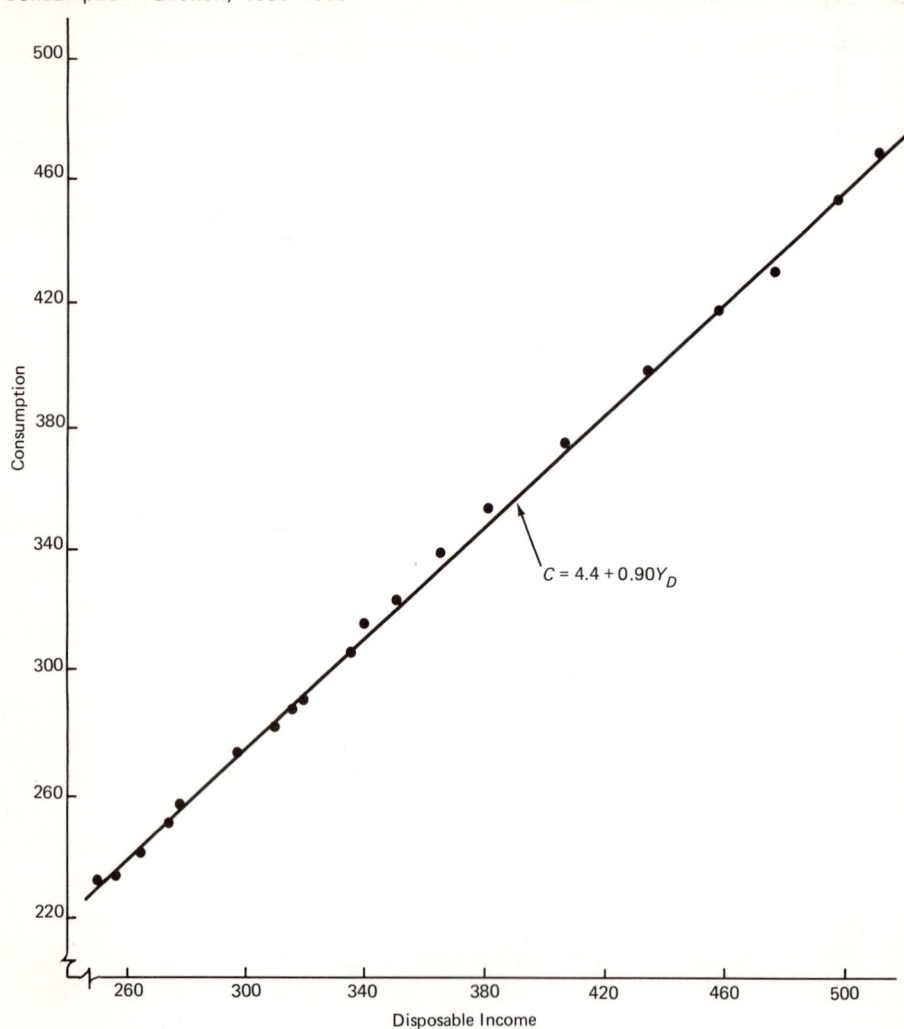

$C = 4.4 + 0.90Y_D$

Source: *Economic Report of the President, 1974.*

entire period. It would seem from this diagram that the absolute income hypothesis stands on fairly firm ground.

However, Figure 8-2 demonstrates the ability of the absolute income hypothesis to predict. The same data for the 1950s and 1960s have been plotted in the diagram, but now two consumption functions were fitted to the data. One was fitted to the data for the whole 1950–1969 period, and the other was fitted to the data for the 1960–1969 period. The equation for the latter period is

FIGURE 8-2
Consumption Functions, 1950–1969

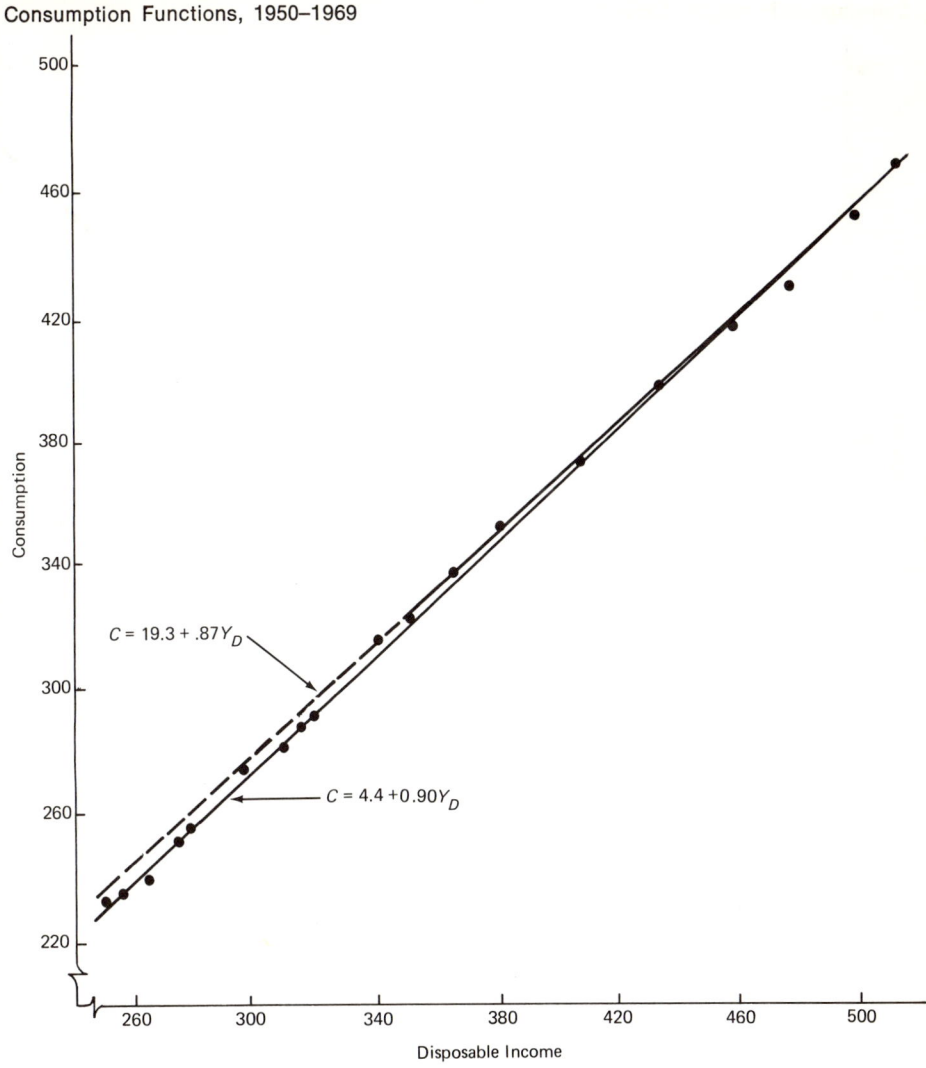

Source: Figure 8-1.

$C = 19.3 + .87 Y_D$. The dashed portion of the latter curve is an extrapolation of that curve to the data period not covered by the curve. Specifically, the consumption function fitted to the 1960s data is extrapolated backward to the 1950s. Note that the two curves do not coincide, and furthermore the scatter of data points around the extrapolated portion of the 1960–1969 curve is not as close as it is for the solid portion. Clearly that consumption function performs less well as a predictive device than as an explanatory device.

Two other characteristics might be mentioned. First, there is an apparent upward shift in the consumption function from the 1950s to the 1960s. Note that the extrapolated portion of the 1960s curve lies above the data for the 1950s. The intercept is 19.3 for the 1960s compared with 4.4 for the full period. Second, the 1960s curve in Figure 8–2 has a more shallow slope than the curve plotted for the entire period (0.87 compared with 0.90). The consumption function appears to have drifted upward over time, and there seems to be a discrepancy between a curve fitted to data over a short period of time (the short run) and a curve fitted to data over a long period of time (the long run).

These empirical problems and others provided considerable impetus to research on the consumption function in the post–World War II period. In fact, the absolute income hypothesis proved to be a particularly poor predictive device in the period immediately following World War II. Disposable income *fell* in the 1944–47 period, but consumption *rose*.

Various reasons might be advanced for the inadequate performance of the hypothesis. For one thing, the income concept used in the model may be incorrect or too simple. In other words, some income measure other than current disposable income might be more appropriate. The function itself might be too simple in the sense that it does not contain a sufficient number of explanatory variables. Variables that have been omitted and should be included might be the interest rate and wealth. Both of these variables in various forms have been suggested for inclusion in the consumption function by various writers. In the remainder of this chapter we shall survey some of the alternative income concepts that have been suggested and also discuss how interest rates and wealth might enter into the consumption function. At the conclusion we shall also examine some of the empirical evidence that bears on the issues raised.

ALTERNATIVE INCOME CONCEPTS

The Relative Income Hypothesis

The relative income hypothesis, introduced by James Duesenberry, attempted to deal with two problems.[2] First, consumption functions

---

[2] James S. Duesenberry, *Income, Saving, and the Theory of Consumer Behavior* (Cambridge, Mass.: Harvard University Press, 1949). A similar approach was introduced independently by Franco Modigliani in "Fluctuations in the Savings-

fitted to time series data were inadequate in explaining the consumption patterns between different income groups. Time series consumption functions tended to be steeper than cross-section functions. Second, there was an observed secular upward drift in the aggregate consumption function, a problem we noted earlier. If the consumption function passes through the origin—that is, the function passes through the point of zero income and zero consumption—then the average propensity to consume (the ratio of consumption to disposable income) will be the same as the marginal propensity to consume (the ratio of *changes* in consumption to *changes* in disposable income). If the consumption function has a positive intercept (at zero disposable income there is some positive consumption), then the average propensity to consume will be greater than the marginal propensity to consume. The implication of the latter type of consumption function is that as income rises and the marginal propensity to consume remains constant, the average propensity to consume will fall.

However, in 1946 Simon Kuznets introduced evidence dating back to the U.S. Civil War that the average propensity to save (and also the average propensity to consume) was virtually constant for the entire period of time under study.[3] On the other hand, a study by Dorothy Brady and Rose Friedman in 1947 using budget study data of households indicated that the marginal propensity to consume was less than the average propensity to consume.[4] Clearly, therefore, there appeared to be a discrepancy between the short-run or cross-section consumption function and the long-run consumption function.

The relative income hypothesis attempts to reconcile this discrepancy by making current consumption expenditures depend not on the absolute level of current disposable income alone, but on current disposable income relative to some ideal or customary level of income. The application to aggregate time series data can be summarized as follows: Aggregate consumption expenditures depend not only on the current level of disposable income, but also on the level of disposable income relative to the previous highest peak level of disposable income attained by the community. If income is rising and above the previous

---

Income Ratio: A Problem in Economic Forecasting," *Studies in Income and Wealth,* Vol. 11 (New York: National Bureau of Economic Research, Inc., 1949).

[3] Simon Kuznets, *National Product Since 1869* (New York: National Bureau of Economic Research, Inc., 1946).

[4] Dorothy S. Brady and Rose D. Friedman, "Savings and the Income Distribution," *Conference on Research in Income and Wealth,* Vol. 10 (New York: National Bureau of Economic Research, Inc., 1947).

118 *Macroeconomic Theory*

high peak, then there is no difference between current disposable income and the previous peak income, and consumption can be simply expressed as a function of current disposable income. However, when income falls below the previous peak, a discrepancy appears between current income and the previous peak income, and current consumption cannot be explained by current income alone. The principle can be illustrated by reference to Figure 8–3.

FIGURE 8–3
The Relative Income Hypothesis

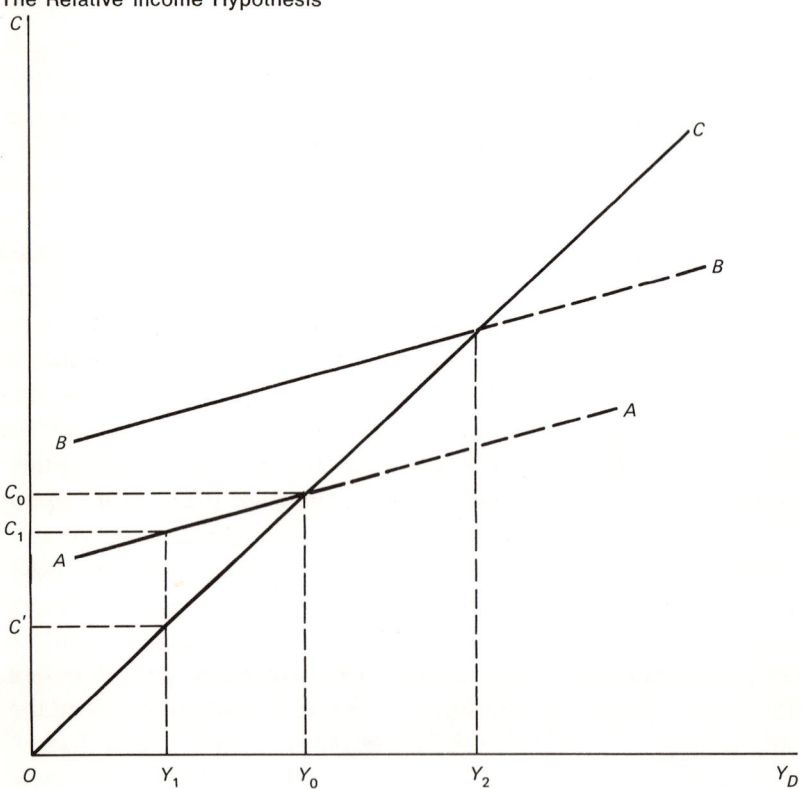

The long-run consumption function in Figure 8–3 is the line segment OC. Suppose the community's income was Y_0, an all-time high. Current consumption expenditures would then be C_0. Now suppose that current income falls from Y_0 to Y_1. According to the relative income hypothesis, consumption would not fall to C', but rather would fall to C_1 along the line segment AA. When income again rises, consumption will rise along line AA until the previous peak income Y_0 is once again reached. Thereafter, further increases in income will cause consumption to rise along the line segment OC. Should income again fall some time in the future, say after having reached income level Y_2, consumption will decline, but along line segment BB rather than along line OC. Thus, the model is consistent with both the shallow consumption functions found from short-run or cross-section data and the steeper consumption function found from long-run data. Note that the long-run function passes through the origin so that the marginal propensity to consume and the average propensity to consume are equal. The short-run functions, on the other hand, would exhibit a marginal propensity to consume that is lower than the average propensity to consume. Moreover, the model would seem to explain the ratchet-like upward drift in short-run consumption functions over time.

The basic rationale behind using previous peak income is that once families become accustomed to a higher standard of living they are willing to give this up in the face of income decreases only reluctantly. Thus, when income falls, consumption falls, but not by as much as it had previously risen. A basic criticism of this type of model is that it appears to be a statistical artifact constructed to fit the peculiarities of the data. In short, the model is not thoroughly grounded in the traditional theory of consumer behavior.

Different approaches have been advanced that take as the starting point the assumption that households maximize utility, with respect to both present and future consumption. In other words, the purpose of household activity is assumed to be consumption. Total utility for the individual or the household is a function of present and future consumption. That utility function is then maximized, subject to the constraint imposed by the household's stock of wealth and its present and future expected income streams. Two major contributions to the literature have been developed from this starting point: the permanent income hypothesis introduced by Milton Friedman and the life-cycle hypothesis introduced by Albert Ando and Franco Modigliani.[5]

---

[5] Milton Friedman, *A Theory of the Consumption Function* (New York: National Bureau of Economic Research, Inc., 1955). Albert Ando and Franco Modigliani, "The 'Life-Cycle' Hypothesis of Saving: Aggregate Implications and Tests," *American Economic Review,* Vol. 53 (March 1963), pp. 55–84. Also see Franco Modigliani and Richard E. Brumberg, "Utility Analysis and the Consumption Function; An Interpretation of Cross-Section Data," in K. K. Kurihara, ed., *Post-Keynesian Economics* (New Brunswick, N.J.: Rutgers University Press, 1954).

The Permanent Income Hypothesis

The central thrust of Friedman's theory is that planned or permanent consumption is proportional to expected or permanent income, where k (see below) is the factor of proportionality. Permanent income itself is dependent upon the individual's stock of wealth and the rate of interest. Permanent income can be viewed as the annual flow of income generated by the individual's estimated stock of wealth at a rate equal to the rate of interest. Alternatively, it is the annual flow of resources that could be spent by the individual without disturbing his estimated stock of wealth. Both permanent income and permanent consumption differ from measured income and consumption by amounts that Friedman calls transitory income and transitory consumption. Current measured consumption (C) is the sum of transitory consumption (C^T) and permanent consumption (C^P), and current measured income (Y) is the sum of transitory income (Y^T) and permanent income (Y^P). The relationships are summarized as follows:

$$C \equiv C^P + C^T$$
$$Y \equiv Y^P + Y^T$$
$$C^P = kY^P$$

Further, Friedman assumes that there is no systematic relationship or correlation between permanent income and transitory income, between permanent consumption and transitory consumption, and between transitory consumption and transitory income. Changes in income that are believed to be temporary do not cause the individual to revise his estimates of permanent income. Moreover, unexpected or transitory changes in consumption spending cause no alteration or modification in permanent consumption expenditures, and finally the marginal propensity to consume out of transitory income is zero. The difficulties with prediction and explanation in empirical studies of the consumption function lay in the fact that we observe relationships between measured income and measured consumption, whereas the relationship we should be observing is between permanent income and permanent consumption.

For example, in Figure 8–4 the permanent consumption function is plotted. Note that the function goes through the origin, consistent with Friedman's hypothesis that permanent consumption is proportional to permanent income. Thus, along the permanent function, the marginal and average propensities to consume are equal. Now

FIGURE 8–4
The Permanent Income Consumption Function

$$C^P = kY^P$$

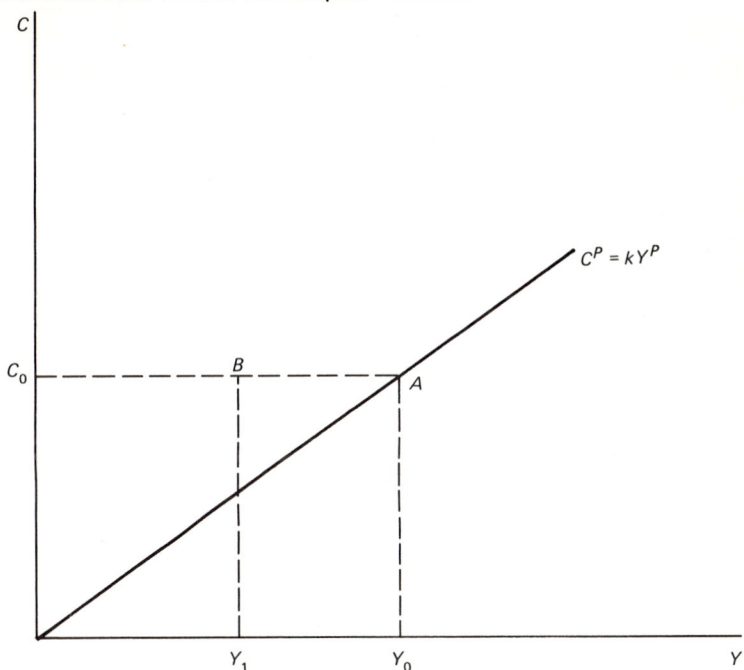

suppose income falls from Y_0 to Y_1, and households perceive this fall in income to be transitory with no change in permanent income. Since there is no correlation, by assumption, between transitory consumption and transitory income and since permanent consumption has not changed because permanent income has not changed, measured consumption will therefore not change. Thus, with the fall in measured income from Y_0 to Y_1, measured consumption remains constant at C_0. The observed data points which result from this would be points A and B. If we were to fit a consumption curve to these and similar data points, we would not be getting an estimate of the "true" consumption function.

One problem, however, is that both permanent consumption and permanent income are not directly measurable. In an attempt to rectify this situation, Friedman has also constructed a model of permanent income determination. On the grounds that our expectations of the future may be largely based upon present and past experience, he has defined permanent income, for empirical purposes, as simply a weighted average of present and past measured incomes. Estimates of permanent income of this type have been used by Friedman and others, not only in studies of the consumption function, but in studies of money demand and investment.

As in the case of the relative income hypothesis, criticism may be levied at the permanent income hypothesis. The permanent income hypothesis comes pretty close to being incapable of refutation. Since the permanent components of the theory are not directly observable, proxies have to be developed to measure them. There is, of course, no way of knowing whether the proxies are good measures of the permanent concepts. Moreover, the proxies themselves may be no more than statistical artifacts. Friedman's statistical definition of permanent income leads to a consumption function that is also consistent with a theory that says that current consumption is a cumulative response to present and past income, with expectations having nothing to do with it.

The use of present and past values of measured income in determining permanent income also violates one of the assumptions made by Friedman. Specifically, since measured income includes both permanent and transitory components and since we use measured income in determining permanent income, then it can no longer be argued that there is no correlation between transitory income and permanent income. Statistical difficulties notwithstanding, the permanent income hypothesis made a major impact on the theory of the consumption function.

The Life-Cycle Hypothesis

The life-cycle hypothesis of Ando and Modigliani also takes individual or household utility maximizing behavior as its starting point. On that assumption, Ando and Modigliani derive a consumption function that makes current consumption proportional to current resources. Current resources, in turn, are defined to be the sum of the previous period's stock of wealth, the current flow of income, and the present value of expected future labor earnings over the remainder of the individual's lifetime. As in the permanent income hypothesis, some elements in the life-cycle hypothesis are not measurable. In particular, the present value of expected future labor earnings is not an observable variable.

In applying the model to time series aggregate data, Ando and

Modigliani make the assumption that expected income can be approximated by current income (specifically that expected income is proportional to current income), so that their aggregate consumption equation makes current measured consumption a linear function of current measured income and the previous period's stock of wealth. Like the permanent income hypothesis, the life-cycle hypothesis (or its empirical counterpart) suffers from statistical difficulties. The treatment of expected income is not altogether satisfactory. It would be preferable to be able to measure expected income. However, until we are able to do so, empiricists will have to remain uncomfortable with statistical approximations.

THE ROLE OF THE INTEREST RATE

Although income has received the greatest recent attention as a determinant of aggregate consumption expenditures, other variables have been considered from time to time. One of these is the interest rate. In fact, the interest rate was considered to be the prime determinant of aggregate saving, and therefore aggregate consumption, long before Keynes introduced income into the function. In classical equilibrium analysis, the economy was assumed to be operating at the full-employment level of income. The choice that households were assumed to face was the allocation of income between present and future consumption (between present consumption and saving). The interest rate, acting as the exchange rate between the present and future, determined how much income was consumed in the present and how much was saved.

However, in looking at the effect of interest rate changes on present consumption, two effects must be carefully distinguished. The first, and the one that concerned the classical economist, is the substitution effect. Interest may be considered the price of present consumption in terms of future consumption. If, for example, I consume \$$x$ today, and if the annual interest rate is represented by i, then to consume those \$$x$ today I must give up consumption equivalent to \$$x(1+i)$ one year from now, or \$$x(1+i)^2$ two years from now and so on. In other words, if the interest rate were 5 percent, then to consume a dollar today, I must give up \$1.05 worth of consumption a year from now.

As the interest rate rises, present consumption becomes more expensive in terms of future consumption. In the foregoing example, if the interest rate rose to 7 percent, a dollar's worth of consumption today would cost me $1.07 one year from now. If the theory of downward sloping demand curves holds, then as the price of present consumption rises I will *consume less* in the present and *save more* in the present so as to consume more in the future. I will shift my consumption expenditures from the present to the future. The implication, then, is that the interest rate has an inverse effect on present consumption.

A second major effect must also be considered—the income effect. Implicit in the discussion of the substitution effect is the assumption of fixed disposable income. However, higher interest rates increase the individual's disposable income. In other words, if I have some accumulated savings (in interest-earning form such as a savings account) and the interest rate increases, then the income I receive from interest payments will also increase. Now if the marginal propensity to consume out of interest income is greater than zero, an increase in the interest rate should increase both present and future consumption and present saving. In other words, if the interest rate goes up, my accumulated past savings will now pay a higher interest income to me, and I should allocate a portion of that to present consumption and a portion to savings which will provide me with a higher future consumption. Thus, the income effect implies that changes in the interest rate and changes in present consumption will be positively correlated.

Another way of looking at the income effect is to note that many savers accumulate to spend, in the future, a specific or fixed sum. For example, a family might save to purchase an automobile that is expected to cost $3,000. Further, they may save at a rate intended to reach that goal of $3,000 in a fixed period of time, say two years. An increase in the interest rate will permit them to reach the goal in two years, while saving less than they had been previously saving. If, out of their given disposable income, they save less, they will consume more. Again, the implication is that the increase in the interest rate will be accompanied by an increase in present consumption.

Whether the income effect or the substitution effect dominates the relationship is an empirical question that must be answered by recourse to the data. Indeed, the two effects may wash each other out, so that for all practical purposes, we might be free in ignoring the effect of the interest rate on consumption.

Furthermore, the effect of the interest rate may be disguised by focusing on total consumption rather than its components. The interest rate may produce a substantial impact on consumer spending on durable goods, but may have virtually no effect on consumer spending on services. This would occur if consumers make a distinction between opportunity cost and cash payments. Interest represents the opportunity cost of present consumption in terms of future consumption, but the consumer may simply ignore this. On the other hand, if a higher interest rate means that he has to pay out higher interest charges on some good, the purchase of which is financed by an installment plan, then he may respond to the higher interest charge. In the case of consumer durables, which are financed in many cases by installment contracts, an increase in the interest rate informs the consumer that he will have to make larger cash payments out of his present and future income in order to finance the purchase of the good. If he considers the interest cost to be part of the price of the product, he may reduce his consumption of that product. Thus, the interest rate and the purchase of consumer durables will be inversely related. On the other hand, consumer services are generally not financed over time, but are usually paid for in the period in which they are purchased. An increase in the interest rate still makes the purchase of those services more expensive in terms of future goods, but the consumer may tend to ignore this opportunity cost, and the relationship between the interest rate and the purchase of consumer services may be nonexistent. Some of the empirical studies discussed later in this chapter will shed light on this issue.

THE ROLE OF WEALTH

Wealth has already been introduced as a determinant of consumption in connection with our discussion of the work by Friedman and Ando and Modigliani. Permanent income, as defined by Friedman, is the flow of income from the individual's estimated stock of wealth. We could just as well substitute into the Friedman consumption function, in place of permanent income, the rate of interest and the estimated stock of wealth. That would make permanent consumption proportional to the product of the interest rate and the stock of wealth, which is identical to saying that permanent consumption is proportional to permanent income.

The approach taken by Ando and Modigliani retains wealth in their empirical consumption function, and they obtain estimates of the propensity to consume out of the existing stock of wealth as well as current income.

Wealth has also been used to explain one of the issues dealt with in the relative income hypothesis—namely, the discrepancy in consumption habits between different income groups. James Tobin has argued that the discrepancy could be explained by the different holdings of financial assets that different income groups (represented by Negroes and whites) have.[6] Moreover, he concluded that such assets, together with absolute income, predicted better than the relative income hypothesis.

However, even before modern refinements in the consumption function were made, wealth was introduced into the consumption function by Pigou.[7] Pigou discussed the idea in order to bring attention to a mechanism by which the economy would tend toward full-employment equilibrium in the face of a temporary disturbance. He argued that should there be a fall in some components of aggregate demand such that the economy fell below full employment, the price level would also fall. As the price level fell, the real value of wealth holdings by individuals would increase. More specifically, financial assets that are stated in fixed nominal terms increase in purchasing power as the price level of commodities falls. This, according to Pigou, would lead to an increase in real consumption expenditures and thus restore aggregate demand to the full-employment level.

More recently, Don Patinkin has zeroed in on one component of the stock of wealth, the stock of real money balances. As in the case of the "Pigou effect," Patinkin argues that the stock of nominal money balances in the economy is determined by the monetary authority. Any change in the price level changes the real value of that money stock and thus alters consumption expenditures. A fall in the price level increases real money balances and therefore increases consumption expenditures, and a rise in the price level has the opposite effect.

As is true of many other economic variables, there is no widespread agreement about what to include in the definition of wealth, or at least financial wealth. Generally, private assets such as corporate bonds are not included because these are offset by liabilities within the private sector. Private assets and liabilities cancel out when we aggregate the balance sheet of the private sector. Notwithstanding this, some writers include both components of money (currency and demand deposits)

---

[6] James Tobin, "Relative Income, Absolute Income, and Savings," *Money, Trade, and Economic Growth: Essays in Honor of John H. Williams* (New York: The Macmillan Co., 1951).

[7] A. C. Pigou, "The Classical Stationary State," *Economic Journal*, Vol. 53 (December 1943), pp. 343–51.

in the definition of wealth, even though demand deposits are offset by the liability of the private banking system.

Federal Reserve Notes (currency) and U.S. government securities are often included in the net wealth of the private sector, on the grounds that these have no offsetting private liability. The use of the latter asset requires that the private sector doesn't fully treat (implicitly) the present value of future tax liabilities to pay off those securities as a private liability.

Other variables may, of course, be suggested for inclusion in the consumption function. However income, the interest rate, and wealth have dominated most of the work in the area. The quantitative importance of each is a subject to which we now turn.

RELATED EMPIRICAL STUDIES

Empirical work on the consumption function is overwhelming in its sheer volume. The most we can hope to do here is sample the studies with the intent of answering three questions:

1. Does the marginal propensity to consume out of income fall between 0 and 1, as assumed in the theory of consumer behavior?
2. Is the interest rate a significant determinant of consumption and is the relationship between the two direct or inverse?
3. Is wealth, however measured, a significant determinant of aggregate consumption?

With respect to the first question, the evidence is quite clear that the marginal propensity to consume is positive, but less than 1, whether income is defined as measured or permanent. All the studies listed in Table 8–1 agree on this. For Duesenberry's relative income hypothesis, the long-run MPC is between 0.93 and 0.95. The short-run MPC—with current income falling, for example, 10 percent below the previous peak income—is about 0.74.

The studies by Hamburger and Zellner also make a distinction between the short and long run, but in a different sense than that assumed by the relative income hypothesis.[8] In both studies, current consumption is a cumulative response to current and past income. In Zellner's study, a $1 change in income induces a $0.375 change

---

[8] Michael J. Hamburger, "Interest Rates and the Demand for Consumer Durable Goods," *American Economic Review,* Vol. 57 (December 1967), pp. 1131–53. Arnold Zellner, "The Short-Run Consumption Function," *Econometrica,* Vol. 25 (October 1957), pp. 552–67.

TABLE 8-1
Empirical Evidence on the Consumption Function

Author(s)	Period Covered	MPC	Wealth Coefficient	Interest Elasticity
Ando-Modigliani	1929–1959	0.52–0.60	0.07	
Hamburger*	1953–1964			
Short run		0.257		−0.85
Long run†		0.71		−2.34
Patinkin	1947–1958	0.447	0.094	
Wright	1929–1959	0.44	0.067	−0.022
Zellner	1947–1955			
Short run		0.375	0.219	
Long run†		0.73	0.42	

* Automobile expenditures only.

† Computed by author from results presented in the study. The short-run elasticity is generally the first quarter's response, where the full response is spread out over many quarters. The full response is the long-run elasticity.

Source: Ando and Modigliani, " 'Life-Cycle' Hypotheses"; Michael J. Hamburger, "Interest Rates"; Don Patinkin, *Money, Interest, and Prices;* Colin Wright, "Some Evidence on the Interest Elasticity of Consumption"; Arnold Zellner, "Short-Run Consumption Function."

in consumption in the current quarter and ultimately a total change in consumption of $0.73. A similar interpretation applies to the Hamburger study, except that his results presented in the table are of expenditures on automobiles only.

The estimated MPCs shown for Ando and Modigliani, Wright, and Patinkin may be interpreted as long run MPCs.[9]

The studies by Hamburger and Wright also provide evidence on the interest elasticity of consumption expenditures. Wright, in examining the substitution effect only, found that a 1 percent increase in the interest rate would induce a reduction in aggregate consumption of 0.022 percent. This may not seem like much until we recognize that a 1 percent change in the interest rate is a small absolute change (for example, from 5.00 percent to 5.05 percent) and that a 0.022 percent change in consumption is a large absolute change (for example, from $800 billion to $799.82 billion, a $180 *million* change).

Hamburger found that consumer durable expenditures were even more sensitive to interest rate changes. The short-run interest elasticity of automobile expenditures was −0.85 and the long-run elasticity was −2.34. On the other hand, a more recent study by Warren Weber concluded that while the interest rate exerts an important influence

---

[9] Ando and Modigliani, " 'Life-Cycle' Hypothesis"; Don Patinkin, *Money, Interest, and Prices,* 2d ed. (New York: Harper and Row, Publishers, 1965); and Colin Wright, "Some Evidence on the Interest Elasticity of Consumption," *American Economic Review,* Vol. 57 (September 1967), pp. 850–55.

on consumer behavior, the substitution effect is swamped by the income effect.[10] On that basis, he concludes that the gross relationship between consumption and the interest rate is direct rather than inverse. The interest rate question, then, is still largely unresolved. Perhaps future research will provide a more definitive answer.

Wealth, in the consumption function, has faired better than the interest rate. Most studies conclude that wealth is a significant determinant of consumption expenditures. Of the studies listed in Table 8–1, the ones by Ando and Modigliani, Patinkin, and Wright measured wealth by the net worth of the private sector (private assets less private liabilities), while Zellner used the liquid assets of the private sector only (money balances plus short-term government securities). The studies using net worth obtained coefficients that are in fairly close agreement.

When Patinkin divided net worth into real money balances and the residual, he obtained coefficients of 0.170 and 0.083, respectively. On the basis of this and a survey of an impressive array of other studies, he concluded that real money balances is an important determinant of consumption.[11] In a recent study of the Canadian experience, J. Ernest Tanner concluded that the real balance effect was significant and relatively large.[12]

Agreement is not unanimous, however: Michael Evans concluded that wealth was unimportant in the post–World War II period.[13] Nevertheless the weight of the evidence seems to argue for the inclusion of wealth, or one of its components, in the aggregate consumption function.

SOME IMPLICATIONS

A number of implications for the basic model follow from the work discussed in this chapter. First, the inclusion of the interest rate in the consumption function means that monetary policy, to the extent that it operates through interest rate changes, will influence aggregate demand by affecting the expenditures of both the household and busi-

---

[10] Warren E. Weber, "The Effect of Interest Rates on Aggregate Consumption," *American Economic Review,* Vol. 60 (September 1970), pp. 591–600.

[11] Patinkin, *Money, Interest, and Prices,* pp. 651–64.

[12] J. Ernest Tanner, "Empirical Evidence on the Short-Run Real Balance Effect in Canada," *Journal of Money, Credit, and Banking,* Vol. 2 (November 1970), pp. 473–85.

[13] Michael K. Evans, "The Importance of Wealth in the Consumption Function," *Journal of Political Economy,* Vol. 75 (August 1967), pp. 335–51.

ness sectors. If the substitution effect on household spending dominates the income effect, monetary policy is made stronger, but if the income effect dominates, monetary policy is made weaker than in the basic model.

Second, the inclusion of wealth has two effects. Statistically, when wealth is added to the consumption function, estimates of the marginal propensity to consume out of *current* income are reduced. This implies a reduction in the autonomous spending multiplier for the current period (sometimes called the *impact multiplier*). The long-run or equilibrium multiplier will not necessarily be altered. A decrease in the MPC implies an increase in the marginal propensity to save. With a larger MPS, wealth is added to (or subtracted from) at a faster rate, with its consequent effect on consumption. Thus, the long-run magnitude in the effect of an autonomous spending change (such as a change in government spending) may not be altered by the inclusion of wealth, but the timing will. The response of income, prices, and employment will be slower.

Similar effects exist when consumption is made a function of permanent income. Current income changes will produce little or no changes in current consumption. Not until the income changes are perceived to be permanent will consumption begin to respond.

The inclusion of wealth has another effect on the basic model. Wealth includes financial assets that are fixed in nominal value (such as money). Price level changes will change the real value of wealth, change consumption, and therefore *shift* the IS curve. An increase (decrease) in the price level decreases (increases) real wealth, which induces a decrease (increase) in consumption, shifting the IS schedule to the left (right). If we include wealth in the basic model and analyze the effect of a fiscal policy change, we shall have to recognize that all three curves (IS, LM, and AS) will shift as the price level changes.

An analysis of monetary policy must recognize a further complication. A monetary policy change initially alters the nominal money stock which is a component of wealth. At the initial price level, a change in the nominal money stock changes real wealth in the same direction. As the economy begins to respond to the policy change, and the price level changes, real wealth will change again, but in the opposite direction. For example, an increase in the money stock initially increases real wealth, shifting the IS curve to the right. The subsequent rise in the price level reduces real wealth and shifts the IS curve back to the left. Whether the two effects cancel out depends on the structure of the model and the precise definition of wealth used.

SUMMARY NOTES

1. The consumption hypothesis of the basic model (current consumption depends on current income) is known as the absolute income hypothesis.
2. The relative income hypothesis makes consumption a function of current income and current income relative to the previous peak income.
3. The permanent income and life-cycle hypotheses make consumption depend on some concept of long-run expected or nomal income (or its present value, expected wealth).
4. The role of the interest rate is ambiguous, depending upon whether the negative substitution effect outweighs the positive income effect. Empirical evidence on the role of the interest rate is mixed.
5. Empirical studies tend to support the use of wealth or one of its components, real money balances, in the consumption function.

APPENDIX

The next few pages are intended only as a review of the statistical jargon relevant to the material in this book. Students who have not studied statistics should by all means do so. It makes reading the literature in economics much more pleasant (and easy). A rigorous, but very appropriate, text is Ralph Beals, *Statistics for Economists* (New York: Rand McNally and Company, 1972).

Economic theory, in the abstract and without verification, is of limited practical usefulness. Natural curiosity may be expected to lead the theorist to construct tests for the hypotheses he has created. Besides checking the internal logic of a theory, testing is usually done by attempting to gather evidence that refutes the theory. Statistics provides methods of gathering and analyzing data with the purpose of critically testing the implications of theory.

If a theory (if you prefer, a model) is operational in the sense that it has successfully resisted repeated attempts at refutation, statistical analysis may be called upon to provide *estimates* of the *parameters* of the model. We might, for example, wish to employ statistical methods to obtain estimates of the parameters C_0 and b in the model of consumer behavior introduced in Chapter 3.

In addition to satisfying our curiosity about the quantitative dimensions of a theory, parameter estimates permit the model to be used in policy formulation and implementation and in prediction. In view of the expanding role of policy, it is not surprising that statistical estimation has become a major focus of economic research.

There are, of course, many methods of estimation which depend on the nature of the model and the characteristics that the researcher wishes the estimates to exhibit. We will consider two methods, one of which has become the workhorse of economic research.

The Scatter Diagram, Freehand, or "Eyeball" Method

If a model contains only two variables, a *dependent* variable and an *independent* or *explanatory* variable, we can make use of a two-dimensional graph. The simple consumption function is a case in point. Data on consumption (the dependent variable) and disposable income (the independent variable) are gathered. Each C, Y_D pair (called an *observation*) is plotted on a graph (Figure 8-1), the result usually called a *scatter diagram*. Now the object is to draw a straight line through the scatter of points in such a way as to group the points as closely about the line as human eyesight will permit.

The slope of the line ($\Delta C/\Delta Y_D$) is the estimate of the marginal propensity to consume (b), and the line's intercept with the vertical axis ($Y_D = 0$) is the estimate of C_0. If you think this is all too simple, you are right. First, if you and I each "eyeball" a line and they differ (be assured they will), how will we know which line is "best"? Second, how do we evaluate the "goodness of fit" of any given line to the data? Third, computing the slope of the curve by reading points off a graph is not the most accurate method. Is there a better way? There is.

The Method of Least Squares

Consider again Figure 8-1. Suppose we call the vertical difference between each observation point and the consumption line an *error*. For each observed level of disposable income we have an *estimated* value of consumption (given by the consumption line) and an *actual* value of consumption. The error is simply the difference between the two. A composite measure of error between the consumption line and the observation points may be obtained by squaring each error (to keep pluses and minuses from canceling each other) and then summing the squared error terms. The result is the *sum of squared errors* (SSE). A "good" line might be defined as one that minimizes the SSE.

The least squares method is a procedure for selecting values of C_0 and b that minimize the SSE. The method is sometimes called *least squares regression* or *simple regression* or *ordinary least squares*. In conducting the procedure, a writer will often say that he has "regressed consumption on disposable income." Minimizing the SSE is not always the best method, but it is a reasonable criterion and the one most frequently used in economic statistics.

As a spin-off, the method provides us with the means for evaluating the quality of the regression line. If we take the average or mean squared error and express that as a percentage of the variance of the dependent variable, we have the percent of the variation in the dependent variable *not explained* by the regression line. Subtracting that figure from one (1) gives us the percent of the variation in the dependent variable "explained" by the regression line. The latter figure is known as the *coefficient of determination* or R^2. The higher the R^2 the better the "fit" of the regression line to the data where $0 \leq R^2 \leq 1$.

Other figures generated by the least squares method enable us to evaluate the quality or reliability of the estimates of C_0 and b. One of the more important is the *standard error* of the estimated coefficient. If we took several different sets of data and estimated a consumption function for each set, we would usually obtain several estimates of C_0 and b. We assume these estimates are scattered about the true values of C_0 and b in a pattern known as a *probability distribution*. The standard error provides information about the nature of that probability distribution.

The standard error is usually used to determine whether the estimated coefficient is different from some hypothesized value of the coefficient (*the null hypothesis*), with a predetermined probability of incorrectly concluding that it is. For example, suppose we estimate b to be 0.75 and we form the null hypothesis that the true value of b is equal to zero. Arbitrarily setting the probability of incorrectly rejecting the null hypothesis at 5 percent, we can use the standard error (in a simple calculation) to tell us to reject or accept the null hypothesis. If we reject the null hypothesis, there is a 5 percent probability of our having drawn the wrong conclusion. When rejecting the null hypothesis, writers normally state that the estimated coefficient is "significant at the 5 percent level."

Least squares estimates are generally evaluated or summarized by statements that attest to the "significance" of the estimated coefficients and the "goodness-of-fit" of the regression line (as measured by the R^2). Estimates of equations containing more than one explanatory variable are handled by a similar procedure called *multiple least squares regression* or, more simply, *multiple regression*. Multiple regression is by far the most common estimating method used in economic statistics, but its use must be exercised with care; for, given an inappropriate environment, the results generated can be misleading. Critical evaluation of the results of empirical research, therefore, requires that the student become familiar with statistical analysis.

DISCUSSION QUESTIONS

1. What is wrong and what is right about the following "theory" of consumption? Household consumption depends on the age and occupation of the family head, size of family, race and nationality, level of education, religion, and type of community (urban, suburban, or rural).

2. Introspection is often a useful method of developing hypotheses about human behavior. In the light of *your own* experience, evaluate the relative income, permanent income, and life-cycle hypotheses.

3. In constructing the aggregate consumption function, disposable income is exogenous to the household sector (although endogenous to the full model). Households are assumed to select the utility-maximizing consumption-saving mix *given* their disposable income. Yet each household is free to attempt to change its income by changing the amount of labor offered for sale (some people do this by taking second jobs). Thus it might be more reasonable to treat consumption *and* disposable income as endogenous to the household sector. Discuss this possibility. What factors might determine the utility-maximizing levels of consumption and disposable income demanded by the household sector?

4. Suppose real wealth is included in the basic model's consumption function in addition to current income. Redefine the IS curve. How do changes in the price level now affect the IS curve? Analyze the effect of changes in government spending, taxes, and the monetary base using your new IS curve in the basic model.

9

Investment

THE HYPOTHESIS OF THE BASIC MODEL

THE investment function used in our basic model has a longer history than the Keynesian type consumption function. Both pre- and post-Keynesian schools of thought treated aggregate investment expenditures as a decreasing function of the interest rate. We noted in the last chapter that the simple consumption function fits the data fairly well, even though more complex functions do a better job. Such, however, is not the case with the investment hypothesis. In Figure 9-1, real gross investment expenditures are plotted against the interest rate on long-term corporate bonds. Note that the scatter of data points does not clearly describe a downward sloping relationship between the interest rate and investment. Another look at a variation of the present value formula discussed in Chapter 3 will help pinpoint some causes of difficulty.

$$P_0 = \sum_{j=1}^{n} \frac{\pi j}{(1+i^*)^i} = \sum_{j=1}^{n} \frac{TRj - TCj}{(1+i^*)^i} \qquad (9\text{-}1)$$

Note that the marginal efficiency of capital, i^*, is computed for a given cost for the capital equipment (P_0) and for a given level of expected total sales (TR), expected total costs other than interest costs (TC) and the difference between the two, expected total profits (π). Now in the aggregate, total sales is nothing more than total nominal income for the economy. This depends, in turn, on the overall

FIGURE 9–1
Investment and the Interest Rate, 1950–1969

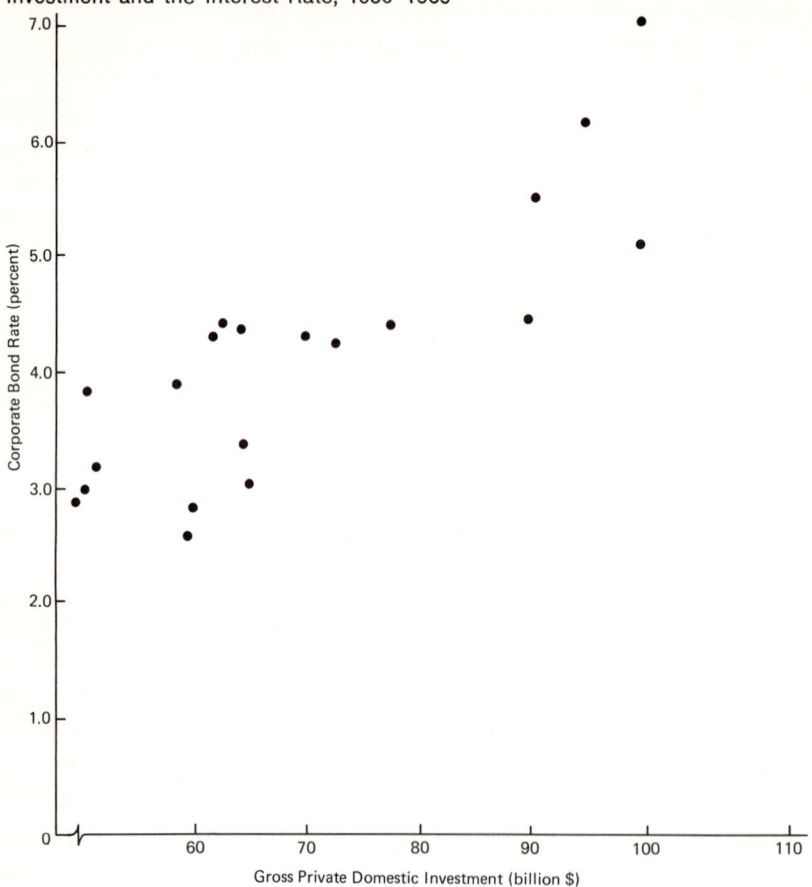

Y-axis: Corporate Bond Rate (percent)
X-axis: Gross Private Domestic Investment (billion $)

Source: *Economic Report of the President, 1972.*

price level and on the level of output in the economy. Neither of these two variables can be considered to be given. In fact, even in our basic model, the price level, total output, and the interest rate were all determined simultaneously. As total sales vary, given total costs, the marginal efficiency of capital will also change. Total costs, however, will also change as total output in the economy changes. Thus, in computing the relationship between the interest rate and investment, account must be taken of the changing level of output and prices. During the period of time covered by the scatter of data points in Figure 9–1, real output in the United States more than doubled, and the price level increased by 50 percent. It should not be surprising, therefore, that no clear-cut relationship can be seen between the level of investment and the rate of interest.

Not only do the items in the numerator of the right side of equation (9–1) depend upon the level of economic activity, but the cost of the capital equipment on the left side of the equation will most likely also vary with a changing economic climate. Consider a situation in which the interest rate falls, say, because of an expansive monetary policy. Business firms will expand their investment spending and in so doing bid up the price of capital goods. This increases the term on the left side of the equation and *ceteris paribus,* lowers the marginal efficiency of capital. Indeed some writers take explicit recognition of this fact and make adjustment for it, calling the resulting schedule a *marginal efficiency of investment* schedule rather than a marginal efficiency of capital schedule.

In the process of trying to develop relationships that can be useful for predicting investment, several variables have consequently been introduced into the investment equation. Some of these, such as total output, expected profits, and of course the interest rate, are suggested by the foregoing discussion. In addition some writers have shifted the focus away from investment to the determination of the firm's optimal stock of capital. The discussion that follows takes this approach.[1]

THE STOCK ADJUSTMENT APPROACH

Capital, like labor, is a factor of production and is desired for the service it yields in the productive process. Given circumstances yet to be discussed, a firm will, in the course of business, adjust its stock of capital and labor with the intent of producing the profit maximizing output using an optimal combination of capital and labor. Investment expenditures—that is, expenditures on capital goods—are simply the means by which the firm adjusts its actual stock of capital goods to the level that it desires.

For simplicity, let us assume that firms adjust their actual stock of capital goods to the desired stock within one time period. Thus the actual stock of capital at the beginning of each period, K_t, is equal to the desired capital stock of the previous period, K_{t-1}^*. Net investment in the current period is the adjustment of the actual capital stock

---

[1] The organization here relies heavily on Dale W. Jorgenson and Calvin D. Siebert, "A Comparison of Alternative Theories of Corporate Investment Behavior," *American Economic Review,* Vol. 58 (September 1968), pp. 681–712.

to the desired capital stock. Put another way, given the assumption of a one-period adjustment, current net investment is the change in the desired capital stock from last period to this period.

$$I_t = K_t^* - K_t = K_t^* - K_{t-1}^* \qquad (9\text{--}2)$$

Given the above hypothesis, a theory that focuses on the determinants of the desired capital stock will also be a theory of net investment. If we add to this a theory of capital replacement, we would then have a theory of gross investment. The discussion in this chapter applies to net investment only. A number of determinants of the desired capital stock have been advanced in the literature.

The Crude Accelerator

One approach introduced as early as 1917 by J. M. Clark states that the desired capital stock is proportional to current output.[2]

$$K_t^* = zY_t \qquad (9\text{--}3)$$

The rationale behind this approach argues that if we assume away substitution between factors of production (capital and labor), then technological considerations dictate a relatively constant ratio of capital to output. In order to produce the currently demanded level of output, producers must maintain a stock of capital equal to the product of the capital-output ratio and the current level of output. If the current desired stock of capital is proportional to current output, the previous period's desired capital stock was proportional to the previous period's output. Given that current net investment spending is defined to be the difference between the current and previous period's desired capital stock, we can derive the following relationship:

$$I_t = K_t^* - K_{t-1}^*$$

Substitute from (9–3):

$$\begin{aligned} I_t &= zY_t - zY_{t-1} \\ &= z(Y_t - Y_{t-1}) \end{aligned} \qquad (9\text{--}4)$$

where z is the accelerator coefficient. Thus current net investment depends upon the current and previous period's levels of output. Alternatively, current investment is proportional to the change in output

---

[2] J. Maurice Clark, "Business Acceleration and the Law of Demand: A Technical Factor in Economic Cycles," *Journal of Political Economy,* Vol. 25 (March 1971), pp. 217–35.

from the previous to current period. Note that unless output is increasing, investment will be nonpositive. Specifically, if output is at an equilibrium level and not changing, net investment will be zero. Should output fall, net investment will not simply decrease; it will be negative. This relationship in various forms has found considerable importance in business cycle theory, a subject to which we will return in a later chapter.

One disadvantage of the approach is that it ignores the effect of changes in the cost or price of capital services. The next approach does, however, take this into account.

The Neoclassical Approach

Neoclassical economic theory assumes that firms maximize profits. This may be accomplished by equating the marginal product of each factor of production to its marginal cost (in real terms). We have already assumed that firms do this with respect to the purchase of labor services. Recall that in Chapter 5, we derived a demand-for-labor schedule by assuming that firms would equate the marginal product of labor and the real wage rate. A similar approach may be taken with respect to capital. The desired capital stock in the current period is the one that makes the marginal product of capital equal to the price of capital services which we approximate by the market rate of interest. Assuming, as we have, that firms do not retain earnings, that all profits are paid out in the form of dividends, that financial markets are perfectly competitive, and that there are no price changes for capital goods relative to other goods, the price of capital services is equal to the interest rate.

Suppose, as an illustration, we have a production function of the Cobb-Douglas form.[3]

$$Y = AK^x N^{1-x}$$

The marginal product of capital is given by the following expression:

$$MP_k = \partial Y / \partial K = \frac{xAK^x N^{1-x}}{K} = xY/K$$

Assuming that firms will desire that stock of capital which equates

---

[3] Paul H. Douglas, "Are There Laws of Production?" *American Economic Review*, Vol. 38 (March 1948), pp. 1–41.

the above marginal product to the interest rate, we can obtain the following expression for the desired capital stock:

$$xY/K = i$$
$$K^* = xY/i \qquad (9\text{--}5)$$

Equation (9–5) can be decomposed still further by recognizing that $Y = AK^x N^{1-x}$ and substituting into (9–5). The result may then be solved for K in terms of N and i. (We leave this as an exercise at the end of the chapter.) However, the empirical studies cited later in the chapter use the form of (9–5) for the desired capital stock.

A word is in order here about the units in which the above variables are expressed. The real capital stock is often expressed in terms of dollars of constant purchasing power as of a point in time. In other words, the capital stock is expressed in dollars with no time dimension. Real output is expressed in terms of dollars of constant purchasing power per unit of time. In other words, we express output as dollars per year. The marginal product of capital is the change in output (change in dollars per year) divided by the change in the capital stock (change in dollars) which is a number with a time dimension (such as 0.10 per year). This can be equated to the interest rate which, in decimal form, is expressed in the same units. For example, a 10 percent annual interest rate is 0.10 per year.

This can be reconciled with equation (9–5) in which x is a number, Y is expressed in terms of dollars per year, and i is a number with a time dimension. Thus xY/i is a number of dollars per year divided by a number per year, which leaves us with a number of dollars with no time dimension, the units in which the capital stock is expressed.

Note that both the current level of output and the current rate of interest are determinants of the current desired capital stock. If we substitute this relationship into the investment definition [equation (9–2)], we conclude that current investment expenditures are proportional to changes in the ratio of output to the interest rate. The relationship implies that an increase in the current level of output induces an increase in current investment expenditures, and an increase in the current interest rate induces a decrease in current investment expenditures.

While this approach handles one problem not dealt with by the crude accelerator approach—namely the role of the rate of interest—it has problems of its own. For one thing, the real world is not perfectly competitive, and thus for any given subset of firms, the profit-maximizing condition we have used may not be the relevant one. Further, the price of capital goods does change, providing capital gains or losses to the owners of capital goods. This, however, may be handled by redefining the price of capital services to include not only the interest rate but also the effect of capital gains and losses.

Finally, large corporations in the real world do retain some earnings, and those firms may not consider the opportunity cost of those retained earnings to be equivalent to the market rate of interest, whether adjusted for capital gains and losses or not. Indeed some writers have gone so far as to suggest, in effect, that large corporations consider the opportunity cost of retained earnings to be zero. If we applied the above approach to those firms, we would arrive at erroneous conclusions about their investment behavior. This last problem has received attention by such writers as John Meyer and Edwin Kuh.[4]

The Role of Liquidity or Internal Funds

Using survey data and statistical analysis, Meyer and Kuh conclude that at least as far as large corporations are concerned, investment is constrained not by the cost and availability of funds external to the firm but by the availability of funds generated internally through retained earnings and depreciation reserves. Large firms treat these internal funds as costless and tend to ignore the external price of capital services—namely, the interest rate. One implication is that firms will invest in capital equipment which on neoclassical grounds would be unprofitable, thus distorting the allocation of resources. Another implication is that monetary policy, to the extent that it operates through interest rates, influences only small firms and is therefore less potent than might otherwise be supposed.

Using this approach to determine the level of investment expenditures, we would make the desired stock of capital a function of internal liquidity, and, applying the definition of investment, we would obtain the result that current investment is a function of changes in liquidity.

One may criticize this approach on the grounds that if we are interested in aggregate investment spending we must consider spending by both large and small firms. The liquidity approach focuses on the

---

[4] John Meyer and Edwin Kuh, *The Investment Decision* (Cambridge, Mass.: Harvard University Press, 1957).

behavior of large firms. Presumably the smaller firms who are forced into the financial markets to obtain funds for investment spending would be subjected to conditions in these markets. Another problem that this approach generates for many economists is that it discards the profit-maximizing assumption so revered for many years. Discarding such an assumption has far-reaching implications for economic theory that extend well beyond the determinants of investment.

The Role of Expected Profits

Returning once again to the present value formula [equation (9–1)], note that if we take the cost of capital goods and the rate of interest as given, the demand for capital goods depends on expected profits. Consequently, some writers have made the desired capital stock a function of expected profits. The chief difficulty with this approach is that expected profits are not measurable. So the theory needs to be supplemented with a model that determines expected profits. The usual approach is to make current expected profits a function of current and past actual profits. Expected profits is also a fairly broad measure, encompassing expected sales, expected costs, and, as a matter of fact, the expected cost of capital services, in addition.

With the desired capital stock a function of expected profits, investment becomes a function of changes in expected profits.

The above summarizes several approaches to the determination of investment spending. However, all of these approaches are generally applied to the determination of expenditures on fixed capital. Aggregate net investment also includes changes in the stock of inventories. Some inventory investment is unintended. If current production is geared to current expected sales and if actual sales in a given period deviate from expectations, then the stock of inventories will rise or fall. However, some portion of inventory investment is intended. Since inventories are not actually used in the productive process, in the same way that plant and equipment are, investment in inventories has received separate attention.

THE SPECIAL CASE OF INVESTMENT IN INVENTORIES

Inventories—that is, stocks of unsold goods—are accumulated primarily to act as a buffer in the face of fluctuations in sales. Customers may be lost if the goods are not readily available to them when ordered. Thus most firms maintain some inventories from which they can immediately supply their customers. If sales are on the uptrend and are expected to continue the trend, then generally firms will increase their buffer stocks of inventories. Unexpected changes in sales will result in changes in inventory holdings also, but we are dealing here with planned rather than unplanned inventory investment.

Most models of inventory behavior apply the stock adjustment approach. The optimal stock of inventories is assumed to be some fraction of total expected sales. Should sales change, then the optimal stock of inventories also changes. Intended investment in inventories is therefore proportional to the change in sales. The relationship is similar to the crude accelerator approach in investment in fixed capital.

There is, however, a cost to holding inventories. Stocks of unsold goods take up warehouse space, thus incurring such costs as insurance, rent, salaries to security guards, and so on. Furthermore, funds which could be earning some interest income become tied up in inventories, and the opportunity cost of holding inventories may, therefore, be measured by the market rate of interest. Thus inventory holding costs include both storage and interest costs. Many models of inventory behavior include both a measure of expected sales and a measure of holding costs, most notably the interest rate.

THE EMPIRICAL EVIDENCE

In applying theory to the real world, some accommodation must be made to the fact that some of the assumptions made in theory are a little too simple. In the case of investment behavior, we earlier made a simplifying assumption about the speed of adjustment between the actual and desired capital stock. We assumed that the firm could adjust its actual capital stock to its desired capital stock in one time period. In the real world this is not likely to be the case—for at least two reasons. First, the firm may not be able to make the adjustment that fast because it takes time to produce capital goods and, depending upon the type of equipment or plant, the production period may be longer than the time period of analysis.

Second, it takes time to plan for the direction and magnitude of the project and to identify the most appropriate sources of finance. To allow for these possibilities, a mechanism has been developed by several writers including Hollis Chenery and L. M. Koyck.[5] The mech-

---

[5] Hollis B. Chenery, "Overcapacity and the Acceleration Principle," *Econometrica*, Vol. 20 (January 1952), pp. 1–28. L. M. Koyck, *Distributed Lags and Investment Analysis* (Amsterdam, North Holland, 1954).

anism, sometimes known as the "flexible accelerator," is a distributed lag which does not constrain adjustment to any specific number of time periods but allows the adjustment to take place as slowly as the data dictate. Most studies of investment behavior have taken advantage of the flexible accelerator or distributed lag approach. However, the essential ingredients are the same as in the case of the one-period adjustment model. The theory is still a theory of desired capital stock, and investment follows as the actual capital stock is adjusted to meet the desired capital stock.

Using this approach, Dale Jorgenson and Calvin Siebert have compared various theories of capital stock determination.[6] In a sample of 15 large firms, Jorgenson and Siebert concluded that the neoclassical approach was superior to all others and that the liquidity approach was the worst. In rejecting the liquidity approach, Jorgenson and Siebert conclude that the profit-maximizing assumption is still the best one that can be made in describing business firm behavior. The expected profits and crude accelerator approaches yielded about the same results, but those results were decidedly inferior to the results obtained with the neoclassical approach.

In a later survey of studies of investment behavior, Jorgenson concluded that real output is the most important single determinant of investment expenditures.[7] As far as the financial constraint is concerned, he concluded that external funds are more important than the availability of internal funds.

Robert Eisner also concluded that changes in output are more important than changes in profits.[8] Profits may affect the timing of investment spending, but output changes determine the total amount.

As far as inventory investment is concerned, Michael Lovell surveyed the literature and concluded that the accelerator approach to inventory investment is a fruitful one, but that the evidence on the role played by financial variables, especially the interest rate, is mixed and inconclusive.[9] However, another study by Paul Kuznets, appearing shortly after the Lovell study, concluded that interest rates, the

---

[6] Jorgenson and Siebert, "Comparison of Alternative Theories."

[7] Dale W. Jorgenson, "Econometric Studies of Investment Behavior: A Survey," *Journal of Economic Literature*, Vol. 9 (December 1971), pp. 1111–47.

[8] Robert Eisner, "A Permanent Income Theory for Investment: Some Empirical Explorations," *American Economic Review*, Vol. 57 (June 1967), pp. 363–90.

[9] Michael C. Lovell, "Determinants of Inventory Investment," in *Models of Income Determination, Studies in Income and Wealth*, Vol. 28, National Bureau of Economic Research (Princeton: Princeton University Press, 1964), pp. 212–24.

stock of liquid assets held by the firm, and the availability of external credit are all significant and important determinants of inventory investment by manufacturing firms.[10]

Recall from Chapter 7 that a crucial parameter in the discussion of the effectiveness of monetary policy was the interest sensitivity of investment. Thomas Mayer has summarized the more recent studies, and these are reproduced in Table 9–1.[11]

TABLE 9–1
Interest Elasticity of Plant and Equipment Expenditures

Author(s)	Elasticity
Stephen Goldfeld (1966)	–0.50 to –0.60
Yehuda Grunfeld (1960)	–0.50
Frederick Hammer (1964)	–0.50 (long run)
	–0.30 (short run)
Dale Jorgenson (1965)	–0.15 (long run)
	–0.56 (short run)
Edwin Kuh and John Meyer (1963)	–0.16
Robert Resek (1966)	–1.00 to –1.40

Note: The short-run elasticity is generally the first quarter's response, where the full response is spread out over many quarters. The full response is the long-run elasticity.

Source: Mayer, *Monetary Policy in the United States*, pp. 122–23.

Except for the Resek study, most authors found that investment spending was interest inelastic. But, while small, the elasticity coefficients are not inconsequential. Thus the interest rate does appear to play an important role in determining investment. However, the magnitude of the response is not nearly large enough to conclude that the IS curve tends toward the horizontal, as we discussed in Chapter 7.

If we were to make a summary statement for purposes of the analysis in this book, it would be that investment is a function of output and the rate of interest. Thus we retain the rate of interest which we used in the basic model but add the level of output to the equation. This addition has implications for the stability of the model which we will discuss in Chapter 13.

---

[10] Paul W. Kuznets, "Financial Determinants of Manufacturing Inventory Behavior: A Quarterly Study Based on United States Estimates, 1947–1961," *Yale Economic Essays* Vol. 4 (Fall 1964), pp. 331–69. The study is based on Kuznets' doctoral dissertation. Interestingly enough, Lowell was a member of Kuznets' dissertation committee.

[11] Thomas Mayer, *Monetary Policy in the United States* (New York: Random House, Inc., 1968).

Algebraically, a revised investment function may be written in the following linear form:

$$I = I_0 - a_1 i + a_2 Y$$

The coefficient, a_2, is sometimes called the *marginal propensity to invest* (MPI). Plotting investment against the interest rate involves not one curve, but many—one for each level of output or income. Representations are shown in Figure 9–2, where $Y_0 < Y_1 < Y_2$.

FIGURE 9-2
Investment Functions for Different Output Levels

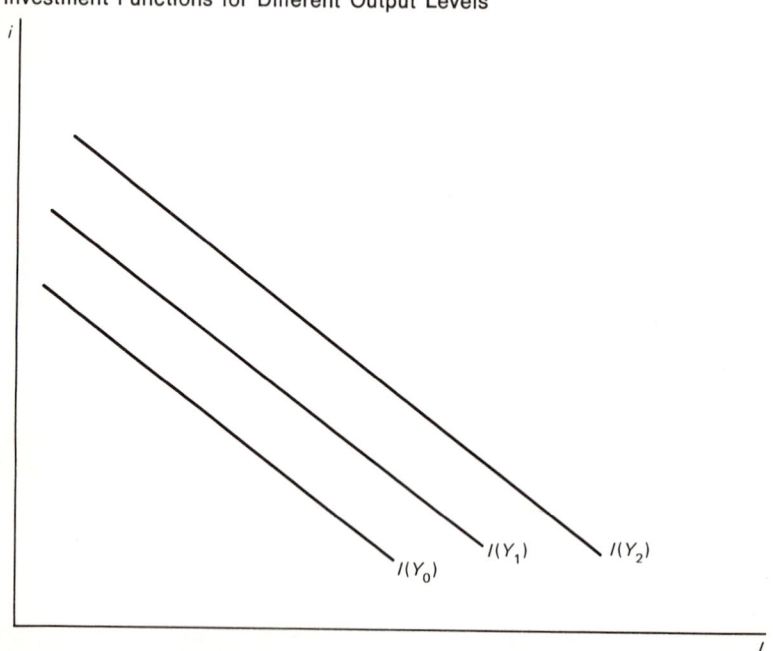

SUMMARY NOTES

1. Modern investment theory attempts to identify the determinants of the firm's optimal capital stock. The change in the actual capital stock from period to period is, by definition, net investment.
2. The crude accelerator approach makes the optimal or desired capital stock proportional to current output. The neoclassical approach makes the desired capital stock proportional to the ratio of output to the interest rate.

3. Other approaches make the desired capital stock a function of the firm's internal liquidity and expected profits.
4. Intended inventory investment is used as a buffer against unexpected changes in sales. Inventory investment is a function of changes in sales and holding (storage and interest) costs.
5. Recent empirical evidence has tended to support the neoclassical approach as the determinant of total investment. The other factors may affect the timing of investment expenditures.

DISCUSSION QUESTIONS

1. It has been argued that the most important factor affecting investment is the "psychology of businessmen." How might we go about fitting the attitudes of businessmen into the various theories of investment discussed in the chapter?

2. In the neoclassical approach, under perfect competition, each factor of production is paid its marginal product. Assuming this to be the case, if the amount of capital employed is K, what is the total payment to capital where the Cobb-Douglas production function is relevant? If total output is ultimately distributed between capital and labor, what is the payment to labor?

3. It was pointed out that equation (9–5) in the chapter could be extended to make the desired capital stock a function of the quantity of labor and the interest rate. Do so. You may find it convenient to convert to logs before solving for K.

10

The Labor Market

LABOR DEMAND

The labor demand schedule used in the basic model was derived in the same fashion as the neoclassical demand for capital introduced in the previous chapter. Under the assumption of competitive markets, a profit-maximizing producer will hire the quantity of labor that is consistent with equality between labor's marginal product and the real wage rate. An illustrative form of the aggregate demand for labor may be derived from the widely used Cobb-Douglas production function. This production function (with constant returns to scale) takes the following form:

$$Y = AK^x N^{1-x} \tag{10-1}$$

where $0 < x < 1$.

Setting the marginal product of labor equal to the real wage rate and solving for the quantity of labor leads to the conclusion that the demand for labor is proportional to the ratio of real output to the real wage rate.

$$\partial Y / \partial N = \frac{(1-x)AK^x N^{1-x}}{N} = W/P$$
$$(1-x)Y/N = W/P$$
$$N = (1-x)\frac{Y}{W/P} \tag{10-2}$$

Since Y is in turn a function of the amount of labor employed, equation (10–2) can be decomposed still further. This is done below. However (10–2), together with the capital demand function derived in the previous chapter, is useful in predicting the shares of total output that will be paid in equilibrium, under perfect competition, to the two factors of production—capital and labor. For example, if we take the quantity demanded (and thus employed in competitive equilibrium) of labor and multiply by the real wage rate (the price commanded per unit of labor), we conclude that the total payment to labor is equal to a fixed percentage of total output. The total payment to capital is the residual.

$$N(W/P) = (1-x)\frac{Y}{W/P} \cdot W/P$$
$$= (1-x)Y$$

For capital we have:

$$\text{capital share} = \text{total output} - \text{labor share}$$
$$= Y - (1-x)Y$$
$$= xY$$

The same conclusion can be reached by multiplying the marginal product of capital (see the previous chapter) by the quantity of capital employed. Thus,

$$MP_k K = (xY/K)K = xY.$$

Put another way, assuming that capital is paid its marginal product, the quantity of capital employed is $K = xY/i$ and the price of capital services is i. Thus,

$$(xY/i)i = xY.$$

Given the Cobb-Douglas production function (or any production function that is homogeneous of the first degree), if every factor is paid its marginal product, the total payment to all factors of production will just equal total output. This is an application of a mathematical theorem known as Euler's theorem.

The parameter x has been estimated to be approximately 0.25.[1] This leads to the conclusion that labor's share of total output would be about 75 percent and capital's about 25 percent. In fact, if we take the total return to all factors of production, national income,

---

[1] See Paul H. Douglas, "Are There Laws of Production," *American Economic Review*, Vol. 38 (March 1948), pp. 1–41 for this as well as for estimates for countries other than the United States.

and distribute professional and farm income between labor and capital, the return to labor out of national income is fairly close to 75 percent. What is even more interesting is that this share has been relatively stable over time in the United States, averaging about 77–78 percent in recent years.

Since output is a function of capital and labor, the demand-for-labor relationship above can be further extended so that the demand for labor can be expressed as a function of the real wage rate and the stock of capital. Making the appropriate substitution and solving for the quantity of labor, we obtain the following demand function:

$$(1-x)AK^xN^{-x} = W/P$$

$$N^x = \frac{(1-x)AK^x}{W/P}$$

$$N = \frac{(1-x)^{1/x}A^{1/x}K}{(W/P)^{1/x}}$$

The relationship may be more conveniently expressed by taking logs of both sides:

$$\ln N = (1/x)[\ln(1-x) + \ln A] + \ln K - (1/x)\ln(W/P) \quad (10\text{–}3)$$

Note that the demand for labor varies inversely with the real wage rate and directly with the stock of capital. An increase in the stock of capital, *ceteris paribus,* increases the marginal product of labor. Thus, increases in the stock of capital shift the demand curve to the right.

This demand function provides us with an estimate of the elasticity of labor demand with respect to the real wage rate. In its present log form, the coefficient for each variable is, in fact, the elasticity. The elasticity of labor demand with respect to the wage rate is $1/x$. Assuming that previous estimates are reasonably accurate so that $x = 0.25$, the elasticity of labor demand is -4. In other words, a 1 percent increase (decrease) in the real wage rate induces a 4 percent decrease (increase) in the quantity of labor demanded.

The size of this elasticity has an interesting implication.[2] It is sometimes argued that the classical prescription for restoring full employ-

---

[2] Lloyd G. Reynolds and Peter Gregory, *Wages, Productivity, and Industrialization in Puerto Rico* (Homewood, Ill.: Richard D. Irwin, Inc., 1965) conclude that the elasticity of demand in Puerto Rico is about -1. However, their quantitative estimate is not comparable to the results outlined above, since different methods were employed. What is important is their confirmation of a downward sloping demand curve for labor.

ment involves a fallacy of composition. The reasoning is as follows: A reduction in the nominal wage rate relative to the price level does indeed increase the demand for labor for an individual firm. However, this reduction in the nominal wage rate does not lead to the same conclusion in the aggregate. The reason is that wages are the dominant source of disposable income for the household sector. A reduction in the nominal wage rate reduces the labor or wages income for the household sector, thus reducing nominal disposable income and consequently nominal consumption expenditures. Thus a reduction in the nominal wage rate results in a decrease in nominal aggregate demand, implying that prices will fall. If the price fall is proportional to the nominal wage-rate cut, no change takes place in employment. If the price fall is greater than the wage cut, it will cause producers to cut back on production and lay off labor rather than the reverse.[3]

Implicit in this argument is the assumption that the demand for labor is inelastic ($e < 1$) with respect to the wage rate. Under that assumption it is true that a reduction in the wage rate will reduce total labor income. However, the implication of work done with the Cobb-Douglas production function is that the demand for labor is elastic ($e > 1$). Thus a fall in the wage rate will raise, not lower, total labor income, resulting in an increase in disposable income, consumption, and aggregate demand.

One major drawback to the foregoing approach to the demand for labor is that it applies to a perfectly competitive economy. For an economy in which not all markets are perfectly competitive, different profit-maximizing conditions prevail. A monopoly firm in the product market will be equating the marginal product of labor to the ratio of the nominal wage rate to *marginal revenue*. Since marginal revenue is lower than the price of the product, as long as the demand curve for the product is downward sloping, the implication is that the monopolist will be hiring a smaller quantity of labor at a higher marginal product than a competitive industry. The U.S. economy contains a mixture of monopolistic, oligopolistic, and competitive elements, and therefore the aggregate demand for labor will not be ex-

---

[3] An example of this argument may be found in Campbell R. McConnell, *Economics: Principles, Problems, and Policies,* 4th ed. (New York: McGraw-Hill Book Co., 1969), pp. 211–12. Even if the demand for labor is inelastic, one must assume that the marginal propensity to consume income from profits is less than the marginal propensity to consume labor income, for the above argument to hold. In that case, a shift of total income from labor to capital would result in a reduction of consumption expenditures.

actly the same as the one that can be derived from the aggregate production function under neoclassical assumptions. However, conformity of the factor shares to those implied under the neoclassical analysis would seem to indicate that the neoclassical assumptions are a sufficiently close approximation to reality.

LABOR SUPPLY

A labor supply function may be derived using the tools of consumer choice theory. The prospective worker is assumed to face a choice between two normal goods—income and leisure. Income is obtained by working, and leisure is the time spent not working. The individual is assumed to maximize satisfaction or utility by selecting an optimal combination of income and leisure. He does, however, face a constraint. The constraint is the number of hours per day that can be devoted either to earning income or to leisure, or some combination of the two. The total constraint is 24 hours per day.

The problem may be illustrated by recourse to Figure 10–1. Income from labor earnings is plotted on the vertical axis, and time, which may be split between work and leisure up to a maximum of 24 hours per day, is plotted on the horizontal axis. Assuming that both income and leisure are normal goods, the indifference curves drawn resemble those drawn for any pair of normal goods. Maximum income may be earned by working 24 hours per day at the current wage rate. This gives us a maximum-income-opportunity point on the vertical axis. Alternatively, no work may be done, and 24 hours of leisure may be chosen. This gives us a maximum-leisure-opportunity point on the horizontal axis. The straight line connecting these points is an opportunity line for the individual.

Two opportunity lines are drawn, AB and AC. The slope of the opportunity line is determined by the wage rate. The vertical distance OB or OC is the total income that can be earned at two different wage rates for 24 hours of work. Thus the wage rate is the distance OB (or OC) divided by the distance OA. The utility-maximizing position is a point of tangency between the opportunity curve and an indifference curve. Income and the wage rate are measured in real terms on the grounds that the rational individual will respond and offer more or less work only to the extent that the purchasing power of his income is affected.

In Figure 10–1, given the opportunity line AB, the individual maxi-

FIGURE 10-1
The Work-Leisure Choice

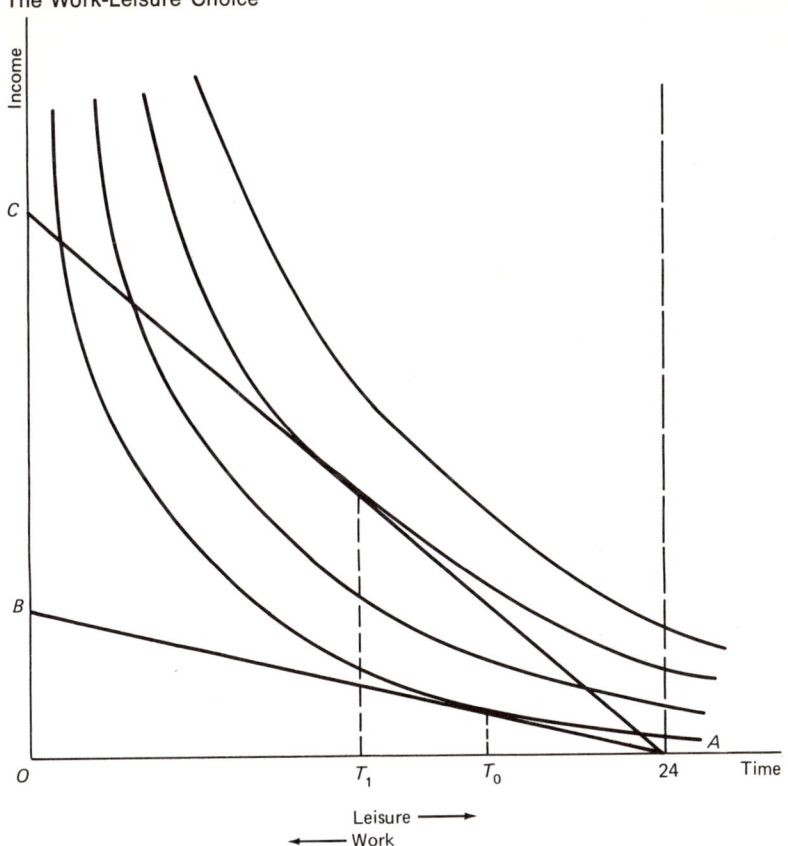

mizes utility by taking leisure equal to the distance OT_0 and by working the remaining number of hours in the day indicated by the distance T_0A. Should the wage rate increase and the opportunity line shift upward to AC, the portion of the day devoted to work increases, and the portion devoted to leisure decreases. Thus at first glance, it would appear that the quantity of labor supplied by the individual and the wage rate vary directly.

However, the conclusion is not quite that clear. Given a higher wage rate, the opportunity cost of leisure is higher, thus implying that the individual will substitute work for leisure. But leisure has been assumed to be a normal good, and, with a rise in total income, we would expect the individual to demand more of that good. Hence, an increase in the wage rate induces the individual to substitute work for leisure and, at the same time, to demand more leisure. The two effects work against each other. In Figure 10–1, it appears that the substitution effect outweighs the income effect, so that the individual offers more work at a higher wage rate; but the reverse could just as well occur. Should the income effect dominate the substitution effect, the supply curve of labor with respect to the wage rate would be downward, rather than upward, sloping. Indeed a hypothesis that is often advanced is that as the wage rate increases, the income effect becomes progressively stronger, and the substitution effect becomes weaker. At some point the income effect swamps the substitution effect, and the labor supply curve bends backwards.

The turning point would, of course, vary from individual to individual; but the expectation is that as the average wage rate increases to high levels, eventually the amount of labor supply forthcoming will decrease with further increases in the wage rate. Thus the labor supply curve that we have drawn in our basic model is not unambiguously upward sloping.

One difficulty with the above analysis is that the individual is forced to dichotomize his time between work and leisure. All nonwork time is leisure; and, furthermore, since we have assumed that leisure is a normal good, all nonwork time is pleasurable. In fact, some nonwork time may be spent in transportation to and from a job, in waiting to consume goods provided with work time income (such as waiting for tee-off time at the golf course), and in doing household chores that may not be pleasant (such as mowing the grass). Individual choice might then be expanded to include work time, nonwork time that yields satisfaction or utility, and nonwork time that yields dissatisfaction or disutility. The three-dimensional choice faced by the individual may modify some of the conclusions reached earlier when the individual had a two-dimensional choice between work and leisure. For example, in the face of a wage-rate increase, the individual may supply more work without giving up leisure by simply giving up unpleasant nonwork time (for example, he hires someone to mow the grass).[4]

All things considered, it is the data that must finally determine the shape of the aggregate labor supply function. The empirical results, however, are not clear-cut. As a general conclusion, the majority of

---

[4] For a further analysis of these possibilities, see Richard Perlman, *Labor Theory* (New York: John Wiley and Sons, Inc., 1969), pp. 13–21.

studies have found that the supply of labor by men varies inversely with the real wage rate, while the supply of labor by women varies directly with the real wage rate. Thus, in the case of men the income effect dominates; and in the case of women the substitution effect dominates. In two separate studies using cross-section data, Marvin Kosters and Sherwin Rosen recently found a negatively sloped supply curve for men. In both cases the measure of quantity supplied was man-hours.[5]

For married women, Glen Cain found that the supply of labor varied directly with the wage rate.[6] Using aggregated data, Cain computed the wage elasticity to be between 0.4 and 1.0. The quantity of labor supplied in this case, however, was measured by the labor force participation rate which is the percent of the eligible population that is actually in the labor force.

A more recent study by Robert Lucas and Leonard Rapping concluded that the aggregate labor supply curve is, in the short run, upward sloping.[7] Lucas and Rapping took as their measure of quantity of labor supplied the number of man-hours in the labor force as a percent of the population. Both men and women were included. Further, they made a distinction between the current measured real wage rate and a long-term "normal" or expected real wage rate. On the assumption that individuals are free of money illusion and do make adjustments for price changes, the expected rate of inflation was also included in the supply function. By including current as well as long-term normal or expected values of the relevant decision variables, Lucas and Rapping were able to make a distinction between a short-run labor supply function and a long-run supply function. They concluded, on the basis of their statistical analysis, that the short-run supply function was indeed upward sloping and had an elasticity with respect to the current wage rate that varied between 0.78 and 3.93, depending on the precise form of the equation used. The elasticity

---

[5] Marvin Kosters, "Income and Substitution Parameters in a Family Labor Supply Model," (Ph.D. diss., University of Chicago, 1966); and Sherwin Rosen, "On the Interindustry Wage and Hours Structure," *Journal of Political Economy*, Vol. 77 (March/April 1969), pp. 249–73.

[6] Glen G. Cain, *Married Women in the Labor Force: A Economic Analysis* (Chicago: University of Chicago Press, 1966).

[7] Robert E. Lucas, Jr. and Leonard A. Rapping, "Real Wages, Employment, and Inflation," *Journal of Political Economy*, Vol. 77 (September/October 1969), pp. 721–54; and Robert E. Lucas, Jr. and Leonard A. Rapping, "Price Expectations and the Phillips Curve," *American Economic Review*, Vol. 59 (June 1969), pp. 342–50.

of labor supply with respect to the long-run or normal real wage rate was computed to be approximately zero.

Much of the foregoing analysis assumes the absence of money illusion on the part of the individual who supplies labor services. But on the contrary, one of the central concerns of Keynesian economics is the possibility that workers may suffer from money illusion, in the sense that they base their well-being upon changes in their nominal wages rather than in real wages. Under the presence of money illusion, workers might be expected to resist a fall in the nominal wage rate, even when it might be accompanied by an increase in the real wage rate, because the price level fell faster. Furthermore, the implication is that workers would not mind a fall in the real wage rate if nominal wages were rising but at a slower rate than the price level. The effect of this is to produce an asymmetrical adjustment pattern in the labor market.

To illustrate, consider Figure 10–2. Labor demand has been plotted against the *nominal* wage rate; thus the demand schedule shifts in response to changes in the price level. Changes in the nominal wage rate given the price level result in a movement along a fixed demand schedule. The supply schedule is drawn under the assumption that workers will resist a fall in the nominal wage rate but will offer more labor when the nominal wage rate rises. Suppose the economy is at full employment, with price level P_1 and nominal wage rate W_1 prevailing. The demand schedule is $D(P_1)$. The equilibrium (full employment) quantity of labor employed is ON_1. Now suppose that aggregate demand falls, resulting in a fall in the price level from P_1 to P_0. The demand schedule shifts from $D(P_1)$ to $D(P_0)$. With the nominal wage rate still at W_1, workers will continue to supply ON_1. However, with the fall in the demand for labor, the quantity of labor hired is reduced to ON_0. Unemployment develops, which is the difference between ON_1 and ON_0. Should the price level thereafter rise and the demand schedule shift to the right, employment will increase from ON_0 to ON_1, after which point an increase in further employment will be accompanied by a rise in the nominal wage rate, although not necessarily in the real wage rate.

Although the idea provides an explanation for variations in unemployment in the face of changes in aggregate demand, it does violence to cherished assumptions about consumer, worker, and firm behavior. Most neoclassical analysis, including that employed in popular textbooks today, assumes the absence of money illusion. Indeed, it would seem that if one is to assume money illusion in the case of the labor

FIGURE 10-2
Labor Market: Money Illusion Case

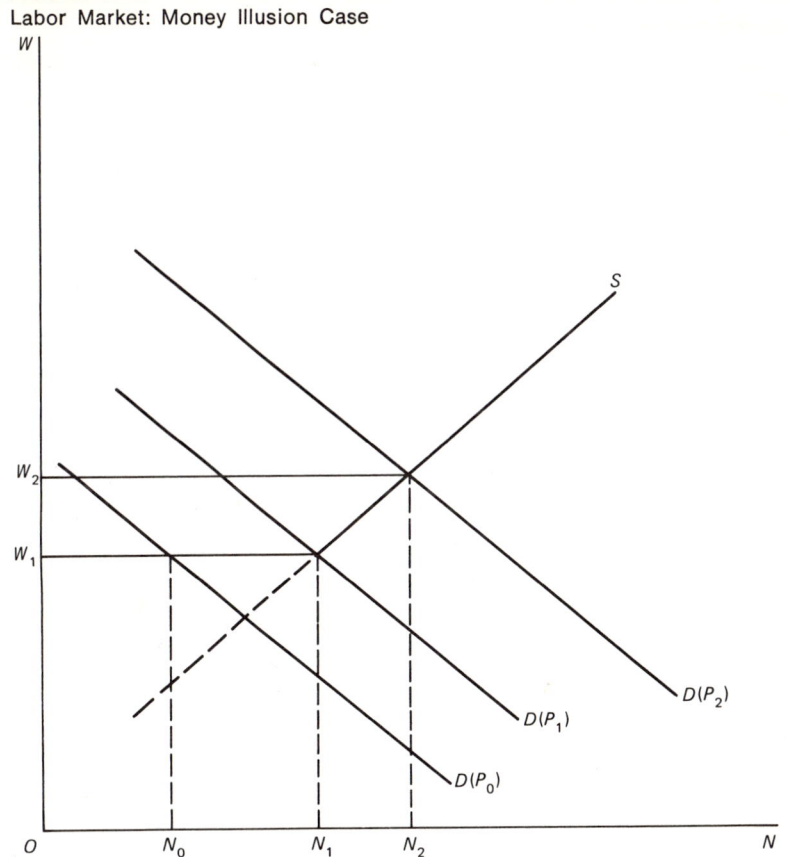

supply function, one should also make the same assumption when considering aggregate consumption because labor income is the main source of disposable income from which consumption expenditures are made. But to the contrary, we usually assume that real consumption expenditures depend on real disposable income, thus implying the absence of money illusion on the part of the household sector.[8]

SUMMARY NOTES

1. The labor demand curve is derived by setting the marginal product of labor equal to the real wage rate, under the assumption

---

[8] However, see the discussion in Thomas F. Dernburg and Duncan M. McDougall, *Macroeconomics,* 4th ed. (New York: McGraw-Hill Book Co., 1972), pp. 233–35.

that firms maximize profits. The approach assumes perfect competition in the factor and product markets.
2. The labor supply schedule is derived from the utility-maximizing choice between income (from wages) and leisure.
3. Assuming that leisure is a normal good, the income effect of an increase in the wage rate is the opposite of the substitution effect. Thus labor supply could vary directly or inversely with the real wage rate.
4. In general, the empirical evidence seems to indicate that the income effect dominates for men and the substitution effect dominates for women.

APPENDIX

The Cobb-Douglas production function can also provide us with some information about the nature of the aggregate supply function in the product market. When constructing the basic model we deduced only that aggregate supply varied directly with the price level and inversely with the nominal wage rate. We can now get some idea about the sensitivity of aggregate supply to changes in those variables.

Consider the labor demand function and the aggregate production function, both in logarithmic terms for convenience.

$$\ln N = (1/x)[\ln (1-x) + \ln A] - (1/x) \ln (W/P) + \ln K$$
$$\ln Y = \ln A + x \ln K + (1-x) \ln N$$

Substituting the demand function into the production function and simplifying, we obtain:

$$\ln = Y \ln A + x \ln K + \frac{(1-x)}{x} [\ln (1-x) + \ln A]$$
$$- \frac{(1-x)}{x} \ln (W/P) + (1-x) \ln K$$
$$= (1/x)[(1-x) \ln (1-x) + \ln A - (1-x) \ln (W/P)]$$
$$+ \ln K$$

Note that as long as $0 < x < 1$, aggregate supply varies inversely with the real wage rate as assumed in the basic model. Given the estimate that $x = 0.25$, the elasticity of aggregate supply with respect to the real wage rate is $(1 - 0.25)/0.25 = 3$. Thus a 1 percent fall in W/P will, *ceteris paribus*, induce a 3 percent increase in real output. A 1 percent fall in W/P may be the result of a 1 percent rise in

P or a 1 percent fall in W or some combination of changes in W and P.

DISCUSSION QUESTIONS

1. The analysis of labor supply in this chapter suggests that workers select their desired leisure-work time mix and their labor income, given their preferences and the real wage rate. Yet we have treated disposable income, of which labor income is a part, as given to, not chosen by, the household sector. Have we contradicted ourselves?

2. Do you know anyone for whom the income effect dominates the substitution effect? Male or female? "High" or "low" income?

3. How do workers become aware of changes in the real value of their earnings due to price level changes? How do we obtain information about price changes? Should the price level in the labor supply function be the *actual* price level or the price level *as perceived by labor?*

4. Figure 10–1 shows the effect of an increase in the hourly wage rate which pivots the opportunity line from AB to AC. However, suppose that an overtime system is used such that one wage rate applies to the first eight hours (per day) of work and a second, higher rate applies to work time in excess of eight hours per day. How would you modify line AB to reflect this? What is the effect on the number of hours offered for work?

11

Money Demand

ISSUES IN MONEY DEMAND

As in the case of consumption and investment, universal agreement does not exist on the determinants of the demand for money. Moreover, agreement does not even exist on the definition of money, and unless we can agree on the definition of money, we cannot agree on determinants of money demand. The "correct" definition of money, then, has been an important issue in monetary economics in the recent past. Is money a medium of exchange or primarily a store of value? Should we view money broadly as a utility-yielding asset? Is it a capital good? Each of these possible definitions of money has found its way into the literature, and each definition implies that a certain set of assets should be called money. As a first step in discussing money demand, we shall have to consider the definition of money.

The second issue at hand is to identify which factors influence the demand for money, however defined. Our discussion in Chapter 4 was confined to the interest rate and income. However, depending upon the definition of money selected, one may also wish to include such things as the price of money substitutes or perhaps some measure of wealth rather than income.

Once one is able to conceptually define those factors that influence the demand for money, the next step requires one to identify the empirical counterparts of those factors. For example, should the interest rate be defined as a long-term or a short-term interest rate? Further, which short-term interest rate or which long-term interest rate is appropriate? If it is generally conceded that the price of money substitutes should be included in the demand relationship, which substitutes will be selected? How will we discover which assets are substitutes for money? And finally, what will we use to measure the income or wealth constraint? Should it be current income, lagged income, permanent income, relative income? If we use a wealth measure, should wealth be defined as total nonhuman wealth or simply capital (nonfinancial) assets or both human and nonhuman wealth?

The literature dealing with these issues is very extensive, and a thorough survey must be left to a course in money and banking. We shall deal in this chapter with representative treatments of various issues.

THE DEFINITION OF MONEY

1. Approaching the problem from a "money-is-what-money-does" perspective, we can identify the functions of money and then identify all those assets in the economy that will fill those functions. Perhaps the narrowest approach is to say that money's primary, if not exclusive, function is to serve as a medium of exchange. That is, money is a good that enables transactions to be carried out in commodities, even though the buyer and seller are not necessarily interested in acquiring or selling each other's goods. For example, money enables the butcher to acquire the shoes from a shoemaker, even though the shoemaker may not want the meat that the butcher sells. The butcher simply sells his meat to any buyer in exchange for money and then exchanges his money for the shoes that he needs.

In the United States there are two assets that fulfill this exchange function of money: currency in the hands of the nonbank public plus the public's demand deposits. The continued use of both as a medium of exchange is, of course, subject to the condition that people are willing to accept these two assets in exchange for goods. At the present time, both currency and demand deposits are generally accepted as means of payment.

A definition of money that is derived from the functions that money is presumed to fill may lead to a particular specification of the demand for money. One might expect that a definition of money that focuses on the exchange medium characteristic would treat transactions, or some proxy for transactions, as a major determinant of the demand for money.

2. A second service that money performs is a value-storage service. Money is a store of value, a temporary abode of purchasing power. Since money can be exchanged for other goods, command over those goods may be accumulated by storing money. Thus, if I store 1,000 one-dollar bills in my mattress, I have stored power over $1,000 worth of goods. However, this command over goods is used in a temporary sense, because it is the goods themselves that we eventually wish to consume.

Viewing the value-storage function as a major one leads us to our first difficulty in defining money. It may well be that money serves as a temporary abode of purchasing power, but then so does virtually every other good in the economy. There is no reason why I cannot accumulate horses and use them to store up purchasing power. Admittedly, taking care of ten thousand dollars worth of horses is somewhat more inconvenient than keeping $10,000 in my checking account, but there is no reason why it could not be done. As might be expected, the focus on the value-storage function has led to a considerable number of definitions of money. The narrowest, and the one advanced by Milton Friedman,[1] would simply add time deposits at commercial banks to the conventional definition of money, and the broadest, advanced by Gurley and Shaw,[2] would add a wide range of financial assets to conventionally defined money. Why have we not added real assets to the definition even though those serve as a store of value? The answer is simply that real assets are not anywhere near as liquid as financial assets. Financial assets are in most circumstances very easily converted into exchange media, whereas real assets are not so easily converted. Consequently, those who focus on the value-storage function in defining money have broadened the definition beyond the conventional definition but have, nevertheless, confined the definition to include only financial assets. Now, of course, there is quite a bit of room for maneuvering, even within the range of financial assets. However, for all practical purposes, most studies have used short-term financial assets such as commercial bank time deposits, savings and loan association shares, and mutual savings bank deposits.

One should expect that the demand for money as a store of value

---

[1] For example, see Milton Friedman and Anna J. Schwartz, *Monetary Statistics of the United States* (National Bureau of Economic Research, 1970).

[2] John Gurley and Edward S. Shaw, *Money in a Theory of Finance* (Washington: Brookings Institution, 1960).

would be strongly influenced by the cost of holding money. The narrowest definition of money—currency plus demand deposits—is the most costly to hold. Neither currency nor demand deposits earn interest. Consequently the cost of using narrow money as a store of value is the full interest earnings that are lost by not using some other store of value such as savings and loan association shares.

3. Rather than segregate the functions of money, one may simply treat money in the same way as one treats any other good. Goods are held and/or consumed because they yield utility or satisfaction. Short-term goods such as food yield satisfaction through present consumption. Long-term goods such as automobiles yield satisfaction for the service (for example, transportation) that they provide over the life of the good. Similarly, money as an asset yields a service—the service of liquidity—and in that sense is unlike any other good. The liquidity service has a cost because while money is held, the utility derived from consuming the goods money can buy is foregone. Under this view, a wide range of assets would qualify as money. Money would include all those assets that are relatively liquid. How liquid an asset should be before it qualifies as money depends on who is defining money. In this case, as in the previous one discussed, a great many definitions of money have been advanced.[3]

4. Finally, from the standpoint of the business firm, money may be viewed as a capital asset, similar to other types of productive capital. This approach has been suggested by such writers as Milton Friedman and Martin Bailey.[4] Money may be viewed as a productive piece of capital in the sense that its usage enables the firm to mobilize other resources in a more efficient manner than would otherwise be possible

---

[3] The literature on definitions of money is extensive. Recent examples include the following: V. Karuppan Chetty, "On Measuring the Nearness of Near-Moneys," *American Economic Review,* Vol. 59 (June 1969), pp. 270–80; George Kaufman, "More on an Empirical Definition of Money," *American Economic Review,* Vol. 59 (March 1969), pp. 78–87; and Richard H. Timberlake, Jr. and James Fortson, "Time Deposits in the Definition of Money," *American Economic Review,* Vol. 57 (March 1967), pp. 190–94. For a survey, see David E. Laidler, "The Definition of Money: Theoretical and Empirical Problems," *Journal of Money, Credit, and Banking,* Vol. 1 (August 1969), pp. 508–25. Data problems may also influence the definition of money. For example, prior to the establishment of the Federal Reserve System, commercial banks did not provide separate series on time and demand deposits. Thus, studies using data prior to 1914 must include time deposits in the definition of money.

[4] Milton Friedman, "The Demand for Money: Some Theoretical and Empirical Results," *Journal of Political Economy,* Vol. 67 (August 1959), pp. 327–51. Martin Bailey, *National Income and the Price Level,* 2d ed. (New York: McGraw-Hill Book Co., 1970), especially Chapter 3.

and, hence, produce a larger output with given resource endowments than would otherwise be possible. Bailey simply argues that given the opportunity cost (the interest rate) of holding narrow money balances, no profit-maximizing firm would hold money if it did not yield some productive service. The fact that business firms do hold money balances is prima facie evidence that it is a productive asset. On this definition, the amount of money held by the firm would vary inversely with the cost of holding money, given the prices of the other factors of production.

Depending on the definition of money, one may include different arguments in a demand function for money. As we already indicated, a definition that identifies the exchange function of money as being the most important would focus on some measure of transactions as the prime determinant of the demand for money. Other definitions that treat money as a store of value or a utility-yielding or capital asset would also include the cost of holding money as a major consideration. In traditional demand theory, income is viewed as the appropriate constraint of the demand for consumer goods. In the case of money, and especially where money is viewed as an asset, the appropriate constraint may be the stock of wealth, rather than the current flow of income. The wide range of literature in money demand theory includes considerable variations on these basic elements. We shall now survey a number of the more important contributions and then examine the empirical studies that relate to those contributions.

SOME THEORIES OF MONEY DEMAND

The beginnings of monetary theory are embodied in the classical quantity theory of money. While the early quantity theory did not focus on the demand for money, it did focus on the relationship between the quantity of money and the general level of economic activity. It, therefore, implied something about the determinants of the demand for money. Adam Smith, for example, recognized money's function as a medium of exchange and referred to it as the lubricant that oils the great wheel of circulation by facilitating the exchange process. The use of money would draw into use resources that might otherwise be unemployed. More recently, Irving Fisher specified clearly the relationship between money and economic activity and embodied this relationship in the famous equation of exchange. The equation, $MV = PT$, is, in the Fisher sense, an identity. It simply states that the quantity of money times its velocity of circulation will be equal to the average price level times the number of transactions. However, one may use the equation of exchange as a framework within which a theory of money demand can be developed. If money is to be used primarily for carrying out transactions, an individual's "need" or want of money balances can be determined, given the level of transactions he wishes to engage in; or, specifically, we might say that the demand for money is a function of the number and value of transactions.

While Fisher did not take this approach, members of the so-called Cambridge school did. In essence, the question that Fisher was asking was: Given the total number and value of transactions that the economy is going to carry out, how much money is needed to carry out those transactions? The answer was that the transactions velocity of money determined how much money was needed. Hence, Fisher's analysis focused on the determinants of the velocity of transactions. The Cambridge economist, on the other hand (most notably, Alfred Marshall, and A. C. Pigou)[5] asked a question that was quite different. Specifically, given that money can be used to carry out transactions, what factors determined the total amount of money that individuals wished to hold? A consideration of interest rates, total wealth, income, and other elements became part of the analysis. But when all was said and done, under the assumption that transactions, income, and wealth were constant proportions of one another, the popular version of the Cambridge demand equation boiled down to making the demand for money a constant percentage of income. The implication was that at least for the short run, the demand for money was sufficiently insensitive to changes in the interest rate that those changes could be ignored, and only changes in income would be of importance. Another implication is that the short-run income velocity of money would also be a constant.

It remained for Keynes[6] to dissent vigorously from these propositions. He did not disagree that the need to carry out transactions formed a major basis for the demand for money. However, he added two additional dimensions which take into account uncertainty about the future, and the fact that money serves as a store of value in addi-

---

[5] A. C. Pigou, "The Value of Money," *Quarterly Journal of Economics,* Vol. 31 (November 1917), pp. 38–65.

[6] John Maynard Keynes, *The General Theory of Employment, Interest, and Money* (New York: Harcourt, Brace and World, Inc., 1936), Chapter 15.

tion to its being a medium of exchange. In the first, future transactions are not known with certainty. Consequently, from time to time unexpected expenditures are made which were not previously planned for. Money, because it does serve as a store of value, could act as a cushion or a reservoir of purchasing power that could be used to make unexpected or unplanned-for transactions as the need arose. Keynes identified this motive, or need, for holding money as the *precautionary motive*.

In addition to the transactions and precautionary motives for holding money, Keynes identified a third motive which also follows from the fact that money is a store of value and that there is uncertainty about the future. A question might be raised as to why individuals hold any money at all as a store of value, or as a reservoir of purchasing power, if there exist alternative forms in which to store value which, in addition, yield some positive rate of return (that is, some rate of interest). The answer is simply that the rate of return, or interest rate, on alternative financial assets is uncertain. Consider the case of marketable bonds. Bonds generally pay a fixed-dollar amount of interest payments per year. Expressing the fixed-dollar interest payments as a percent of the price that one pays for the bond, gives us the effective interest yield for that bond. For example, if I pay $100 for a bond that pays $5 annually, the interest return on the bond is 5 percent. However, suppose I hold the bond for one year, receive one $5 interest payment, and then sell the bond. And suppose no one is willing to pay me $100 for the bond, but instead the highest price I can sell the bond for is $95. I will have suffered, in that case, a capital loss of $5, since I paid $100 for the bond and could only sell it for $95. I received a $5 interest payment, hence the bond paid 5 percent interest; but I suffered a 5 percent capital loss, and therefore my net return was zero.

Now, suppose I was faced with a choice of buying a bond today or not, and suppose I had a strong expectation that I would want to sell the bond a year from now, if I did buy it today. And once more I strongly suspected that the price of the bond would fall between the time I purchased it and the time I sold it. Would I buy the bond? Probably not. For if I strongly expected to incur a capital loss that might exceed the interest rate I would receive on the bond, I would lose overall if I went ahead and purchased the bond. On the other hand, if I held onto the money instead, my return (although zero) would be certain. At least I would not expect a negative return. So, given that I expect bond prices to fall, which is the same as saying I expect interest rates to rise, I would prefer a higher degree of liquidity—that is, I would prefer to hold onto money. (We are abstracting from changes in the value of money due to changes in the price of goods.)

This liquidity preference forms Keynes' *speculative motive* for holding money. With respect to the individual, once the transactions and precautionary motives are satisfied, any further holding of money balances becomes an all-or-nothing proposition. Either I expect the capital loss, or I do not expect a capital loss; and hence I will hold either bonds or money.

Now *my* expectations about future interest rates may be different from the expectations of other individuals. While I may consider a 2 percent interest rate to be the lowest possible interest rate, someone else may consider the lowest possible interest rate to be 1.5 percent, a third person may consider the lowest possible interest rate to be 1.8 percent, and so on. If we aggregate all of our individual liquidity preference schedules, we obtain a smooth curve that is downward sloping on a graph with the rate of interest on the vertical axis and desired cash balances on the horizontal axis, as in Figure 11–1. That is, the aggregate speculative demand for money varies inversely with the rate of interest.

Thus Keynes introduced the rate of interest as a major determinant of the demand for money, and this factor has tended to dominate post-Keynesian thinking about money demand. We saw earlier in the development of the basic model that the extent to which money demand is sensitive to the rate of interest strongly influences the efficacy of monetary policy. Much of the postdepression downgrading of monetary policy followed the belief that the demand for money was highly sensitive to the rate of interest. In fact, it was argued that at certain low rates of interest, the preference for liquidity would become absolute so that the interest rate could not be depressed any further. This occurs at i^* in Figure 11–1. Increases in the money stock beyond $(M/P)^*$ would result in no reduction in the interest rate. Consequently, monetary policy would be powerless to stimulate investment spending by business firms.

The Keynesian trichotomy provided the framework for much of the work in money demand theory over the last 30 years. Both William Baumol and James Tobin expanded the analysis of the transactions demand for money and included the interest rate as a determinant

FIGURE 11–1
The Speculative Demand for Money

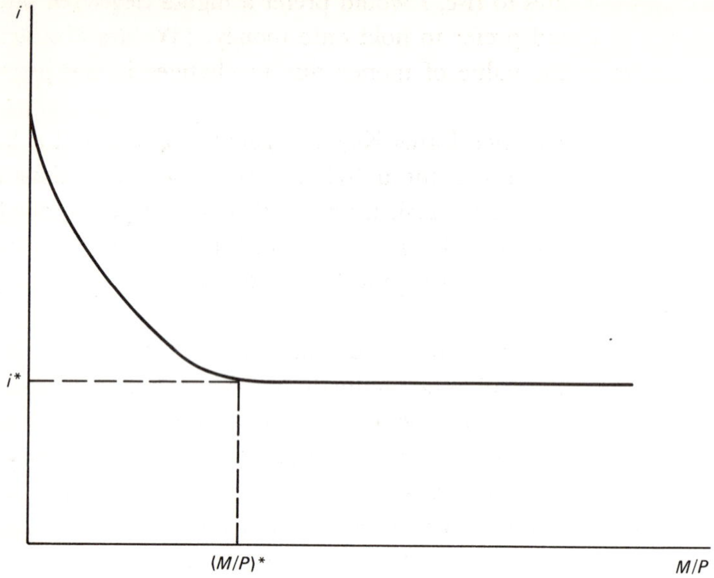

of the transactions demand.[7] In particular, their analyses point out that money is held to bridge the gap between the receipt of payments, so as to be able to finance expenditures on goods in the interim period. However, the total expenditures for a given period are not all made at the beginning of the period but are, instead, spread out over the entire period. Consequently, not all of the money balances accumulated at the beginning of the period are needed. It would therefore be to the benefit of the individual to purchase interest-earning assets with the excess money balances until such time as they are needed to carry out transactions.

Suppose, for example, I received a payment of $1,000, and I planned to spend $250 each Wednesday for the next four weeks—at the end of which time I would receive another $1,000. If I took the thousand dollars and placed it in my checking account, then until the first Wednesday I would be holding $1,000 in idle cash balances which are earning no interest. I would then spend $250, and from that period until the second Wednesday I would be holding $750 in idle money

---

[7] William Baumol, "The Transactions Demand for Cash: An Inventory Theoretic Approach," *Quarterly Journal of Economics*, Vol. 66 (November 1952), pp. 545–56. James Tobin, "The Interest-Elasticity of Transactions Demand for Cash," *Review of Economics and Statistics*, Vol. 38 (August 1956), pp. 241–47.

balances earning no interest, and so on. Since I only need $250 in my checking account to finance the first week's expenditures, it would pay me to place $750 into some form of interest-earning asset. In the second week, when I needed the second $250, I would cash in $250 of this interest earning asset in order to make the expenditures, leaving the remaining $500 to still earn interest. Of course, the interest earnings are to some extent offset by the brokerage costs of converting money into interest-earning assets and the assets back into money. From these considerations, one might derive an optimal average cash balance to be held, given the total dollar volume of transactions that are planned to occur, the interest rate on the financial asset, and the brokerage cost.

Let Y be real income per period which will be spent in its entirety over the period. The individual receives Y at the beginning of each period, converts all of Y into bonds, and cashes C dollars (in real terms) worth when needed to make expenditures. The number of withdrawals is therefore Y/C per period. If each withdrawal is subject to a brokerage cost of b dollars, total brokerage fees are $b(Y/C)$. Assuming that the expenditure of C is done uniformly, the average real cash balance held is equal to $C/2$. The opportunity cost of holding $C/2$ is $i(C/2)$, where i is the interest rate. The total cost of the process is then:

$$TC = b\frac{Y}{C} + i\frac{C}{2}$$

The size of C that will minimize TC can be found by setting $\frac{\partial TC}{\partial C} = 0$ and solving for C.

Thus:

$$\frac{\partial TC}{\partial C} = \frac{-bY}{C^2} + \frac{i}{2} = 0$$

$$C^2 = \frac{2bY}{i}$$

$$C = \sqrt{\frac{2bY}{i}}$$

Since the average real money holdings (M/P) is equal to $C/2$, we have:

$$M/P = \frac{1}{2}\sqrt{\frac{2bY}{i}}$$

The implications of the above analysis, which is representative of the approach taken by Baumol and Tobin, are the following: The transactions demand for money varies inversely with the square root of the interest rate and directly with the square root of the volume of transactions and the square root of the brokerage fee. In particular, note that if the volume of transactions is a constant proportion of the level of income (as assumed above), then the demand for money is implied to vary directly with the square root of income. Should income increase, say, by 4 times, the demand for money would simply double. In other words, the income elasticity of the demand for money is $\frac{1}{2}$. Compare this with, say, the Cambridge equation, which implies that the income elasticity of the demand for money is one. We will see later how the empirical evidence bears on this distinction. The analysis also concludes that the interest elasticity of the demand for transaction balances is $-\frac{1}{2}$, a proposition that can also be subjected to empirical verification.

The precautionary demand for money and the speculative demand for money, like the transactions demand, have been treated separately and extended by various writers since Keynes first introduced the ideas. The Baumol methodology has been applied to the precautionary demand by Tsiang.[8] More recently, Weinrobe[9] has treated the demand for precautionary balances as simply the necessity of accommodating uncertainty in the demand for transactions balances. As in the case of the transactions demand for money, these analyses have included variables other than income in the demand equation. They may be considered a generalization of Keynes work within the Keynesian framework.

One treatment of the speculative demand for money as simply liquidity preference deserves special attention. The work by James Tobin[10] in this area is important because it leads to a much broader treatment of the demand for money than was employed by either Keynes or many of his antecedants. Specifically, Tobin deals with the individual's decision to allocate his wealth between two different kinds of assets. One asset yields a potentially positive rate of return

---

[8] S. C. Tsiang, "The Precautionary Demand for Money: An Inventory Theoretical Analysis," *Journal of Political Economy,* Vol. 77 (January/February 1969), pp. 99–117.

[9] Maurice D. Weinrobe, "A Simple Model of the Precautionary Demand for Money," *Southern Economic Journal* Vol. 39 (July 1972), pp. 11–18.

[10] James Tobin, "Liquidity Preference as Behavior Towards Risk," *Review of Economic Studies* Vol. 25 (February 1958), pp. 65–87.

but has some risk associated with it; the other asset yields a zero rate of return but has no risk associated with it. The asset with risk is bonds. Holding bonds implies a risk for the reasons discussed earlier. Bond prices are subject to fluctuations in the marketplace and should one buy a bond today, there is no certainty that the bond can be sold for the same price, or any other given price, at any point before the bond matures. Consequently, the bond's yield is equal to the interest rate plus the percent change in its price or, what is the same thing, minus the percent change in the interest rate. The other asset that may be held is money. This asset yields no interest return and has no fluctuation in its price. Consequently, it yields a zero, but certain, return. If an individual allocates all of his wealth to money holdings, then his total return is zero and his risk is zero. If he allocates all of this wealth to bonds, then he encounters a maximum possible return and also maximum risk. The question that Tobin deals with is what percentage of an individual's wealth holdings will be held in the form of money, and what percentage will be held in the form of bonds, given the interest rate on bonds and their risk level?

The answer is obtained by employing conventional indifference curve analysis. Risk is measured by the standard deviation of percent changes in bond prices. The greater the fluctuation in bond prices, the greater the standard deviation and, thus, the greater the risk. In Figure 11–2 we have plotted on the horizontal axis the standard deviation of percent changes in bond prices (σ). The standard deviation varies from zero up to σ_0, which is the maximum variation that can be experienced in bond prices under the assumption that one holds all his wealth in the form of bonds. On the vertical axis, the individual's wealth (W) is plotted. The indifference curves, I_0, I_1, and I_2 are drawn under the assumption that individuals are risk avoiders. That is, higher levels of risk are associated with lower utility levels. On the other hand, higher levels of wealth are associated with higher utility levels.

Let the individual's wealth holdings be denoted by W_0 and the interest rate paid on bonds be denoted by i. We can then plot a budget constraint as follows: If the individual holds all money and no bonds, then his wealth holdings at the end of one year would be the same as they are now. Hence we plot W_0 on the vertical axis. If the individual held all bonds and no money, then his wealth holdings at the end of the year would $W_0(1+i)$. This is shown plotted on the vertical line drawn at risk level σ_0. The budget constraint line connects

FIGURE 11-2
Portfolio Optimization

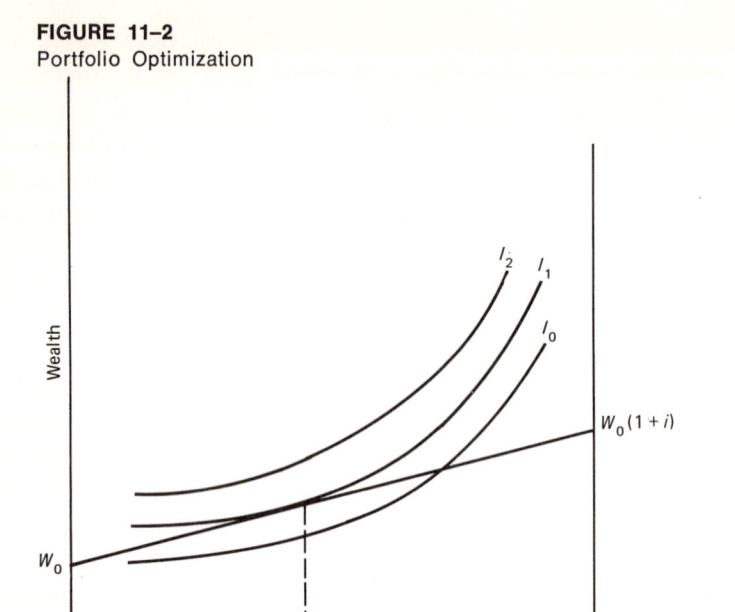

these two points. The individual will maximize satisfaction if he holds money and bonds in such a ratio as to make the budget constraint line tangent to the highest indifference curve. In the above figure, this would occur at risk level σ_1, and that risk level would have associated with it a particular distribution of wealth between bonds and money. The apparatus can be used to derive propositions about the effect on desired money holdings of changes in the interest rate, total wealth, and risk.

But the importance of Tobin's analysis extends far beyond this. What Tobin has done is to apply conventional utility-maximizing behavior to the problem of distributing one's financial wealth over a number of different assets. In the two asset case, illustrated above, the choice was made on the basis of the relative yields of the two assets, given the total wealth to be distributed and the riskiness of the interest-earning asset. The procedure may be generalized to include a whole range of financial assets. Demand curves for each individual asset may then be derived in the process. The results should be no different than in the case of choice among real goods. In particular, the demand for any single asset would vary directly with its own yield and inversely with the yield on substitutes, given the total level of wealth and the risk structure of all the assets. The demand for money is treated no differently than the demand for any other financial asset.

This approach, commonly referred to as the *portfolio balance approach,* has profound implications for monetary policy. In particular, it is argued by its proponents that monetary policy, formulated in terms of changes in the money supply only, may well prove to be an ineffective tool of stabilization policy. What is relevant is financial control, rather than simply money supply control.

At this juncture one might be led to ask why the demand for money is an element in the theory of choice among financial assets. Rather, shouldn't the demand for money be treated as an element in the theory of choice among all assets, financial and real? As a matter of fact, this approach has been taken by the so-called modern quantity theorists. Milton Friedman, in particular, makes the demand for money depend not only on its own yield and the yield of financial substitutes but also on the yield on real goods, as measured by the rate of change in the prices of those goods. Thus the demand for money would vary directly with its own yield, inversely with the yield on substitute financial assets, and inversely with the rate of change in the price of goods.

Friedman also broadens the definition of the wealth constraint to include human wealth. What distinguishes the modern quantity theory from the portfolio balance approach and makes it more kin to the earlier quantity theory is the uniqueness that money is considered to have. Generally, the advocates of the portfolio balance approach do not consider money to be uniquely different from any other financial asset. The quantity theorist, on the other hand, ascribes a unique character to money and a casual relationship between changes in the quantity of money and changes in the level of economic activity, the strength of which is not agreed to by the portfolio economist. In particular, those who promote the portfolio balance approach would argue that the equilibrium quantity of money in the economy is a result of many utility-maximizing and profit-maximizing decisions made in the economy, together with some influence from the central bank. The modern quantity theorist, on the other hand—in particular, Friedman—treats the nominal money stock as being exogenously determined by the central bank; and the public, through its actions, causes interest rates and prices to adjust to accommodate to that stock of money. The two approaches, then—although sharing considerable common ground on the determinants of money demand—nevertheless are far apart on the policy implications of their respective analyses.

The reader may have gotten the impression that many of the competing theories have equally persuasive arguments on their side and that in the final analysis resolution of the disagreements must rely upon recourse to empirical data. Many economists would agree with that assessment, and it is in that spirit that we turn now to consider some of the empirical studies of money demand.

RELATED EMPIRICAL STUDIES

Two questions might be asked with respect to the role the interest rate plays in determining money demand.

1. Is the relationship between the interest rate and money demand a negative relationship?
2. Does the demand for money become more elastic, with respect to the interest rate, at lower interest rates than at higher interest rates?

No monetary economist quibbles over the first question. The empirical evidence strongly indicates a negative and significant relationship between the rate of interest and money demand. The second question is more crucial—for on the answer to the second question hinges the success or failure of monetary policy in the view of many economists. You may recall that back in Chapter 7 we discussed the conditions under which monetary policy would be negated. Specifically, monetary policy becomes ineffective if the LM schedule approaches a horizontal position. This could result from one of two sources: Either the demand for money could be perfectly elastic with respect to the interest rate, or the supply of money could be perfectly elastic with respect to the interest rate. In this chapter we will look at the evidence that bears on the first source. We save until the next chapter the evidence that bears on the second possibility.

This question was examined as early as 1947 by James Tobin.[11] Tobin defined idle money balances, which is roughly the analogy of the speculative demand for money, as the difference between total money demanded and that portion held for transaction purposes. Having obtained estimates of such idle money balances, he then plotted

---

[11] James Tobin, "Liquidity Preference and Monetary Policy," *Review of Economics and Statistics,* Vol. 29 (May 1947), pp. 124–31.

those against the average interest rates of commercial paper for the years 1922 to 1945. The results were quite striking. The scatter of points is negatively sloped and, at about a 1 percent interest rate, flattens out and becomes horizontal. These results would seem to confirm the liquidity trap hypothesis. However, Tobin's definition of transactions balances may be flawed because his measure of transactions includes only those for which payment was made by check. Transactions involving cash were ignored for a very practical reason, no records exist. Moreover, the assumption was made that in 1929 no idle balances were held and that the total amount of money demanded in 1929 was for transactions purposes only.

It is generally argued by those who support the liquidity trap hypothesis that this was a reasonable explanation for why monetary policy allegedly did not work during the depth of the depression during the 1930s.

However, virtually all of the scatter points in Tobin's analysis that fall into the range of the liquidity trap occurred during the World War II years, from 1940 through 1945, not during the depression. During that time the Federal Reserve Bank, through its own actions, pegged interest rates at very low levels and held them there. In short, we may have had a liquidity trap on the supply side rather than on the money demand side. We will return to this point in the next chapter.

At the opposite end of the spectrum, Milton Friedman, writing in 1959, could find no discernible relationship between money demand and the rate of interest.[12] However, Friedman's analysis may be flawed by the definition of money he chose to use. He defined money broadly as consisting of currency in the hands of the public, the public's demand deposits, and time deposits at commercial banks. Moreover, the movements he observed were long-term movements occurring over the course of business cycles. Now on the one hand, the demand for money should vary inversely with the yield on substitutes; on the other hand, it should vary directly with its own yield. Money narrowly defined to include only currency in the hands of the public, plus demand deposits, has a yield of zero. Consequently its demand should vary inversely with the interest rate on some alternative assets. However, time deposits have a positive and safe yield, and if over a period of time the interest rate on time deposits and interest rates on alternative

---

[12] Friedman, "The Demand for Money."

assets vary proportionately, then there is no reason on this ground alone that the demand for time deposits should change. By defining money broadly to include those time deposits, the interest rate effect may be washed out.

As might be expected, most other studies of money demand arrive at interest rate elasticity estimates that fall somewhere between those implied by Tobin's work and Friedman's work. In 1960 Bronfenbrenner and Mayer set out to test the liquidity trap hypothesis.[13] In so doing, they defined idle balances in a manner analogous to the definition used by Tobin. Assuming a logarithmic relationship between the demand for idle balances and the interest rate, they estimated the interest elasticity of idle balances to be -1.16. Unfortunately the logarithmic form of the demand equation could not test for the existence of higher elasticities at lower interest rates because such a form implies a constant elasticity at all interest rates.

The work by Tobin, Friedman, and Bronfenbrenner and Mayer either found or assumed the elasticity of one variable and then proceeded to attempt to determine the elasticity on the residual variable. Modern high-speed computers and multiple regression analysis have made it possible to estimate both the income and interest elasticities simultaneously. One early attempt along these lines was conducted by Allan Meltzer.[14] The time covered by Meltzer was 1900–1958. He used three different definitions of income and wealth and three definitions of money. The interest rate was a long-term interest rate. Meltzer found a negative relationship between the demand for money and the interest rate with all definitions of income, wealth, and money. The average elasticity was about -0.7.

However, all of these and similar studies suffer from what econometricians call the "identification problem."

The identification problem arises because the interest rate and the quantity of money demanded and supplied are jointly determined by the interaction of the demand function and the supply function. As long as one is willing to permit the nominal supply of money to vary directly with the interest rate (as we have done earlier in this book), then one cannot treat the equilibrium nominal money stock as an exogenous variable. The real money stock is endogenous because the

---

[13] Martin Bronfenbrenner and Thomas Mayer, "Liquidity Functions in the American Economy," *Econometrica,* Vol. 28 (October 1960), pp. 810–34.

[14] Allan H. Meltzer, "The Demand for Money: The Evidence from the Time Series," *Journal of Political Economy,* Vol. 81 (June 1963), pp. 219–46.

11 / Money Demand

price level is endogenous. In our basic model, both the real and nominal money stocks are endogenous. However, the studies discussed above have treated the nominal money stock as exogenous.

The problem can be illustrated by recourse to Figure 11–3. In Figure 11–3A several money demand and supply functions are plotted. Nominal money is shown on the horizontal axis, so changes in real income *and* the price level result in shifts in the demand curve. The supply curve shifts in response to changes in the nominal monetary base. The number attached to each function identifies the period to which that function applies. The observed interest rate and money stock values will be the equilibrium values for each one of those periods. The scatter of points derived from Figure 11–3A is plotted in Figure 11–3B.

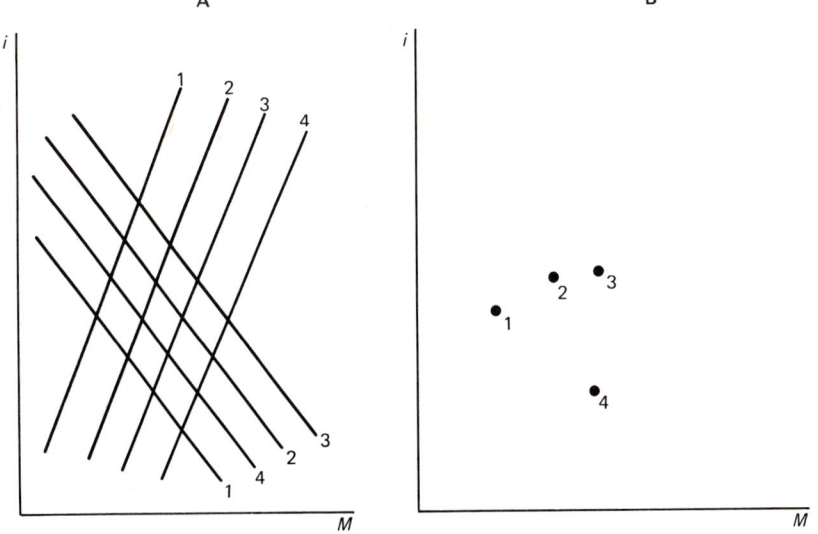

FIGURE 11–3
The Identification Problem in the Money Market

Note that it would be very difficult to fit a single freehand line through those points, and it should be clear that whatever single line is fitted represents the influence of shifts in both the money demand and money supply functions. Therefore that single, fitted line cannot be taken to be either a demand or supply function. Consequently, a more appropriate technique would be one that takes cognizance of the simultaneous (two-equation) determination of the money stock and the interest rate.

Attempts to deal with this problem were undertaken by Brunner and Meltzer and by Teigen.[15] The former, using a long-term interest rate, obtained an interest elasticity estimate of −0.7. Teigen, on the other hand, used a short-term interest rate and got an elasticity of −0.15.

The two studies are not necessarily inconsistent over the normal course of the business cycle. Percentage fluctuations in short-term interest rates are usually greater than those in long-term interest rates. Given the definition of the interest elasticity—namely, the percent change in the quantity of money demanded divided by the percent change in the interest rate—any study using a long-term interest rate will yield larger elasticity coefficients than studies using short-term interest rates. What is of importance, however, is that the elasticity coefficient that Teigen obtained using a different estimating technique was only slightly different from the elasticity obtained using the single-equation estimating technique on the same set of data. Apparently the identification problem is not very severe, at least in the money market.

Controversy over the interest elasticity of money demand has stemmed directly from the issue of the effectiveness of monetary policy. Hence considerable attention has been devoted to answering the question of whether or not money demand is responsive to the rate of interest and, further, just how responsive. However, most money demand studies have also yielded information about the income and wealth elasticities. In general, studies have found that the income and wealth elasticities of money demand are approximately equal to one. Friedman did find a higher income elasticity, 1.8. However, this may be due to his inclusion of time deposits in the definition of money. Time deposits are generally perceived to be a luxury good and hence would have an income elasticity greater than one.

When discussing the demand for money in Chapter 4, we assumed that money holders were free of money illusion. The implication is that the demand for nominal money balances is proportional to the price level—that is, the demand for nominal money balances has a

---

[15] Karl Brunner and Allan Meltzer, "Some Further Investigations of Demand and Supply Functions for Money," *Journal of Finance,* Vol. 19 (May 1964), pp. 240–83. Ronald L. Teigen, "Demand and Supply Functions for Money in the United States: Some Structural Estimates," *Econometrica,* Vol. 32 (October 1964), pp. 476–509.

price elasticity equal to one. Various studies (for example, one done by Meltzer in 1963) have borne this out.[16]

There remains the question of the substitutability amongst financial assets, including money, that is implied by the portfolio balance approach. Recall that the portfolio balance approach argues that the demand for any financial asset, of which money is only one, should depend upon its own price and the price of substitutes as well as either income or wealth constraints. This means that money conventionally defined, for example, should be sensitive to interest rates on time deposits, savings and loan association shares, and other potential substitutes. One study done by Feige in 1964 estimated the cross elasticities among demand deposits, time deposits, and savings and loan shares for the period 1949–1958.[17] While statistically significant, the elasticities were low—in all cases, less than one. Tom Hun Lee conducted tests to determine the extent to which money and other financial assets were substitutes and came to the conclusion that a definition of money that ignores other financial assets is likely to be in error.[18] His results were vigorously disputed by Michael Hamburger in subsequent work.[19] On the basis of the empirical evidence to date, this issue is still largely undecided.

Summarizing the empirical evidence:

1. The demand for money has been found to be inversely related to the interest rate, as postulated by Keynes. But the responsiveness, as measured by elasticity coefficients, is rather low. No evidence has been found, using United States data for the last 70 years, of the Keynesian liquidity trap.
2. Income and wealth appear to play almost equally important roles in money demand, and their elasticities conform to the neoclassical assumption of unitary elasticity.
3. Virtually all studies have found that the demand for nominal money balances is proportional to the price level, consistent with the idea that money holders are free of money illusion.

---

[16] Meltzer, "The Demand for Money."

[17] Edgar Feige, *The Demand for Liquid Assets: A Temporal Cross-Section Analysis* (Englewood Cliffs, N.J.: Prentice-Hall, 1964).

[18] Tom Hun Lee, "Alternative Interest Rates and the Demand for Money: The Empirical Evidence," *American Economic Review*, Vol. 57 (December 1967), pp. 1168–81.

[19] Michael J. Hamburger, "Alternative Interest Rates and the Demand for Money: Comment," *American Economic Review*, Vol. 59 (June 1969), pp. 407–12.

4. No definite and universal conclusions have been reached about the extent to which money and other financial assets are substitutes.

SUMMARY NOTES

1. Money serves as a medium of exchange and a store of value. The latter use implies a great many definitions for money. The narrowest definition consists of the public's holdings of currency and demand deposits. Broader definitions would include other financial assets.
2. Keynes identified three motives for holding money: the transactions, precautionary, and speculative motives. The transactions and precautionary motives are a function of income. The speculative motive is a function of the interest rate.
3. Tobin applied utility-maximizing behavior to the choice between bonds and money to derive the speculative demand for money. The analysis formed the basis for the portfolio balance approach to the demand for financial assets.
4. The modern quantity theory treats the demand for money as an element in the theory of choice among all assets, including real assets.
5. Empirical evidence supports the hypothesis that the demand for money varies inversely with the interest rate. The interest elasticity has been found to be very low. The demand for money also appears to be proportional to the price level and to real income (or wealth).

DISCUSSION QUESTIONS

1. Consider an economy without money. How would transactions be carried out? How would you measure the "overall price level"?
2. In Tobin's analysis of the speculative demand for money, interest can be obtained only by acquiring assets that entail risk. Suppose we postulate an interest-bearing asset that is risk free (for example, ordinary savings accounts). How would this affect Tobin's speculative demand for money? What is the implication for the interest elasticity of the total demand for money?
3. Why do you hold money balances? If you found yourself with larger money balances than you wished to hold at some point in time, how

would you dispose of the excess? What factors might determine the method of disposing of the excess? Have any of those factors been left out of the discussion in this chapter?

4. No mention was made of the role played by credit in this chapter. Yet credit cards do play a role in the exchange process. Can credit cards be considered a money substitute? What is the function of credit cards in the exchange process?

12

Money Supply

THE development of money supply theory is a relatively recent phenomenon in the history of economic analysis. The pure *mechanics* of the money supply process were usually covered in standard textbooks prior to the 1960s. During the 1960s a number of writers began to add propositions about the behavior of the bank and nonbank public to the money supply framework by assuming that the nonbank public adjusts its holdings of financial assets so as to maximize utility and by assuming that banks adjust their assets so as to maximize profits.[1]

The money supply, previously treated as an exogenous, policy controlled variable, now became an endogenous variable reflecting both the behavior of the private sector and the input provided by the monetary policy makers. The starting point is the accounting framework of the nonbank public, the private banking system, and the central bank. With the accounting framework specified, appropriate behavioral hypotheses can be incorporated so as to provide the life of theory to the money supply process.

In this chapter we shall first derive a money supply framework

---

[1] Much of the seminal work appears in Karl Brunner, "A Schema for the Supply Theory of Money," *International Economic Review*, Vol. 11 (January 1961), pp. 79–109. For a survey of several alternative models, see David I. Fand, "Some Implications of Money Supply Analysis," *American Economic Review*, Vol. 57 (May 1967), pp. 380–400.

from the appropriate balance sheets. We shall then examine the ways in which utility- and profit-maximizing behavior alters the elements in these balance sheets and thus alters the money supply. Following that, we will examine some of the implications for policy that follow from an endogenous treatment of the money supply, and we will also examine some of the empirical studies that have been done on the money supply process.

THE MONEY SUPPLY FRAMEWORK
Balance Sheets of the System

In deriving the following money supply framework, we will concentrate only on the elements of the financial system relevant to our analysis. This abstracts somewhat from the real world, but the principal thrust of money supply theory can be gleaned from what we have here.

The financial status of any accounting unit—at a point in time—is represented by the unit's balance sheet. The balance sheet lists on the left side the assets of the accounting unit and on the right side the unit's liabilities. The difference between total assets and total liabilities, usually called net worth, is also listed on the right side. Balance sheets, by definition, must balance. That is to say, the sum of the items on the left side must equal the sum of the items on the right side.

Generally, an asset of an accounting unit is anything to which the unit has legal title or which is owed to that unit. Liabilities represent claims of others on the unit. Finally, net worth is the difference between the two. For an individual, typical assets might include one's house, car, checking account deposits, cash, diamond rings, and loans advanced to other people. An individual's liabilities might include the mortgage on the house, the installment loan on the car, and other assorted debts.

In discussing the money supply process, however, we shall be mainly concerned with financial assets rather than with real assets. The transactions that follow in the balance sheets of the bank and nonbank public and the central bank include only financial assets and liabilities. Nevertheless, the *changes* must balance out. For a given unit, if an asset is increased, some liabilities must also increase or some assets decrease or some combination of the two, so that after the changes are made, the balance sheet is still in balance.

The pertinent assets and liabilities of the private banks are shown below:

BALANCE SHEET ITEMS OF PRIVATE BANKS

Assets	Liabilities
Vault cash	Demand deposits
Deposits with Federal Reserve	Time deposits
Loans to the public	Borrowing from Federal Reserve
U.S. government securities	

Some of the items listed above are self explanatory, but others may require explanation. "Deposits with Federal Reserve" represents sums placed on deposit with the Federal Reserve Bank by the private banks. These are analogous to the deposits made by individuals in the private banks. In this sense, the Federal Reserve Bank (affectionately known as the "Fed") is often called a bank for bankers. These deposits are listed as an asset of private banks because the funds are owed to the banks by the Fed. "U.S. government securities" represents holdings of bonds, notes, and bills issued by the U.S. Treasury.

Private banks that are members of the Federal Reserve System have the privilege of borrowing on a short-term basis from the Fed. These funds are then owed to the Federal Reserve Bank and are listed as the private bank's liability. There are other financial items, such as deposits made by the U.S. Treasury in the private bank, but these are relatively minor and we shall ignore them.

The important balance sheet items of the Federal Reserve Bank are shown below:

BALANCE SHEET ITEMS OF THE FEDERAL RESERVE BANK

Assets	Liabilities
U.S. government securities	Federal Reserve notes outstanding
Loans to banks	Deposits of banks
	Treasury deposits

Note that like the private banks, the Fed also owns government securities. The borrowings by the private banks show up as an asset of the Federal Reserve Bank, and deposits made by private banks with the Fed show up as a liability of the Fed. The U.S. Treasury also makes deposits with the Fed which become the Fed's liability.

Federal Reserve Notes are the green pieces of paper that we all covet, and these are a liability of the Fed. The Federal Reserve Bank may issue Federal Reserve Notes in order to acquire assets such as U.S. government securities. However, the usual impetus to the issuance of Federal Reserve Notes comes from the nonbank public through a process that we shall observe shortly. Before we do that, we need to consider the balance sheet of the nonbank public.

BALANCE SHEET ITEMS OF THE NONBANK PUBLIC

Assets	Liabilities
Currency (cash)	Loans from banks
Demand deposits	
Time deposits	
U.S. government securities	

The assets and liabilities shown above for the nonbank public have already been identified in the accounts of the other two units. Note that demand and time deposits—liabilities of the private banks—are assets of the nonbank public. Similarly, loans from banks—a liability of the nonbank public—is an asset of the private banks. Finally, the currency held by the public consists mainly of Federal Reserve Notes which are liabilities of the Fed.

The picture would be rounded out if we also included the U.S. Treasury. However, the Treasury's role in the money supply process is a relatively minor one, and we shall abstract from its influence. Of the total of vault cash held by private banks and currency held by the public, over 90 percent is supplied by the Fed and the remainder by the Treasury. Moreover the dominant thrust of monetary policy is exercised by the Federal Reserve Bank.

You may have already noticed that the three units are linked through their balance sheets. It would be difficult for one unit to alter the composition of its balance sheet without one or both of the other units altering their balance sheets. By way of illustration, consider two cases.

Case 1. Suppose some members of the nonbank public decide to increase their currency holdings, for some reason, by $100. They might do this by simply cashing checks drawn on their own personal checking accounts (demand deposits) for $100. This would have the effect of reducing the demand deposits of the public by $100 and increasing its currency holdings by the same amount. The private banks, on the other hand, would pay out the $100, reducing their vault cash and their demand deposit liabilities by $100. Should the private banks wish to retain their previous level of vault cash, they now have the option of going to the Fed and withdrawing $100 in Federal Reserve Notes. The Fed will receive payment for this by reducing the accounts of those banks by $100. The three balance sheets and the changes that result from these transactions are shown below:

NONBANK PUBLIC

Assets		Liabilities
Currency	+100	
Demand deposits	−100	

PRIVATE BANKS

Assets		Liabilities	
Vault cash	−100	Demand Deposits	−100
Deposits with the Fed	−100		
Vault cash	+100		

FEDERAL RESERVE BANK

Assets	Liabilities	
	Federal Reserve Notes	+100
	Deposits of banks	−100

Case 2. Suppose the Federal Reserve wishes to buy $200 worth of U.S. government securities that are currently outstanding. Further suppose that it buys the securities from private banks. The transaction will appear as an increase in the Fed's holdings of government securities and a decrease in the private bank's holdings. The Federal Reserve will pay for the government securities by increasing the deposit accounts of the banks from whom it purchased the securities. This will show up as an increase in deposits with the Fed on the balance sheet of the private banks. The transactions are shown below:

PRIVATE BANKS

Assets		Liabilities
Deposits with the Fed	+200	
U.S. government securities	−200	

FEDERAL RESERVE BANK

Assets		Liabilities	
U.S. government securities	+200	Deposits of banks	+200

Are there further repercussions from these sample transactions? As a matter of fact, there are! In each of the cases, the relationship between the reserves of the private banks and their deposit liabilities was altered. These alterations may cause them to engage in further operations that result in changes in such things as loans to the nonbank public and their demand deposits. To show these effects, we need to restate some concepts presented earlier in Chapter 4.

We pointed out at that time that banks were required to hold reserves behind their deposit liabilities. The specific items in the banks' balance sheet that can serve as legal reserves are vault cash and deposits with the Federal Reserve Bank. Banks are required to maintain some minimum level of reserves for every dollar of deposits. This ratio (the ratio of required reserves to deposits) is called the *required reserve ratio*. Suppose the ratio were 20 percent. This means that behind every dollar of deposits the banks are required to keep $0.20 in reserve in the form of vault cash or on deposit with the Fed or some combination of the two. With a reserve ratio of 20 percent, every time deposits increase by $1, the minimum amount of reserves held must increase by $0.20. When deposits decrease by $1, minimum reserves can decrease by no more than $0.20.

Note that in Case 1 above the deposit liabilities of the banks decreased by $100, but their reserves also decreased by $100. Had they been maintaining only the required minimum reserves previously, the transactions would have placed them in a deficit position—they would be holding less than the minimum. In Case 2 the banks experienced a $200 increase in their reserves and no increase in their deposits. Had they previously been holding just the required amount of reserves, they now would have reserves in excess of the amount required.

Bank response, predicated upon profit-maximizing behavior, to such changes in reserve position constitutes a central element of money supply theory. In addition, the nonbank public's desire to alter its holdings of assets, such as altering the amount of currency held relative to demand deposits, adds additional elements to the development of money supply theory. Most frameworks for the money supply process link some concept of bank reserves with the money supply and incorporate both the behavior of the public and the behavior of private banks into the process. The framework that we will use links together the money supply and a reserve concept called the monetary base which we introduced in Chapter 4.

The Money Supply Identity[2]

We have defined the money stock as consisting of currency in the hands of the nonbank public plus the nonbank public's demand deposits. Note that these two items can be obtained from the balance sheet of the nonbank public. The monetary base can be defined using the balance sheet of the Federal Reserve Bank. The monetary base consists of the total reserves of the private member banks of the Federal Reserve System plus currency in the hands of the nonbank public. The source of the monetary base can be derived from the Fed's balance sheet. Both components of the base appear on the liability side of the balance sheet. The reserves of member banks consist of the deposits of those banks with the Federal Reserve Bank plus a portion of the Federal Reserve Notes outstanding (held as vault cash). The remainder of the Federal Reserve Notes outstanding is held by the nonbank public. The total of these items can be obtained by adding all of the assets of the Federal Reserve and subtracting all of the liabilities other than those items. In short, it is the assets of the Fed that are the principal source of the monetary base. The monetary base and the money stock are linked by the following definition:

$$M = mB \qquad (12\text{-}1)$$

In the above equation, M is the money stock, m is a money supply multiplier, and B is the monetary base. The precise form that the multiplier takes may be obtained from the definitions of the money stock and the monetary base. From (12-1)

$$m = \frac{M}{B} = \frac{C_p + D}{C_p + TR} \qquad (12\text{-}2)$$

C_p and D are the public's currency and demand deposits, and TR is total member bank reserves. Total reserves can be divided between required reserves (R) and excess reserves (E). The ratio of total reserves to total deposits [demand plus time (T)] can be expressed as

---

[2] The particular framework used here was introduced by Robert Weintraub, "The Stock of Money, Interest Rates, and The Business Cycle, 1952–1964," *Western Economic Journal*, Vol. 6 (June 1967), pp. 257–70. Considerably more detail is provided in Weintraub's *Introduction to Monetary Economics* (New York: Ronald Press, 1970). A similar, and widely used, model is found in Karl Brunner and Allan H. Meltzer," Some Further Investigations of Demand and Supply Functions for Money," *Journal of Finance*, Vol. 19 (May 1964), pp. 240–382.

the sum of the required reserve ratio $[r = R/(D + T)]$ and the excess reserve ratio $[e = E/(D + T)]$. It follows that:

$$TR = (E + R)(D + T)/(D + T)$$
$$= (r + e)(D + T)$$

Substituting this into (12–2) yields the following:

$$m = \frac{C_p + D}{C_p + (r + e)(D + T)}$$

Finally, dividing the numerator and denominator by D and letting $c = C_p/D$ and $t = T/D$, we have:

$$m = \frac{c + 1}{c + (r + e)(1 + t)} \qquad (12\text{–}3)$$

This result now provides us with a framework or model within which we can incorporate both the behavior of the nonbank public and the private banks, as well as the policy tools of the Federal Reserve. The ratio of currency to demand deposits (c) and the ratio of time to demand deposits (t) are under the control of the nonbank public. Presumably these are altered to reflect the preferences of that group. The ratio of excess reserves to total deposits (e) is under the control of the private banks.

The ratio of required reserves to total deposits (r) as well as the magnitude of the monetary base itself are under the control of the Federal Reserve Bank, and both of these can be considered to be policy instruments. The core of money supply theory consists in identifying those economic stimuli that influence the currency, time deposit, and excess reserve ratios. Having identified those, we would have identified the determinants of the money supply. Thus we turn now to a brief discussion of the determinants of these ratios.

Before doing so, however, it may be instructive to reconcile the foregoing framework with the simple deposit expansion framework usually presented in introductory courses. In the simple framework it is assumed that the nonbank public holds no currency, that there are no time deposits, and that banks hold no excess reserves. With these assumptions, $c = t = e = 0$. Further, since $C_p = 0$, the monetary base consists solely of total reserves. Substituting these assumptions into equation (12–3), we get the following multiplier:

$$m = 1/r$$

Equation (12–1), with M consisting now only of demand deposits, becomes the following:

$$D = 1/r \cdot TR.$$

MONEY SUPPLY THEORY
The Currency Ratio

Both components of the currency ratio are assets of the nonbank public. Both yield utility to the holder, due partly to the liquidity service they provide. Under utility-maximizing assumptions, the relative quantities held of these two assets will vary inversely with the relative cost of holding them. While there is no explicit cost to holding currency, there is to holding demand deposits, since many banks levy a service charge on demand deposits.[3] Should the service charge be increased (decreased), we might expect people to reduce (increase) their holdings of demand deposits relative to currency, thus increasing (decreasing) the currency ratio.

As we indicated in the last chapter, the opportunity cost of holding money is the market rate of interest. Unless the interest elasticity of both currency and demand deposits is the same, a change in the interest rate will induce a change in the currency ratio. The same argument applies to changes in income. Both assets are money assets, and, by the discussion in the previous chapter, the demand for each should be positively related to income. The two assets are not perfect substitutes, however, and their income elasticities are likely to be different. Intuitively, we might expect that as income rises people make relatively greater use of checking accounts as compared with cash. This would imply an inverse relationship between the currency ratio and income. However, when we survey the empirical evidence later, we will see that the available evidence is mixed.

The Time Deposit Ratio

The determinants of the time deposit ratio are essentially the same as those for the currency ratio. The t ratio should vary inversely with the cost of holding time deposits relative to the cost of holding demand

---

[3] Service charges may consist of a fixed monthly maintenance charge and/or an activity charge that depends on the number of checks written and the number of deposits made.

deposits. The opportunity cost of holding time deposits is the market rate of interest *less* the interest rate paid on time deposits. The cost of holding demand deposits is the market rate of interest plus the service charge on demand deposits. Thus the time deposit ratio should vary directly with the rate paid on time deposits and directly with the service charge on demand deposits.

As in the case of the currency ratio, income changes will induce changes in the time deposit ratio as long as the components of the ratio have different income elasticities. However, in this case it is possible to be more definite about the direction of change. There is widespread agreement that the demand for time deposits is more income elastic than the demand for demand deposits. If so, the time deposit ratio should vary directly with the level of income.

The Excess Reserve Ratio

Unlike the previous ratios, the excess reserve ratio is not a ratio of assets. It is, instead, the ratio of an asset (excess reserves) to a liability (total deposits). Thus relative prices analogous to the previous cases are not a factor in determining the excess reserve ratio. Instead, the profit-maximizing desire of private banks, as it affects excess reserves, is assumed to play a major role.

If an individual bank increases its loans by $1, the increase in total revenue for the bank is $1 $\times i$, where i is the market rate of interest applicable to the period of the loan. Additional reserves against which additional loans can be made can be obtained by borrowing from the Fed and paying $1 $\times i_d$, where i_d is the Fed's discount rate. Thus i may be considered an index of the marginal revenue obtained from lending, and i_d may be considered an index of the marginal cost of obtaining additional reserves. Should i increase, given i_d, a profit-maximizing bank can be expected to increase its loans and reduce its excess reserves. Should i_d increase, given i, the same bank can be expected to hold a larger stock of excess reserves to avoid being forced to borrow from the Fed. Other things being equal, an individual bank can be expected to expand its loans as long as i is greater than i_d.

As the banking *system* expands its loans (and reduces its excess reserves), it expands the money supply; and the market rate of interest will fall until $i = i_d$ and no further expansion takes place. Usually, however, expansion stops short of this because banks are constrained by uncertainty in their need for liquidity. If deposits and withdrawals, loans and repayments could be timed perfectly, the bank could make do with zero excess reserves. This is not the case, and the bank is forced to maintain some level of excess reserves to reduce the probability of having deficient reserves or of borrowing excessively from the Fed.

The implications of the foregoing are that the excess reserve ratio varies inversely with the market interest rate, directly with the discount rate, and directly with the need for liquidity.

We may summarize the above arguments by writing the ratios as functions of their determinants:

$$c = c(i, sc, Y)$$
$$t = t(i, i_T, sc, Y)$$
$$e = e[(i - i_d), L]$$

where c, t, e, i, and Y retain their earlier definitions. Further, sc = service charge on demand deposits; i_T = interest rate on time deposits; i_d = Federal Reserve discount rate; and L = index of liquidity need.

If these behavioral relationships are substituted into the money multiplier definition, we obtain a behavioral model of the money multiplier and, given the monetary base, of the money supply. In Chapter 4 we plotted the money supply against the interest rate so that changes in the interest rate result in a movement *along* the money supply curve. Given the analysis of this chapter, we can translate changes in the monetary base, the required reserve ratio, and the variables listed above into *shifts* in the money supply function. The responsiveness of the money supply to the interest rate is determined by the responsiveness of the c, t, and e ratios to the interest rate.

One Application: A Money Supply Liquidity Trap?

We noted earlier (Chapter 7) that a highly interest responsive money supply could frustrate monetary policy even if money demand was unresponsive to the interest rate. While investigation has not discovered a liquidity trap for money demand, little investigation has been done on the supply side for the 1930s, during which time a liquidity trap was often assumed to exist.[4]

---

[4] Two studies that do approach this issue are: George Horwich, "Effective Reserves, Credit, and Causality in the Banking System of the Thirties," *Banking and Monetary Studies,* ed. Deane Carson (Homewood, Ill.: Richard D. Irwin, Inc., 1963), pp. 80–100; and Peter A. Frost, "Banks Demand for Excess Reserves," *Journal of Political Economy,* Vol. 79 (July/August 1971) pp. 805–25.

In order to illustrate the possibilities, consider the scatter diagram in Figure 12–1 in which the excess reserve ratio has been plotted against a short-term interest rate for the 1929–1939 period. The scatter of points is downward sloping as we would expect from our discussion

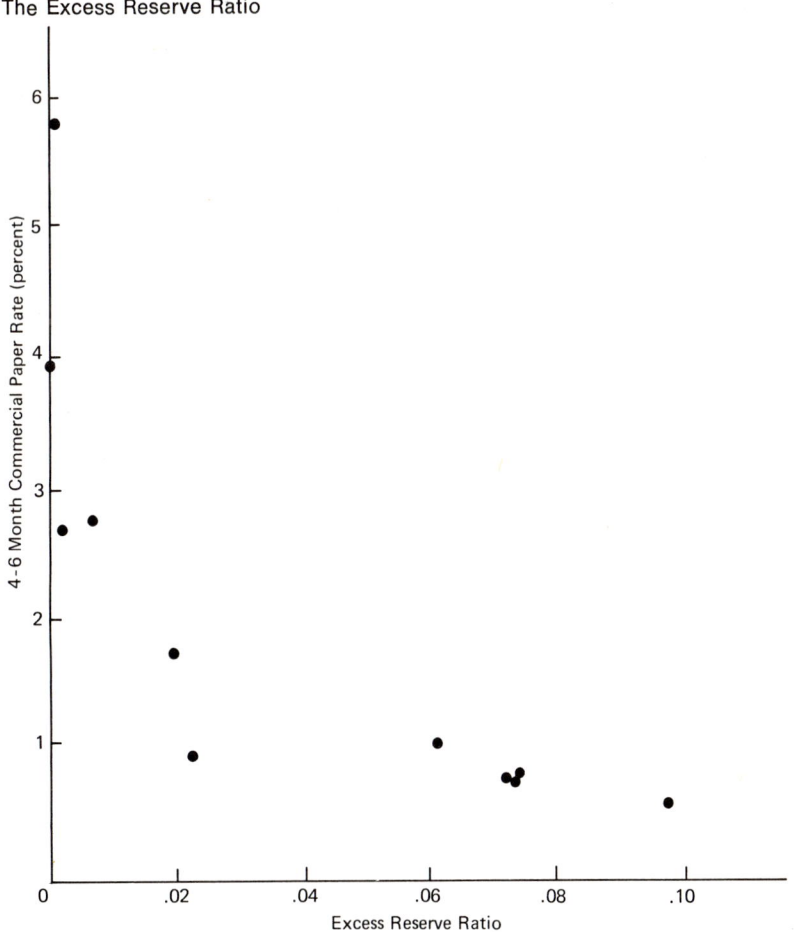

FIGURE 12–1
The Excess Reserve Ratio

Source: Robert Weintraub, *Introduction to Monetary Economics*, p. 185; and the *Economic Report of the President, 1973*.

in this chapter. A logarithmic curve "fit" to the data yields the following result:

$$\ln e = 3.40 - 2.79 \ln i$$
$$R^2 = 0.84$$

The interest elasticity of e for this period was therefore -2.79, a fairly high value.

This does not mean, however, that the money supply itself was highly interest elastic. Indeed, for the same period, a logarithmic regression of m on the interest rate yielded an interest elasticity of 0.31. The reason for this is simply that the excess reserve ratio is such a small component of the multiplier that even large percent changes in the excess reserve ratio will result in only small percent changes in the multiplier.

RELATED EMPIRICAL STUDIES

Empirical work in money supply theory is not as extensive as it is for money demand theory. However, the studies that do exist indicate that such variables as income and interest rates are significant determinants of the money supply. Studies by Goldfeld, Hess, and Hosek imply that the income elasticity of the demand for currency is greater than that of the demand for demand deposits.[5] Thus the currency ratio varies, *ceteris paribus,* directly with income. The opposite conclusion was implied, however, in a study by Phillip Cagan.[6] The conflict may be due in part to the use of different definitions of income in the various studies.

On the other hand, on both a priori and empirical grounds there is widespread agreement that the income elasticity of the demand for time deposits is greater than that for demand deposits.

In addition to the authors listed above, Teigen, Brunner and Meltzer, and de Leeuw have examined the sensitivity of the money supply or its components to the interest rate.[7] Representative elasticities from

---

[5] Stephen M. Goldfeld, *Commercial Bank Behavior and Economic Activity* (Amsterdam, North Holland, 1966); Alan C. Hess, "An Explanation of Short-Run Fluctuations in the Ratio of Currency to Demand Deposits," *Journal of Money, Credit, and Banking,* Vol. 3 (August 1971), pp. 666–79; and William R. Hosek, "Determinants of the Money Multiplier," *Quarterly Review of Economics and Business,* Vol. 10 (Summer 1970), pp. 37–46. Hess and Hosek used a "permanent income" measure.

[6] Phillip Cagan, "The Demand for Currency Relative to the Total Money Supply," *Journal of Political Economy,* Vol. 66 (August 1958) pp. 303–28.

[7] Brunner and Meltzer, "Further Investigations of Demand and Supply Functions,"; Frank de Leeuw, "A Model of Financial Behavior," *The Brookings Quarterly Econometric Model of the United States,* ed. James S. Duesenberry et al. (Chicago: Rank McNally & Co., 1965) pp. 465–532; Ronald Teigen, "An Aggregated Quarterly Model of the United States Monetary Sector, 1953–1964," *Targets and Indicators of Monetary Policy,* ed. Karl Brunner (San Francisco: Chandler Publishing Co., 1969), pp. 175–218; and Ronald Teigen, "Demand and Supply Functions for Money in the United States: Some Structural Estimates," *Econometrica,* Vol. 32 (October 1964), pp. 476–509.

these studies are summarized in Table 12–1. Note that like money demand, the elasticities are fairly low which would tend to discount the possibility of a liquidity trap on the supply side even where the long-run adjustment of the money supply to the interest rate is estimated.

TABLE 12–1
Money Supply Interest Elasticities

Author(s)	Elasticity	Adjustment Period
Brunner-Meltzer	0.660	long run
DeLeeuw	0.172	long run
Goldfeld	0.042	short run
	0.222	long run
Hosek	0.043	short run*
Teigen	0.195	short run
Zahn-Hosek	0.176	short run

* Inferred from the interest elasticities of the components of the money multiplier.
Source: All except Hosek and Zahn-Hosek are reported in Robert H. Rasche, "A Review of Empirical Studies of the Money Supply Mechanism," *Review*, Federal Reserve Bank of Saint Louis, Vol. 54 (July 1972), pp. 11–19. The Hosek elasticity was computed from the results reported in Hosek, "Determinants of the Money Multiplier." The remaining elasticity can be found in Frank Zahn and William R. Hosek, "Impact of Trade Credit on the Velocity of Money and the Market Rate of Interest," *Southern Economic Journal*, Vol. 40 (October 1973), pp. 202–9.

By the same token, the evidence also indicates a weakness in Federal Reserve control over the equilibrium nominal *money stock*. By the money stock we mean the quantity of money determined by the intersection of the money supply and money demand functions. The Fed's control over the monetary base is only one input into the money supply function. In short, given the evidence, the Fed could act to determine precisely the money stock only if interest rates and income were held constant. But the actions taken would themselves induce changes in interest rates and income, making very precise control extremely difficult—if not impossible.[8]

One further point may be mentioned in this connection. With influences other than the Fed entering into the money supply function, a given change in the money stock may or may not reflect the intent of the policy makers. Thus the recognition that the money supply is influenced by interest rates and income implies that the money stock

[8] A good summary of these problems is found in David I. Fand, "Can the Central Bank Control the Nominal Money Stock," *Review*, Federal Reserve Bank of Saint Louis, Vol. 52 (January 1970), pp. 12–16.

is not a completely reliable indicator of the stance of monetary policy. This bears directly on the "indicator problem" which we shall discuss in the next chapter.

SUMMARY NOTES

1. The preferences of the public (as regards its holdings of currency, demand, and time deposits), the preferences of the private banking system (as regards its holdings of excess reserves), and the Federal Reserve System determine the money supply.
2. The money supply varies inversely with the ratio of currency to demand deposits, the ratio of time to demand deposits, and the ratio of excess reserves to total deposits.
3. The behavior of the private sector implies that the money supply varies directly with the interest rate. Estimated interest elasticities have been rather low.

DISCUSSION QUESTIONS

1. Assume that the relationship between the money multiplier and the interest rate can be approximated linearly (for example, $m = a + bi$). Using the definitions of this chapter, compute the multiplier for the past ten years and plot on a scatter diagram against some interest rate (for example, the yield on three-month Treasury bills). Does the scatter of points appear to conform to the idea of a positive relationship between the multiplier and the interest rate?
2. If the Federal Reserve is to exercise control over the nominal money stock, it must be able to control the position of the money supply function. What information should the Fed obtain about the supply function? What desirable characteristics should the supply function itself possess?
3. Derive a money supply multiplier for the following situations: (*a*) The system contains currency, demand deposits, and excess reserves, but no time deposits; (*b*) the monetary base is defined to *exclude* member bank borrowing from the Federal Reserve. Note that excess reserves minus member bank borrowing equals "free reserves."

13

Stabilization Policy: A Second View

POLICY EFFECTIVENESS: THE EMPIRICAL EVIDENCE ON THE FORM OF THE BASIC MODEL

The IS Schedule

ONE CONCLUSION reached in the policy discussion of Chapter 7 was that the relative strength of fiscal and monetary policy depended on the relative slopes of the IS and LM schedules. It might be useful to review how the material of the last few chapters bears on this issue, beginning with the IS schedule. The IS slope in the basic model is the following:

$$\Delta i/\Delta Y = -(1-b)/a,$$

where b is the marginal propensity to consume, and a is the change in investment induced by a change in the interest rate. Summarizing the foregoing chapters, we noted that:

1. Estimates of a are fairly low (but not zero), implying a steep IS schedule.
2. Some components of consumption (especially durable goods) seem to respond inversely to the interest rate, tending to make the IS curve less steep.
3. The addition of wealth to the consumption function reduces estimates of b, and this tends to make the IS schedule steeper.

4. The marginal propensity to invest out of current income is positive and significant, and this works toward a less steep IS schedule.

The general thrust of all factors is not clear-cut. The slope of the IS schedule could be anything, depending on the relative magnitudes of the above elements. The evidence on the LM schedule, however, is a little clearer.

The LM Schedule

From the basic model we have the following LM slope formula:

$$\Delta i/\Delta Y = 1/(\beta/Pk + g/k)$$

where β and g represent the change in money supply and money demand, respectively, with respect to a change in the interest rate. Both money demand and money supply have been found to be rather insensitive to the interest rate. The implication of both cases is that the LM curve tends to be steeply sloped. But how steep the LM curve is, compared with the IS curve, is not clear.

Rather than infer the slopes of the schedules from the underlying functions, one might attempt to estimate the two curves directly. One study has attempted to do just that. Robert Scott, employing a basic model very similar to the model of Chapter 4, estimated the IS schedule and the LM schedule for the period 1951–1964.[1] The following slopes were computed from his results.

$$\text{IS;} \quad \Delta i/\Delta Y = -0.00065$$
$$\text{LM;} \quad \Delta i/\Delta Y = 0.0233$$

It can be seen from the absolute values of the slopes that the LM curve is considerably steeper than the IS curve. Thus, if we shifted each curve, in turn, horizontally an equal distance, the shift in the LM curve would produce a larger change in equilibrium income than the shift in the IS curve. Does this mean that monetary policy is implied by Scott's results to be more powerful than fiscal policy. Not necessarily. The extent to which the IS schedule shifts in response to a change in government spending depends on the magnitude of the marginal propensity to consume (see Figure 6–1). Similarly, the extent to which the LM curve shifts in response to a change in monetary policy depends upon the magnitude of certain parameters in the

---

[1] Robert Haney Scott, "Estimates of Hicksian IS and LM Curves for the United States," *Journal of Finance*, Vol. 21 (September 1966), pp. 479–87.

money demand and money supply functions (see Figure 6–3). Thus it might take a massive change in monetary policy to shift the LM curve the same distance that a small change in fiscal policy shifts the IS curve.

The IS and LM curves may, of course, be solved simultaneously to obtain multipliers that reflect the change in income with respect to a unit change in a fiscal policy or monetary policy variable. Using Scott's results, we obtain the following relationship:

$$Y = -47.32 + 1.92M + 1.35G$$

Note that the numerical value of the money multiplier ($\Delta Y/\Delta M = 1.92$) is larger than the numerical value of the government spending multiplier ($\Delta Y/\Delta G = 1.35$). Again, does this mean that monetary policy is more powerful than fiscal policy? And again, the question cannot be definitely answered. The principal reason is that the two multipliers are not strictly comparable. The monetary policy multiplier measures the change in income *flow* with respect to a change in the *stock* of money balances. While the government spending multiplier measures the change in income *flow* with respect to a change in government spending *flow*.

Other problems intervene. For example, the IS and LM schedules indicate only the level of *aggregate demand*. Whether *aggregate supply* (real output) responds to shifts in aggregate demand depends upon the responsiveness of aggregate supply to the price level. For a shift in aggregate demand, resulting either from a shift in the IS schedule or the LM schedule, to result in an equal change in aggregate output, aggregate supply must be perfectly elastic with respect to the price level. The sequence described in the basic model was as follows: Aggregate demand initially increases, causing the price level to rise. The rising price level induces an increase in output, but at the same time the rising price level moderates the increase in aggregate demand by shifting the LM curve somewhat to the left. Were aggregate supply perfectly elastic with respect to the price level, then no price rise would be necessary to induce an increase in output, and the change in output would be the same as the initial increase in aggregate demand. At the opposite pole, a perfectly inelastic supply (for example, at full employment) means that an increase in aggregate demand is fully absorbed by a price rise, with no expansion in output.

Using the Cobb-Douglas production function we were able to derive an aggregate supply function. With commonly accepted estimates of certain parameters in the function, we deduced that the price elasticity of aggregate supply was about 3. Thus an increase in aggregate demand would have to be accompanied by some increase in the price level in order to induce an increase in aggregate output. Moreover, the increase in output would not be as great as the initial increase in aggregate demand.

The Problem of Stability in the Model

According to the evidence discussed in Chapter 9, income most definitely does belong in the investment schedule. The effect of adding income is to reduce the slope of the IS schedule. In fact, there is a possibility that the IS schedule could become upward sloping instead of downward sloping. If the sum of the marginal propensities to consume and invest exceeds 1 in numerical value, the slope of the IS schedule will be positive. There are no a priori grounds for assuming that the sum of these propensities exceeds 1 or not. In the study cited earlier, Scott assumed that both consumption and investment were responsive to changes in income. His direct estimate of the IS schedule nevertheless yielded a negative slope.

A differently structured model might, however, yield an IS schedule with a positive slope. A positively sloped schedule changes some of the conclusions we have reached with our basic model. Further, a positively sloped IS schedule introduces the potential for instability in the model. Consider Figure 13–1A. The AS and the LM schedules have been plotted as they were in previous chapters. The IS schedule is upward sloping, but its slope is not as steep as that of the LM schedule. The initial equilibrium is at interest ratio i_0 and income Y_0.

Now suppose that there is an increase in government expenditures on goods and services, with no change in taxes and no change in monetary policy. The *increase* in government spending will in this case shift the IS schedule to the *left,* say, to IS'. Recalling the adjustment mechanisms which were discussed in Chapter 6, the sequence of events is as follows: The increase in government expenditures is an increase in aggregate demand. In response, the price level should begin to rise. With a rising price level, aggregate supply increases and the real value of the monetary base decreases, shifting the LM schedule to the left. With the AS schedule moving to the right and the LM schedule to the left equilibrium will be restored along the

13 / Stabilization Policy: A Second View   201

FIGURE 13–1
The Upward Sloping IS Schedule

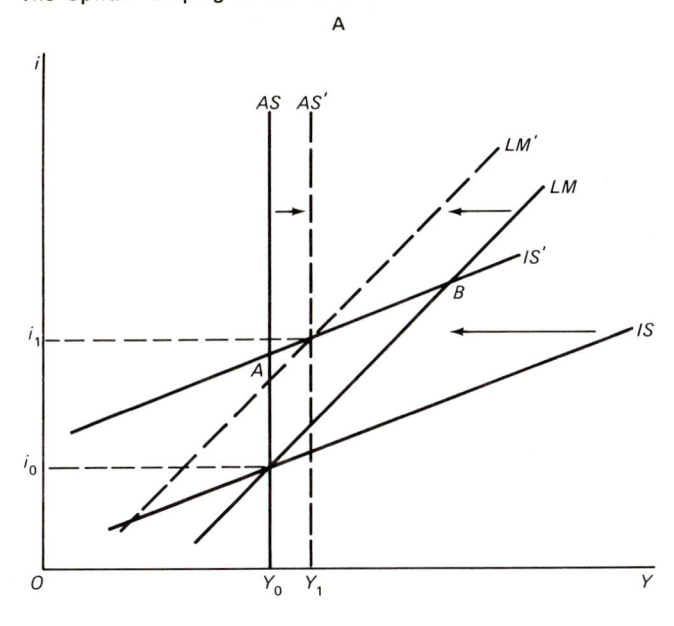

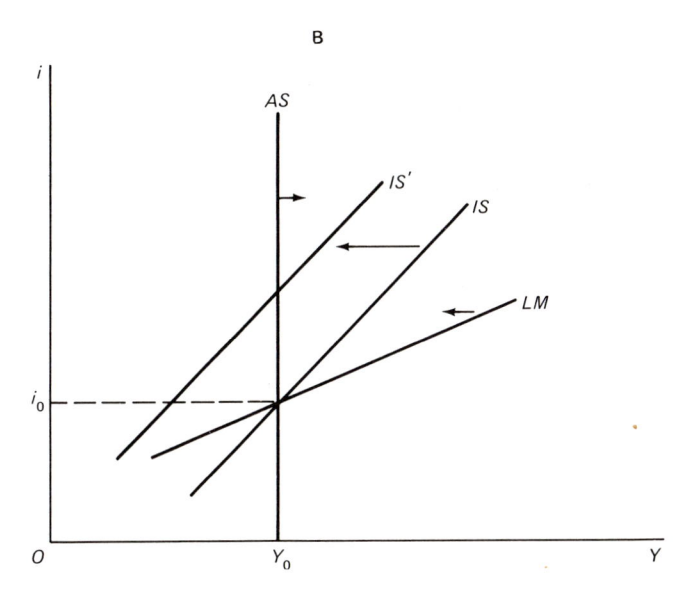

A

B

IS' schedule someplace on the line segment AB, perhaps at interest rate i_1 and income level Y_1. Thus, an increase in government expenditures leads to an increase in the equilibrium level of income and to an increase in the equilibrium interest rate, just as we obtained in the case of a downward sloping IS schedule.

However, in the case of a change in monetary policy, the results will be slightly different. If the monetary base is increased, the equilibrium level of income will rise and so to will the equilibrium level of the interest rate. This is the opposite of the basic model result in which income rises, but the interest rate falls. Note, however, in both cases that the equilibrium point moves toward the general direction of the intersection of the IS and LM schedules. In the case cited in Figure 13–1A, the new equilibrium moves towards point B, where point B indicates a higher interest rate and a higher level of income than the initial starting point.

Consider now Figure 13–1B. In this case, the slope of the IS schedule is greater than that of the LM schedule. Again, suppose there is an increase in government expenditures which shifts the IS schedule to the left. The increase in aggregate demand resulting from expanded government spending forces the price level upward, with the result that aggregate supply increases, shifting the AS schedule to the right, and the real value of monetary base decreases, shifting the LM schedule to the left. Rising money demand due to the increased income and the falling money supply function due to the rising price level both assure that the interest rate will be rising. So from the initial equilibrium point, we shall be moving upward to the right. However, it is not clear that a new equilibrium will be reached. A little experimentation will indicate that if the AS schedule moves rapidly to the right and the LM schedule moves slowly to the left, the intersection point of these two curves will move further away from the IS' schedule.

The explanation is straightforward. A steeply upward sloping IS schedule indicates that consumer and investment spending taken together are extremely sensitive to changes in income. If income is rising, aggregate demand will, on that account, be rising very rapidly. In Figure 13–1A and in the case where the IS schedule is downward sloping, the rising interest rate chokes off a sufficient amount of investment expenditures so that aggregate supply is able to catch up to aggregate demand and equilibrium is restored. In the case of Figure 13–1B, the interest rate may not rise rapidly enough to choke off aggregate demand. Thus, aggregate demand will grow rapidly and more rapidly than aggregate supply, with the result that the system explodes—prices, income, and the interest rate rising continuously.

The possibility of the IS schedule being more steeply sloped than the LM schedule is probably pretty slim, however. The LM schedule, itself, appears to be rather steeply sloped. In addition, when wealth is included in the consumption equation the marginal propensity to consume out of current income seems to be fairly low, in the neighborhood of 0.4 to 0.6. Thus it would take a fairly large marginal propensity to invest to result in an upward sloping IS schedule to begin with, let alone to make the slope steeper than the slope of the LM schedule.

MEASURING POLICY CHANGES: THE INDICATOR PROBLEM[2]
Appropriate Indicator Qualities

In discussing the influence of stabilization policy on the economy, we need first to determine how policy is measured. In the context of our basic model, we used government expenditures and taxes as indicators of fiscal policy and the monetary base as an indicator of monetary policy. Changes in these variables signal expansive or contractionary policies, depending on the direction of the change.

Generally, an indicator should fulfill three properties. First, the indicator should be an exogenous variable in the system. If we select an endogenous variable as an indicator, we cannot distinguish between system induced changes in the indicator and policy induced changes. Moreover, if the indicator is endogenous, we cannot tell whether changes in the system are causing changes in the indicator or the reverse.

Second, an appropriate indicator should reflect policy actions only. Whatever variables are selected will need to reflect the intentions of the policy makers. A variable suggested as an indicator may be exogenous, but changes in it may be the consequence of both policy changes and other exogenous influences. If we are to use the indicator as a reflection of policy movements, then only the policy maker must have control over that variable.

---

[2] The papers of an entire conference devoted to this problem may be found in Karl Brunner, ed., *Targets and Indicators of Monetary Policy* (San Francisco: Chandler Publishing Co., 1969).

Third, an indicator should consistently reflect the thrust of policy on the economy. If an increase in an indicator sometimes leads to an expansion in the economy and other times leads to a contraction, then the indicator does not consistently show us in which direction policy will drive the economy. Not only should the qualitative thrust be consistent but it is desirable that the quantitative thrust be consistent also. In other words, we would like to select an indicator in such a way that its influence on the endogenous variables of the system is consistently predictable, both as to direction and magnitude of change.

Possible Fiscal Policy Indicators

Although we have used government expenditures and taxes as indicators of fiscal policy, both measures may not adequately fulfill the previously stated criteria. In particular, both taxes and transfer payments are endogenous variables. This is especially true of taxes. In the U.S. economy the bulk of federal taxes is received through personal or corporate income taxes. Both personal and corporate income (profits) are endogenous variables in the economy. That is to say, they are determined by the level of economic activity. If the total tax burden is, in part, a function of personal income and corporate profits, then total taxes will also be an endogenous variable. Thus, a decrease in total taxes may signal an expansionary fiscal policy, or it may simply reflect the fact that the economy has fallen into a recession and incomes have fallen.

The same problem applies to transfer payments, although in this case the problem is not quite as severe. While only government expenditures on goods and services add directly to aggregate demand in the product market, changes in government transfer payments may indirectly influence aggregate demand. Changes in unemployment and welfare benefits influence the disposable income of the household sector and thus influence the household sector's consumption expenditures. Thus, in the real world, an expansive or contractionary fiscal policy may be introduced through government transfer payments as well as through expenditures in the product market. However, changes in transfer payments may reflect changes in the level of economic activity as well as changes in policy stance. For example, when the economy moves into a recession, unemployment increases and government outlays on unemployment benefits also increase. This does not necessarily indicate a discretionary policy change by the government but simply reflects an automatic change in transfer payments resulting from the reduction in the level of economic activity.

To overcome these difficulties, a measure of fiscal policy has been developed that is known as the "full-employment" or "high-employment" budget. In this concept, both government expenditures and taxes are computed as they would be if the economy was at full employment. The difference between the two is the high-employment surplus or deficit. Changes in that surplus or deficit reflect only discretionary changes in the tax structure or in expenditures and do not reflect changes in the level of economic activity. Thus, the high-employment budget becomes a useful measure of the stance of fiscal policy.

The concept may be illustrated by reference to Figure 13–2. Two

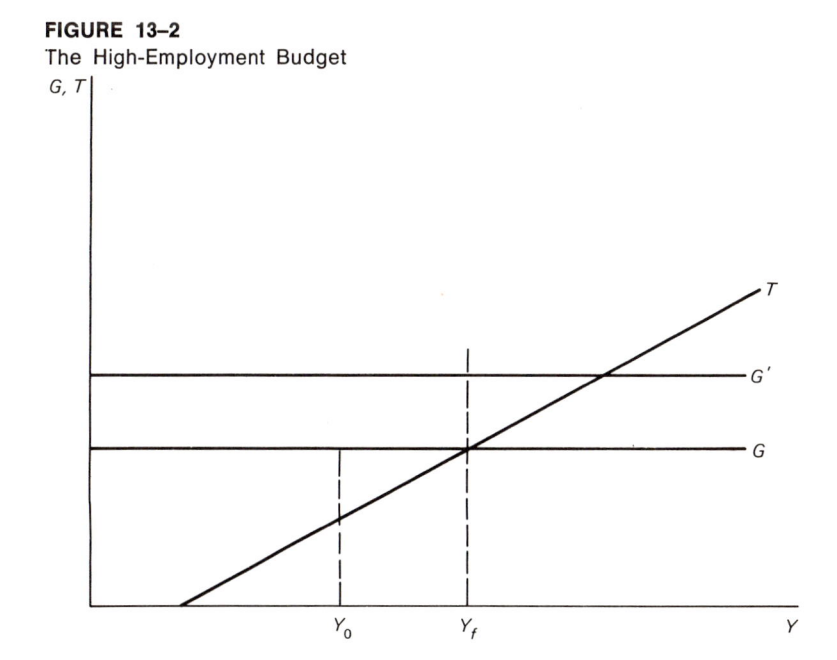

FIGURE 13–2
The High-Employment Budget

functions are drawn in the diagram: a tax function net of transfer payments and a government expenditure (on goods and services) function. The tax function rises as income rises, reflecting the fact that many taxes are based on income or income related expenditures and that transfers such as unemployment insurance and welfare vary inversely with income. Expenditures on goods and services are assumed to be constant as income varies.

As drawn, the budget is in balance at full employment (Y_f). Should there be a recession and income fall from Y_f to Y_o, net taxes would fall. Thus a current deficit would develop. However, we would not be correct in stating that government fiscal policy had become expansionary because net taxes fell. For these changes are the result of a fall in income rather than a conscious decision on the part of the government to employ an expansionary policy.

On the other hand, if there had been an attempt to move to an expansionary policy, say, by increased public works expenditures, shifting the G line to G', this would show up as an increase in the high-employment budget deficit. Thus, by looking at the high-employment budget we can tell whether there has been a discretionary policy change or whether the change in the deficit was the result of a change in the level of economic activity. On these grounds, many economists consider the high-employment budget concept to be a superior indicator of the stance of fiscal policy.

Possible Monetary Policy Measures

The two most frequently used measures of the stance of monetary policy are the money stock and the interest rate. Unfortunately, both variables are endogenous variables in the system. Further, an increase in the interest rate may reflect a contractionary monetary policy *or* an expansionary fiscal policy. In the conventional IS-LM framework, we note that the interest rate rises when either the LM curve is shifted to the left or when the IS schedule is shifted to the right. Therefore, not only is the interest rate an endogenous variable in the system, but also it does not give a consistent indication of the thrust of policy.

Many "monetarists" treat the money stock as an indicator of monetary policy on the grounds that its value is determined solely by the monetary authority. However, on the basis of our discussion in Chapter 12, it seems likely that the money stock is influenced by endogenous elements in the model as well as by Fed.

More recently, some writers have suggested that the monetary base be used as an indicator of policy on the grounds that the major source of the monetary base is the Fed's portfolio of U.S. government securities and, further, that the Fed can make the base any value it wishes by simply offsetting other influences on the base. This is acceptable as long as the Federal Reserve believes it can control the magnitude of the base and, in fact, seeks to make the base its policy decision variable. If the Fed has some other target in mind and pays no attention to the magnitude of the base, then changes in the base will reflect changes in other exogenous factors and will not reflect changes in monetary policy. Thus, the base may fulfill two of the criteria that an indicator needs to possess but fail the third. The base is an exogenous variable and therefore is not determined by the system, and the base consistently indicates the thrust of monetary changes on the economy (increases in the base always shift in the LM curve to the right and decreases in the base always shift the LM curve to the left). But the base may not reflect policy changes, simply because the Federal Reserve Bank may not have chosen the base as its target for policy purposes.

In an attempt to compensate for the deficiencies that individual indicators show, some writers suggest that a variety of indicators be used, including current government expenditures and taxes, the high-employment budget, the interest rate, the monetary base, the money supply, total bank credit, and so on. By surveying a variety of different indicators, it is hoped that some clear picture may emerge as to the stance of policy at any particular point in time.

THE STRENGTH OF POLICY

The Transmission Mechanism

Whatever indicators may be used to measure fiscal and monetary policy, the choice of one or the other under different sets of circumstances depends in great part on the impact that that policy has on such ultimate objectives as full employment and growth. Of the two types of policies, fiscal and monetary, the most controversy rages over the way in which monetary policy affects the economy. The transmission mechanism through which fiscal policy operates is subject to less controversy. It is generally agreed that a change in government expenditures on goods and services directly affects aggregate demand in the product market.

What is subject to question, however, is whether or not fiscal policy actions of this type tend to "crowd out" private expenditures. From the framework of our basic model, we have seen that an increase in government expenditures in the product market (without a change in taxes and without any change in monetary policy) tends to bid up interest rates. Higher interest rates will, in turn, tend to retard private investment expenditures and perhaps also private consumption expenditures. The impact of this fiscal policy measure depends upon the relative magnitudes of these changes. How much investment and consumer spending will be crowded out with a given increase in government spending?[3] The answer depends upon the interest sensitivity of money demand and supply and, also, upon whether the household sector treats an increase in government debt as an increase in net wealth.

On the other hand, the use of tax changes and changes in government transfer payments involves somewhat more controversy. Under our basic model assumptions, a change in total taxes changes disposable income by the same amount (but in the opposite direction) and thus induces a change in consumer spending. However, suppose that consumers behave according to the permanent income hypothesis. If so, the marginal propensity to consume out of current measured income will be extremely low. A change in taxes under this condition will affect current measured disposable income but will produce only a slight, if any, impact on permanent disposable income. Thus, consumer spending will not be affected. In the case of a tax cut, the increased measured Y_D will be taken up by increased savings; and in the case of a tax increase, by decreased savings. The same argument applies to the use of changes in transfer payments to stimulate or retard the economy. If the transfer payment changes are perceived to be of a temporary nature, then consumers may not react in the way that the policy makers expect.

We might classify the transmission mechanisms for monetary policy as the "indirect" mechanism and the "direct" mechanism.[4] The indirect mechanism is the one embodied in the basic model. Changes in the monetary base shift the money supply function, resulting in changes in the interest rate; and those changes in the interest rate induce changes in investment spending. The change in investment

---

[3] For a survey of crowding-out theories, see Roger W. Spencer and William P. Yohe, "The 'Crowding Out' of Private Expenditures by Fiscal Policy Actions," *Review,* Federal Reserve Bank of Saint Louis, Vol. 52 (October 1970), pp. 12–24.

[4] For a recent survey, see Yung Chul Park, "Some Current Issues on the Transmission Process of Monetary Policy," *IMF Staff Papers,* Vol. 19 (March 1972) pp. 1–43.

spending is a change in aggregate demand in the product market. Those who have disputed the effectiveness of monetary policy argue that shifts in the money supply function will have little effect on the rate of interest and, furthermore, changes in the rate of interest produce only a slight effect on aggregate investment.

Opponents of this point of view argue that whether the indirect mechanism is strong or not is of little consequence because the important mechanism is the direct effect that monetary changes have on aggregate spending. According to this point of view, the indirect mechanism posits an unrealistic dichotomy for money-holding decision makers. A change in money balances is assumed to be split between purchases of securities and holdings of cash. However, the money holder faces a third choice. He can choose to hold an increase in money balances, or he can buy financial assets with the increase, *or he can buy real goods*. If he buys real goods, aggregate demand is directly affected; and the increase in aggregate demand bids up prices, resulting in changes in aggregate output and so on.[5]

However, in the monetarist view it is important to distinguish between the short run, in which monetary changes can affect output, and the long run, in which monetary changes can only affect prices. The monetarist assumption of price flexibility does not imply that all prices adjust instantaneously. Given a monetary disturbance, it takes time for information to become available about the new market-clearing price structure. Prices must adjust on all assets—real and financial—as well as on current output, before equilibrium can be reestablished.[6]

During the period of *disequilibrium,* current output and employment will be changed. After all prices have adjusted and a new equilibrium has been reached, output and employment will have returned to their former levels. In driving the economy from one equilibrium point to another, monetary effects are felt in all markets, whether real or financial.

---

[5] One attempt to test the relative importance of the direct and indirect mechanisms was done by Burton Zwick, "The Adjustment of the Economy to Monetary Changes," *Journal of Political Economy,* Vol. 79 (January/February 1971), pp. 77–96. He concluded that both were important. For an analysis of the effect of the addition of a direct mechanism on a model's multipliers, see William L. Silber, *Portfolio Analysis of Financial Institutions,* (New York: Holt, Rinehart, and Winston, 1970).

[6] See Karl Brunner and Allen H. Meltzer, "Money Debt, and Economic Activity," *Journal of Political Economy,* Vol. 80 (September/October 1972), pp. 951–77 for a model that makes these changes explicit.

Thus, a demonstration that the indirect mechanism is weak is not sufficient to argue that monetary policy is weak. One must also show that the direct mechanism is also weak. However, even if one could demonstrate on empirical grounds that fiscal and monetary policy were equally strong, or weak for that matter, one may still prefer one type of policy to the other—on other economic grounds.

The Lag in Effect

No policy takes effect instantaneously. Most fiscal and monetary actions require some time between the policy decision and the policy effect. In the case of fiscal policy, discretionary changes in taxes or spending must first be channeled through the legislative process and, if approved, through the executive branch before they are even implemented. After they are implemented, some time may pass before the spending or taxing policy produces its impact in the product market.

The same argument applies to monetary policy. It takes time for the Federal Open Market Committee (FOMC) of the Federal Reserve Bank to formulate plans for policy change. Once the plans have been formulated, the manager of the System Open Market Account at the New York Federal Reserve Bank must implement the changes proposed by the FOMC. Since the policy is likely to be introduced through a change in open market operations by the Fed and since open market operations generally influence, in the first instance, member bank reserves, we must then wait for banks to respond to changes in their reserve position by increasing or decreasing their loans to the nonbank public. Finally, it takes time for people to become aware of the increased availability of funds or lowered interest rates and to revise their plans accordingly.

Now the lag in effect in policy changes might not be so troublesome, except for two additional problems. First, the lag may not be consistently of the same length. If the length of the lag is highly variable, uncertainty will be introduced into the policy-making process, and policy action may be, as a result, ill-timed. Second, if the lags are unduly long, then precise forecasting techniques must be used in order to pinpoint the proper time for policy change. While computers and large-scale econometric models have improved our forecasting ability, forecasting is still not quite that precise. It may then happen that because of long lags and poor forecasting ability a policy decision may be made at an inappropriate time. For example, a policy decision to fight a recession may be made too late so that its impact is not felt until after the economy has left the recession and is now in an inflationary period. The policy impact would simply aggrevate the inflation.

Up to this point the discussion has proceeded under the assumption that stabilization policy was desirable and the only issue involved was which policy to use. This may not, however, be the case.

POLICY PROPOSALS

While there is widespread agreement that the federal government should use its discretionary powers to promote such stabilization objectives as high employment, there is by no means unanimity in this. It has been argued that the role of government ought to be to provide for society as a whole those needed goods and services that individuals in society cannot feasibly provide for themselves. Examples might include a military establishment for purposes of national defense and a judicial system. This group might also argue that in conducting its affairs the government should maintain stability rather than try to be conscious controller of the direction in which the economy will move. Proposals exist for conducting monetary policy by an automatic rule, such as making the money supply grow at a fixed annual rate year after year whether the economy fluctuates from boom to recession or not.[7]

Another issue is the role of coordination between fiscal and monetary policy. By establishing a quasi-independent Federal Reserve Bank, the Congress opened the way for the monetary authority to pursue an independent stabilization objective. The result is that there may be times when the monetary and fiscal authorities will pursue opposite goals, perhaps because their interpretations of economic affairs differ at the moment. If the object of the fiscal authority is to increase the level of aggregate demand so as to reduce unemployment, it may act by an expansionary policy which shifts the IS schedule to the right. If, at the same time, the monetary authority feels that no change

---

[7] The classic statement on rules is by Henry Simons, "Rules versus Authorities in Monetary Policy," *Journal of Political Economy,* Vol. 44 (February 1936), pp. 1–30. For a present-day survey of opinion among monetary economists, see the *Compendium on Monetary Policy Guidelines and Federal Reserve Structure,* Committee on Banking and Currency, U.S. House of Representatives (Washington: U.S. Government Printing Office, 1968), especially the statement by Milton Friedman.

should take place in the economy, it may offset the fiscal policy move by a leftward shift of the LM schedule. This may lead to a political confrontation that works to the detriment of the stabilization objectives of both sides. On the other hand, if the monetary authority consistently accommodates every change in fiscal policy, then no check is provided to any mistakes the fiscal authorities might make.

The issues are, in any case, complex. While the economist may be in a position to evaluate the impact and effect of various alternative policies, much of the policy making is made in the political arena. Congressmen may agree that some policy change is necessary but may, as individuals, disagree as to the type of change. For example, on what goods should an increase in government expenditures be spent?[8] Moreover, in which states will the bulk of these goods be purchased?

It is not likely that these issues will be settled quickly. This is unfortunate, for while the issues remain unresolved, policy making will continue to be inconsistent and confusing.

SUMMARY NOTES

1. The empirical studies surveyed in the book imply a steep LM schedule. However, the evidence on the slope of the IS curve is not clear-cut.
2. An income responsive investment function raises the possibility of an upward sloping IS curve. This may result in unstable equilibria in the model if the slope of the IS curve is greater than that of the LM curve.
3. An appropriate indicator of policy should be an exogenous variable, should reflect policy actions only, and should consistently indicate the direction of policy. The high-employment budget is such an indicator for fiscal policy. The monetary base fulfills two of the three criteria as an indicator of monetary policy.
4. Monetary policy may work through a direct mechanism in addition to the indirect mechanism employed in the basic model. Excess money balances may be disposed of by lending *or* spending on real goods.

---

[8] One congressional committee even argued that the government should undertake no project that yields a rate of return less than the private rate of return. See "Economic Analysis of Public Investment Decisions: Interest Rate Policy and Discounting Analysis," Joint Economic Committee, United States Congress (Washington: U.S. Government Printing Office, 1968).

DISCUSSION QUESTIONS

1. Some politicians and laymen argue that "government deficits" are inflationary. Under what circumstances is this true? False?

2. Suppose that the appropriate income variable in both the consumption and investment functions is permanent income. Further, let there be no correlation between current and permanent income. Redefine the IS curve accordingly and analyze the effect of changes in government spending and the monetary base.

3. Many writers include government debt in the definition of wealth because, when held by the private sector, it is part of the private sector's assets, with no offsetting private liabilities. As such, changes in government spending unaccompanied by tax changes or money creation result in changes in privately held wealth. Assuming that there is a significant wealth effect in the consumption function, analyze all the effects of an increase in government spending, holding taxes and the monetary base constant.

4. Modify the basic model by adding the interest rate and wealth to the consumption function, and current income to the investment function. Derive a new IS schedule. Derive the slope of the IS schedule and determine the conditions necessary to make the IS schedule upward sloping.

part four

SPECIAL TOPICS

14

International Economics

ALTHOUGH the foreign sector plays a relatively small role in the U.S. economy, it plays a large role in U.S. policy formulation. In fact during the 1960s, balance of payments problems for the United States may have reached the same status in policy priority as unemployment and inflation. It is therefore appropriate that we consider, in more detail than we have previously, the role of the foreign sector and indicate how the foreign sector may be incorporated into our basic model.

THE FOREIGN SECTOR AND THE BASIC MODEL

The Balance of Trade and Aggregate Demand

The flow diagram in Figure 1-1 indicates where the balance of trade enters into U.S. gross national product. Purchases of U.S. goods and services are made by foreigners as well as U.S. residents. The purchases by foreigners must be added to the flow of spending by the domestic sector, which consists of the household, business, and government sectors. Thus we add total exports to the other expenditure items in the product market. On the other hand, the three other expenditure categories contain some expenditures on foreign produced goods and services. Since these expenditures are not made in the U.S. product market, they must be deducted from the total flow of consumption, investment, and government spending. Thus we subtract total imports of goods and services. These two items are generally netted against each other and are shown as a single item—net exports of goods and services. Product market equilibrium now requires that total output be equal to the sum of consumption, investment, government expenditures, and net exports.

$$Y = C + I + G + (X - F),$$

where X is exports and F is imports.

Product market equilibrium may be rewritten so that equilibrium occurs when saving by the household sector is equal to investment spending plus the government deficit plus net exports of goods and services.

$$S = I + (G - T) + (X - F),$$

or alternatively:

$$S + F = I + X + (G - T).$$

The addition of net exports to the other flows in the product market means that our IS schedule must be redefined. We shall do so later on in this chapter after the determinants of imports and exports are discussed.

The Capital Account Balance and Other Items

While only the balance of trade (net exports) enters into the flow of spending in the product market, other elements must be added to this to make up the total U.S. balance of payments. Dollars enter or leave the country for reasons other than the purchase or sale of currently produced goods. U.S. business firms and individuals buy the securities of foreign companies or make direct investments in foreign countries, and these represent an outflow of dollars from the United States. Similarly, foreign nations purchase securities and make direct investments in the U.S. economy, resulting in an inflow of dollars. These items do not represent current flows of income and expenditure and therefore do not enter into net exports of goods and services. They do, however, influence the net flow of dollars into or out of the country and therefore are of concern in computing the total balance of payments.

In addition, unilateral transfers and U.S. government gifts and grants do not enter into current product market flows but do result in a flow of dollars out of the United States. Unilateral transfers are included in the current account balance, along with net exports, even though they do not involve purchases of current output. U.S. government gifts and grants are included in the capital account balance. Both unilateral transfers and gifts and grants result in a flow of dollars between countries and therefore enter into the balance of payments.

The total balance of payments consists of two major categories: the current account balance and the capital account balance. We can now turn to the specific items in each category.

BALANCE OF PAYMENTS ACCOUNTING

Table 14-1 details the U.S. balance of payments for 1973.

TABLE 14-1
U.S. Balance of Payments, 1973 (billions of dollars)

Current Account:		
Total exports		$76.3
Merchandise	$67.0	
Military sales	1.8	
Net investment income	9.0	
Net travel expenditures	−2.4	
Other services, net	.9	
Total imports		−72.3
Merchandise	−67.7	
Military expenditures	−4.6	
Balance of trade		$ 4.0
Remittances, pensions, and other unilateral transfers		−3.6
Current Account Balance		$ 0.4
Capital Account:		
Private capital, net		−2.2
Long term	1.8	
Short term	−4.0	
U.S. Government		−0.8
Capital Account Balance		$−3.0
Errors and omissions		−6.4
Balance of Payments		$−9.0

Source: *Economic Report of the President, 1974.*

The Current Account

The largest elements in the current account are the exports and imports of merchandise. As examples, these would include the purchase of Toyota automobiles by U.S. residents and the sale to foreign residents of U.S. television sets or washing machines. The Department of Commerce does tabulate a separate merchandise balance. Its use is somewhat dubious as a measure of product market flows, since the exports and imports of services also enter into current flows in the product market.[1] *Investment income* under total exports represents net payments of interest and dividends to U.S. residents by foreign individuals, business firms, and governments. *Other services* would include expenditures by tourists.

The balance of trade is equal to total exports minus total imports, which in 1973 amounted to $4 billion. *Remittances, pensions, and other unilateral transfers* amounted to $3.6 billion. This item represents gifts by U.S. residents to individuals and organizations in foreign countries as well as pensions received by former employees of U.S. firms or of the U.S. government who are now living in foreign countries. Thus the current account balance, $0.4 billion, represents a net flow of dollars *into* the U.S. economy.

The Capital Account

Capital flows include direct investment and both long- and short-term financial investment. Direct investment includes the building of plants and factories in foreign countries. Financial items include the purchase of stocks and bonds of foreign businesses and governments. Such items represent an outflow of dollars from the United States and would be a negative item in the balance of payments. Similar flows result from foreign investment in the U.S. economy. Foreign private investment in the United States in 1973 was exceeded by U.S. private investment in the rest of the world by $2.2 billion. Adding U.S. government capital outflows of $0.8 billion results in a capital account balance of $—3.0 billion.

Since records are not kept of many expenditures, particularly tourist expenditures, some errors and unrecorded transactions arise. These are shown as a separate item. Such errors and omissions amounted to $—6.4 billion in 1973. This amount, together with the current and capital account balances, resulted in a net outflow of $9 billion from the United States in 1973.

---

[1] See the comments by Charles P. Kindleberger, *International Economics,* 5th ed. (Homewood, Ill.: Richard D. Irwin, Inc., 1973), p. 306. For a balance of payments framework different from the one discussed here, see Delbert A. Snider, *Introduction to International Economics,* 3d ed. (Homewood, Ill.: Richard D. Irwin, Inc., 1963), pp. 143–49.

For simplicity in the analysis to follow, we shall neglect the influence of transfer payments and consider only the trade and private capital flows. These are the items which we expect to respond to changing economic conditions. Thus, in what follows, the current account balance consists only of net exports (balance of trade), and the capital account consists only of *private* capital flows.

DETERMINANTS OF THE COMPONENTS OF THE BALANCE OF PAYMENTS

The Influence of Income

Income influences the consumption of foreign goods in the same way that it influences the consumption of domestic goods. As income rises, the household sector will consume more domestic goods and will also consume more foreign goods. Thus, *ceteris paribus,* imports should vary directly with the level of domestic income. This relationship is shown in Figure 14-1 where total imports of goods and services are plotted against U.S. GNP, both expressed in real terms.

While imports in Figure 14-1 were plotted against current income, a better relationship might be obtained by using wealth, relative income, or permanent income—on the grounds that these alternative income concepts produce better relationships for total consumption expenditures. Indeed the discussion in Chapter 8 applies with equal force to the consumption of imported goods. For our purposes, however, the use of current income will suffice.

Influence of Relative Prices

Income, or some variant of income, may determine the total level of household expenditures on consumer goods, both foreign and domestic. However the allocation of those expenditures between domestic and foreign goods is largely influenced by the relative prices of foreign and domestic goods. Given the level of domestic income, we might expect that imports will vary inversely with the price of foreign goods and directly with the price of domestic goods. Put another way, imports should vary directly with the *ratio of domestic to foreign prices.* This *ratio* is often referred to as the *terms of trade.* In Figure 14-2, imports, expressed as a percentage of GNP (to abstract from the influence of income), are plotted against the terms of trade. The scatter

FIGURE 14–1
Imports and GNP, 1950–1970

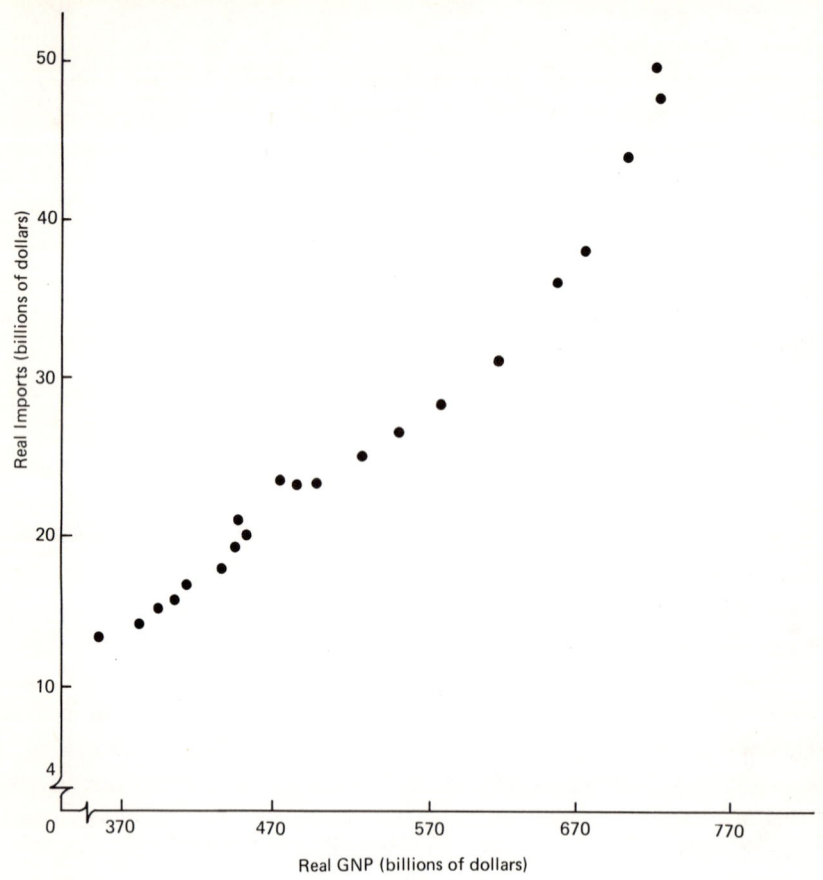

Source: *Economic Report of the President, 1973*.

of points represents a direct (upward sloping) relationship, as we should expect.

On the same grounds, purchases of U.S. goods by foreigners—that is, U.S. exports—should vary inversely with the terms of trade, given the level of foreign incomes. It follows, therefore, that given the level of domestic and foreign incomes, the balance of trade will vary inversely with the terms of trade (the ratio of domestic to foreign prices).

The Influence of Relative Interest Rates

Under the assumption that business firms and individuals will allocate their resources so as to obtain the highest rate of return or maxi-

FIGURE 14-2
Imports and the Terms of Trade, 1950–1970

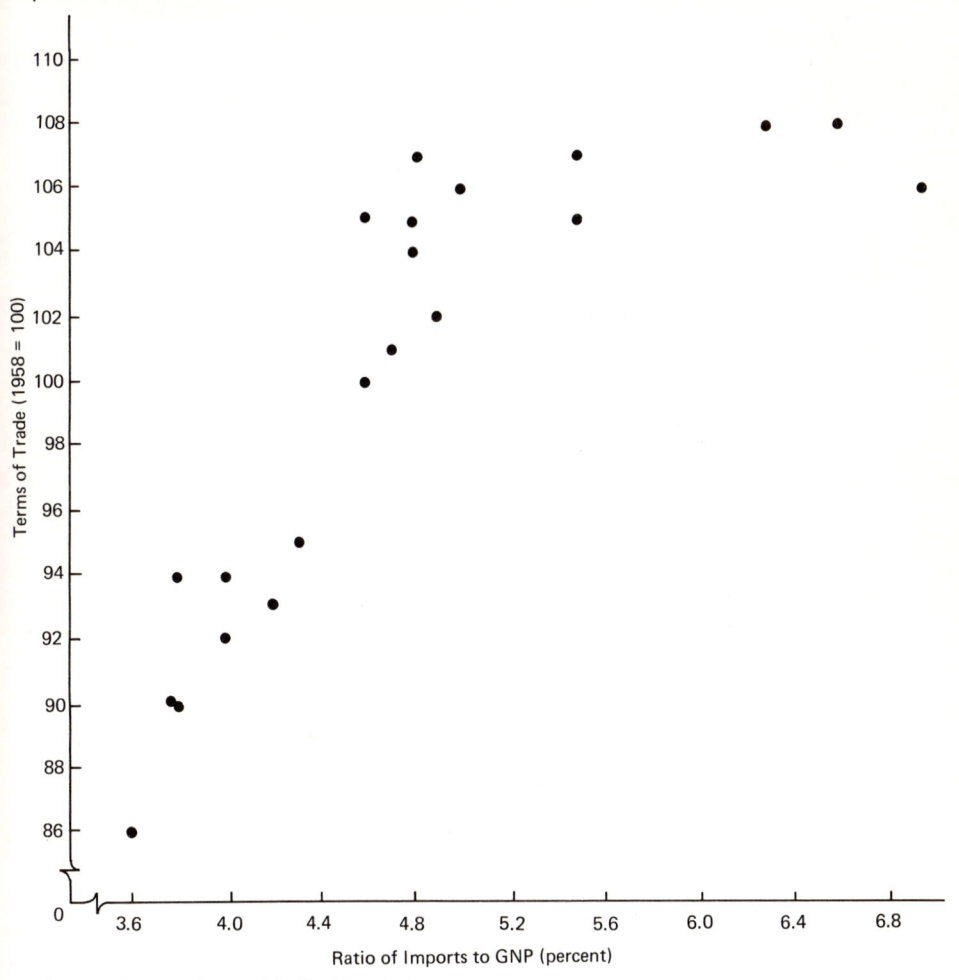

[Scatter plot: Terms of Trade (1958 = 100) on y-axis (86 to 110) vs. Ratio of Imports to GNP (percent) on x-axis (3.6 to 6.8)]

Source: *Economic Report of the President, 1973.*

mum utility, direct and financial investment will be allocated toward that activity which provides the highest yield. Given a choice of buying two types of securities of equal risk, one a foreign security and one a domestic security, we should expect individuals and firms to buy the security that has the highest yield or interest rate. Thus U.S. capital outflows will vary inversely with domestic interest rates and directly with foreign interest rates. Similarly, capital inflows from foreigners will vary directly with the U.S. interest rate and inversely with foreign interest rates. The net capital flow (capital outflows minus capital inflows) will vary inversely with the U.S. interest rate and directly with the foreign interest rate, or inversely with the ratio of domestic to foreign interest rates.

The Influence of Exchange Rates

When a U.S. resident buys goods manufactured in the United States, only one price need be considered—namely, the price of the good in terms of U.S. dollars. However when a U.S. resident buys foreign goods, two prices must be considered: the price of the foreign good in terms of the foreign currency and the price of the foreign currency in terms of U.S. dollars. In other words, in order to determine the price of a foreign good in terms of dollars we need to know the price of the foreign good in terms of its own currency and the price of the foreign currency in terms of dollars. For example, if the price of a Rolls Royce (in terms of British pounds) were to increase by 10 percent and, at the same time, the price of the British pound (in terms of dollars) were to fall by 10 percent, then no change would have taken place in the price of the Rolls Royce (in terms of dollars).

Given the terms of trade and foreign and domestic incomes, we should expect that U.S. imports will vary inversely with the price of foreign currencies (in terms of dollars) or directly with the price of U.S. dollars (in terms of foreign currencies). In other words, if it takes more (less) dollars to buy foreign currencies, then U.S. imports will decline (increase). The reverse occurs for U.S. exports. For purposes of discussion in this chapter, we will define the *exchange rate* as the price of foreign currencies in terms of dollars. Thus the exchange rate between British pounds and U.S. dollars may be stated as $2.40 per pound, for example.

Now in the domestic economy, the price of goods changes in response to disequilibrium between the supply of goods and the demand for goods. Similarly in the foreign market, if there is a discrepancy between the demand for and supply of a particular currency, the exchange rate should adjust to help resolve the discrepancy. The exchange rate can be considered to be the adjustment mechanism in the market for currencies.

Discrepancies between the supply of and demand for individual currencies arise as a result of disequilibrium in the balance of payments. If the United States is running a balance of payments deficit (surplus), there will be a surplus (deficit) of dollars on the international market.

As an illustration, consider the case of disequilibrium in the balance of trade between two countries. For the sake of argument let us assume that capital flows are in equilibrium and that there are no transfer payments or other unilateral transfers. Further we assume that the domestic income levels are constant in both countries. The two countries are the United States and the United Kingdom. On the basis of the above discussions, imports from the United Kingdom into the United States would be a function of U.S. income, the terms of trade, and the exchange rate between pounds and dollars. Exports from the United States to the United Kingdom would be a function of the terms of trade and the exchange rate given the level of income in the United Kingdom.

These two functions are plotted in Figure 14–3A. The terms of

FIGURE 14–3
The Balance of Trade and the Foreign Exchange Market

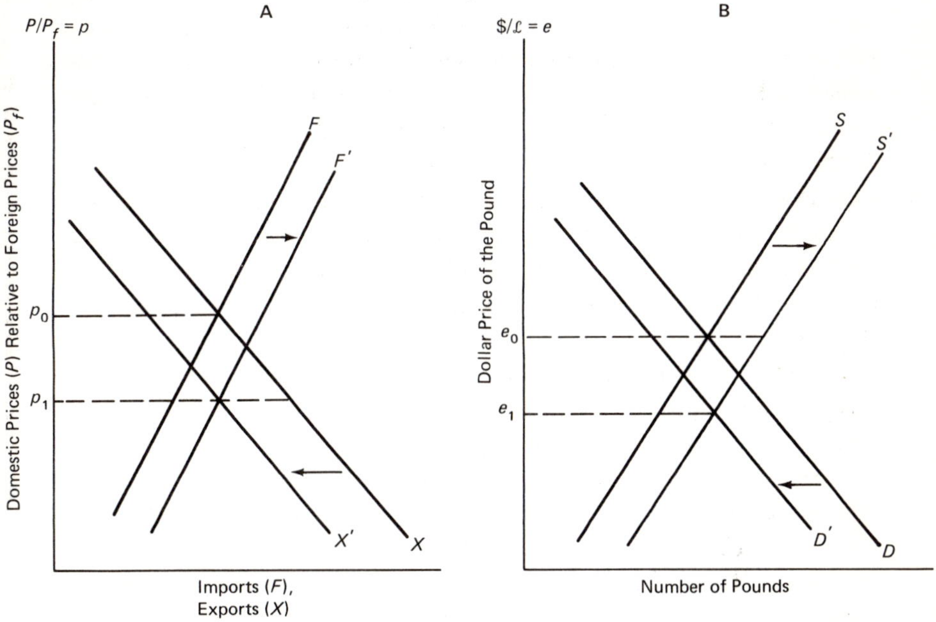

trade are plotted on the vertical axis and the real values of exports and imports are plotted on the horizontal axis. Note that consistent with our assumptions, the import function slopes upward with respect to the terms of trade, and the export function slopes downward. The market for pounds between the two countries is plotted in Figure 14–3B. The exchange rate is plotted on the vertical axis and the number of pounds demanded or supplied is plotted on the horizontal axis. The exchange rate indicates the number of dollars that can be purchased per British pound, or the number of dollars it would take to buy one pound. Thus as the exchange rate increases, the pound becomes more valuable (more costly in terms of dollars) and the demand for pounds decreases. As the exchange rate falls, the pound becomes less costly in terms of dollars and the demand for pounds increases. The supply of pounds varies directly with the exchange rate. More pounds are supplied, therefore the more valuable pounds become in terms of dollars.

For the sake of argument, we treat the price of U.S. goods and the price of British goods as being exogenous to the import-export market and to the foreign exchange market. Assume initially that the market for imports and exports is in equilibrium at p_0. Corresponding to this is equilibrium in the market for pounds at exchange rate e_0. Suppose there is an exogenous increase in the price of British goods which reduces the terms of trade from p_0 to p_1. This increases the demand for U.S. goods by British residents and reduces the demand for British goods by U.S. residents. Thus we have an excess of exports over imports (the gap between X and F at p_1). The increased demand for U.S. goods shifts the supply curve for pounds to the right, and the decreased demand for British goods shifts the demand for pounds to the left—creating, at the old exchange rate, an excess supply of pounds (the gap between S' and D' at e_0).

In response to the excess supply of pounds, the value of the pound falls relative to the dollar. The exchange rate falls. A fall in the exchange rate, given the terms of trade at p_1 and given the level of income in the United States, shifts the import function to the right. The same fall in the exchange rate, given the terms of trade and income in the United Kingdom, shifts the export curve to the left. As long as there is disequilibrium in the market for pounds, the exchange rate will continue to fall; and as long as the exchange rate continues to fall, the import schedule will move to the right and the export schedule will move to the left. Once exports and imports are equal at the new terms of trade, p_1, excess supply will no longer exist in the market for pounds and the exchange rate will stop falling. Equilibrium will be restored at p_1 and exchange rate e_1.

The exchange rate, if flexible, becomes the equilibrating mechanism, even if we include a consideration of the capital account and transfers. As long as a balance of payments surplus results in an excess supply of other currencies, their value will fall relative to the dollar. This will stimulate imports, retard exports, stimulate capital inflows, and retard capital outflows until balance is once again restored.

However, a striking feature of international markets is that at least until recently, the adjustment mechanism, working through flexible exchange rates, did not exist. By both international agreement and by choice of individual countries, exchange rates were generally fixed in value. Thus disequilibrium was resolved through other mechanisms. Since prices, income, and interest rates affect the relevant schedules, much of policy directed towards restoring international equilibrium has attempted to affect prices, income, and interest rates. These policies can be identified and analyzed by incorporating the balance of payments into our basic model.

EXTERNAL EQUILIBRIUM AND THE BASIC MODEL

The IS Curve with the Addition of the Balance of Trade

As we noted earlier, net exports of goods and services, which involves expenditures on current output, affects the IS schedule. On the basis of the foregoing arguments, we allow imports of goods and services to vary directly with the level of domestic income, directly with the terms of trade, and inversely with the exchange rate. Thus if domestic income rises (falls), imports increase (decrease). If the price of domestic goods rises (falls) relative to foreign goods, imports increase (decrease). If the price of other currencies in terms of the dollar falls (rises), imports increase (decrease). Exports, on the other hand, will vary inversely with the terms of trade and directly with the exchange rate. Linear representations of these two functions are presented below:

$$F = \gamma_0 + \gamma_1 Y + \gamma_2 (P/Pf) - \gamma_3 e$$
$$X = x_0 - x_1 (P/Pf) + x_2 e,$$

where Pf is a price index of foreign goods and e, the exchange rate, varies directly with the value of foreign currencies in terms of the dollar.

Adding the difference between exports and imports to our old equilibrium condition for the product market results in the following IS schedule:

$$Y = C + I + G + (X - F)$$
$$Y = C_0 + b(Y - T) + I_0 - ai + G + x_0$$
$$\quad - x_1(P/Pf) + x_2 e - \gamma_0 - \gamma_1 Y - \gamma_2(P/Pf)$$
$$\quad + \gamma_3 e$$
$$(1 - b + \gamma_1)Y = C_0 + I_0 - bT - ai + G + x_0 - \gamma_0$$
$$\quad - (x_1 + \gamma_2)(P/Pf) + (x_2 + \gamma_3)e$$
$$Y = \frac{1}{1 - b + \gamma_1}[C_0 + I_0 + x_0 - \gamma_0 - bT - ai$$
$$\quad + G - (x_1 + \gamma_2)(P/Pf) + (x_2 + \gamma_3)e]$$
$$\tag{14-1}$$

An examination of the equation for the new IS schedule (14–1) indicates the following:

1. A rise (fall) in the domestic price level will shift the IS schedule to the left (right). The coefficient on the terms of trade variable is negative.
2. A rise (fall) in the exchange rate shifts the IS schedule to the right (left). The coefficient on the exchange rate variable is positive.
3. The slope of the IS schedule is made more steep by the inclusion of an income responsive import function. The slope of the new IS schedule is:

$$\Delta i / \Delta Y = -(1 - b + \gamma_1)/a$$

As long as the marginal propensity to import is positive, the slope of the new IS schedule will be greater, in absolute value, than the slope of the IS schedule for the basic model.

Of importance in the analysis to follow is the extent to which the IS schedule shifts in response to changes in the domestic price level and in response to changes in the exchange rate. Changes in the domestic price level will now shift all of the curves of our basic model—the IS, LM, and AS curves. How much the IS schedule shifts in response to changes in the price level and in the exchange rate depends upon the responsiveness of the import and export functions, which, in turn, may depend on the size of the foreign sector relative to GNP.

The changes we have made in the IS schedule incorporate only the balance of trade because it is only the balance of trade that affects current flows of spending in the product market. A complete picture of the balance of payments may be shown by constructing an external equilibrium relationship and superimposing it over the IS-LM-AS diagram.

The External Equilibrium Function[2]

In constructing this relationship, we will abstract from unilateral transfers by governments, pensions, unrecorded transactions, etc. and focus only on the trade balance and net private capital flows. Using the import and export functions derived earlier, the balance of trade becomes the following:

$$X - F = x_0 - \gamma_0 - (x_1 + \gamma_2)(P/Pf) + (x_2 + \gamma_3)e - \gamma_1 Y \quad (14\text{--}2)$$

On the basis of our earlier discussions, capital inflows are assumed to be a positive or direct function of the ratio of domestic to foreign interest rates, and capital outflows are assumed to be an inverse function of that ratio. We have then the following expressions for capital inflows and capital outflows.

$$K_{in} = f_0 + f_1(i/if)$$
$$K_{out} = j_0 - j_1(i/if)$$

The capital account balance is defined to be the difference between capital outflows and capital inflows.

$$\begin{aligned} K_n &= K_{out} - K_{in} \\ &= j_0 - f_0 - (j_1 + f_1)(i/if) \end{aligned} \quad (14\text{--}3)$$

Finally the full balance of payments is in equilibrium if the trade balance minus net capital flows equals zero. This requires that a balance of trade surplus be offset by net capital outflows or that a balance of trade deficit be offset by net capital inflows. The above expressions for the balance of trade (14-2) and net capital flows (14-3) together

---

[2] For an early attempt to incorporate an external equilibrium function into an IS-LM framework, see Dwayne Wrightsman, "IS, LM, and External Equilibrium: A Graphic Analysis," *American Economic Review*, Vol. 60 (March 1970), pp. 203–8. See also the advanced treatment in William H. Branson, *Macro-Economic Theory and Policy* (New York: Harper & Row, Publishers, 1972), pp. 297–317.

230   Macroeconomic Theory

with the balance of payments equilibrium condition provides us with a relationship for an external equilibrium.

$$(X - F) - K_n = 0$$
$$x_0 - \gamma_0 - (x_1 + \gamma_2)(P/Pf) + (x_2 + \gamma_3)e - \gamma_1 Y - j_0 + f_0 + (j_1 + f_1)(i/if) = 0$$
$$\gamma_1 Y = x_0 - \gamma_0 - j_0 + f_0 - (x_1 + \gamma_2)(P/Pf) + (x_2 + \gamma_3)e + (j_1 + f_1)(i/if)$$
$$Y = \frac{1}{\gamma_1}[x_0 - \gamma_0 - j_0 + f_0 - (x_1 + \gamma_2)(P/Pf) + (x_2 + \gamma_3)e + (j_1 + f_1)(i/if)] \quad (14\text{--}4)$$

Equation (14–4) can be interpreted as showing combinations of domestic income and domestic interest rate that are consistent with equilibrium in the balance of payments.

This external equilibrium or EE curve can also be derived graphically. The left side of Figure 14–4 shows the net capital balance as

FIGURE 14–4
Derivation of the External Equilibrium (EE) Curve

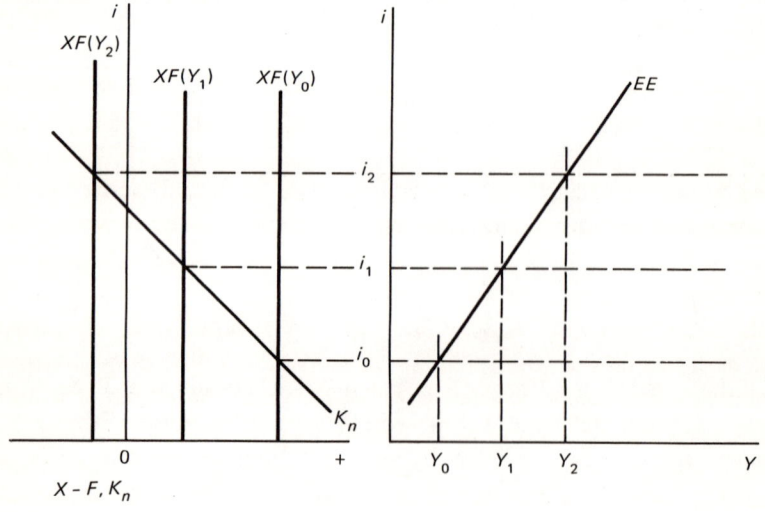

a function of the interest rate. Capital outflows increase relative to capital inflows as the interest rate falls. Thus the capital balance schedule is downward sloping. The interest rate does not enter into the balance of trade relationship. Instead, the balance of trade function *shifts* in the diagram as the level of domestic income changes. Increases in income increase imports relative to exports, decreasing the trade balance and shifting the trade balance function to the left.

The trade balance function is drawn for three levels of income. External equilibrium requires that the trade balance and the capital account balance be equal. If the domestic income level is equal to Y_1, then the relevant trade balance curve is $XF(Y_1)$, and the interest rate would have to be equal to i_1 in order to make the capital account balance and the trade balance equal. If we transfer this and other equilibrium interest rate and income combinations to the right side of Figure 14-4 and connect the points, we obtain an external equilibrium curve which shows the combinations of interest rate and income that result in equilibrium in the balance of payments. The curve is upward sloping, and this is confirmed by noting that the coefficient on the interest rate in equation (14-4) is positive.

Changes in income and/or the interest rate result in movements along the EE curve. The EE curve also shifts in response to changes in certain variables. Specifically, a change in the terms of trade will shift the external equilibrium curve. A rise in the domestic price level, given the foreign price level, will shift the EE curve to the left. Similarly, an increase in the exchange rate will shift the EE curve to the right. These conclusions can be verified by observing the signs of the coefficients of the relevant variables in the external equilibrium equation.

The EE curve can be superimposed over the basic model diagram which contains the IS-LM-AS schedules. The equilibrium domestic interest rate and income combination is determined by the latter three curves. More often than not, the equilibrium income and interest rate combination will not lie on the external equilibrium curve. Thus the balance of payments will be in deficit or surplus, depending upon the position of the (i,Y) combination. If the domestic equilibrium point lies above or to the left of the EE curve, the economy will experience a balance of payments surplus because the interest rate will be too high or income too low, making the net capital account balance less than the balance of trade. By a similar argument, interest rate-income combinations that lie below or to the right of the EE curve will produce a balance of payments deficit. (See Figures 14-5 and 14-6.)

The external equilibrium curve in conjunction with the other curves of the model can be useful in analysing policy problems where external equilibrium is one concern of the policy makers.

POLICY ISSUES

Analysis of Policy Effects

To illustrate the use of the external equilibrium curve in policy analysis, we shall consider two cases. The first case is one that troubled the United States in most of the post–World War II period—namely, the one of combined unemployment and a balance of payments deficit. The second case involves a situation in which the Federal Republic of Germany found itself—namely, that of overfull employment coupled with a balance of payments surplus.

Case 1. Assume that the exchange rate is fixed. Under this assumption there is no automatic tendency for equilibrium to be restored in the balance of payments through exchange rate adjustment. External equilibrium can only be obtained by altering the interest rate-income combination determined by domestic factors. Figure 14–5 shows the unemployment-balance-of-payments-deficit case. The equi-

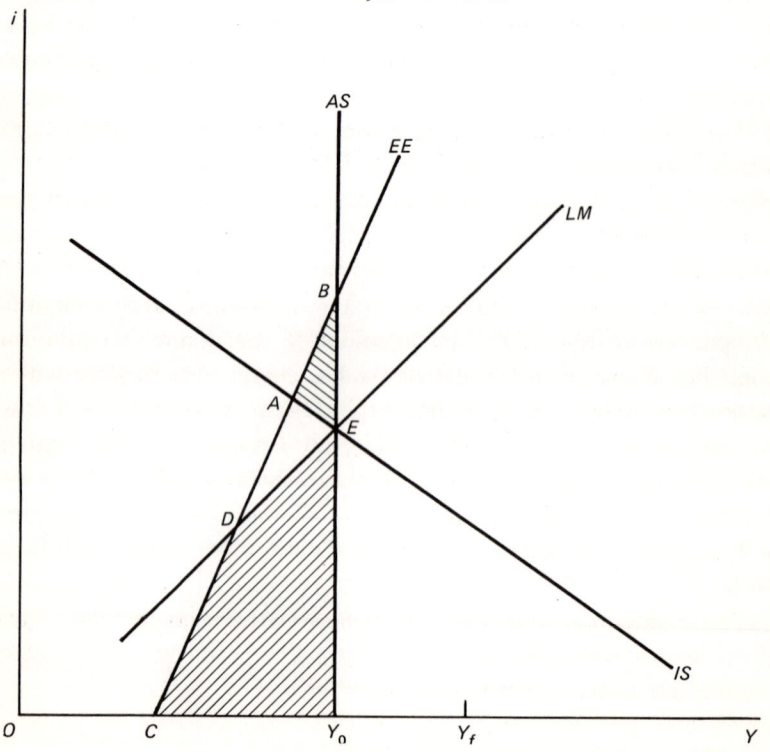

FIGURE 14–5
Unemployment with a Balance of Payments Deficit

librium level of income is at Y_0 which is less than the full-employment level of income. The equilibrium lies to the right of the EE curve, implying a balance of payments deficit. In the absence of any action on the part of the policy makers, the situation will be self-correcting. The balance of payments deficit will normally result in a gold outflow from the United States. As the surplus of dollars is redeemed (exchanged for gold), this reduction in the domestic gold stock reduces the monetary base unless offsetting action is taken by the Federal Reserve Bank.

As the base decreases, the LM curve is shifted to the left. This raises the domestic interest rate, choking off domestic investment expenditures and reducing aggregate demand. The result is that the price level begins to fall. As the price level falls, the AS schedule shifts to the left and the IS and EE schedules shift to the right. This action continues as long as there is a gold outflow and the monetary base decreases. A little experimentation will show that convergence takes place in the shaded area *ABE* in Figure 14–5. Balance of payments equilibrium is restored but only with an increase in unemployment. The monetary authorities, by not offsetting the gold outflow, conduct the equivalent of a contractionary monetary policy. Thus a contractionary monetary policy, by raising domestic interest rates and lowering the domestic price level and domestic income, reduces imports relative to exports and increases capital inflows relative to capital outflows. These actions restore balance-of-payments equilibrium, but the cost is increased unemployment.

Balance-of-payments equilibrium may also be restored through a contractionary fiscal policy. In this case assume that the monetary authorities act to offset the gold outflow, say, by open market purchases of government securities so that the nominal value of the monetary base remains unchanged. Contractionary fiscal policy may be implemented either through a tax increase or a reduction in government expenditures or some combination of the two. Either action lowers aggregate demand and shifts the IS schedule to the left. In response to the decreased aggregate demand, the price level falls, shifting the AS schedule to the left. The falling price level also tends to move the EE and LM curves to the right. Some experimentation with these shifting curves will indicate that the new domestic equilibrium, coupled with equilibrium in the balance of payments, will take place in the lower shaded area $CDEY_0$.

In the case of a contractionary monetary policy, changes in income, interest rates, and the price level all work toward reducing the balance-of-payments deficit. Income falls, and this reduces imports. The falling price level both reduces imports and increases exports; and the rising interest rate increases capital inflows and decreases capital outflows. In the case of a contractionary fiscal policy, the price and income changes tend to reduce the balance-of-payments deficit, but the fall in the domestic interest rate tends to aggravate the capital account balance. Thus in the case of fiscal policy, the price and income changes must be sufficiently large to offset the detrimental fall in the interest rate. It seems likely, therefore, that equilibrium in the balance of payments can be restored only with a larger increase in unemployment than in a case of contractionary monetary policy. In this sense, given the combined external deficit and unemployment situation, a contractionary monetary policy can be said to have a comparative advantage over a contractionary fiscal policy. That is, the cost—in terms of increased unemployment to restore balance of payments equilibrium—is less in the case of a contractionary monetary policy than it is in the case of a contractionary fiscal policy. This conclusion has led many economists to prescribe monetary policy for external disequilibrium and fiscal policy for internal problems.[3]

Equilibrium can also be restored by making exchange rates flexible. In the case illustrated, assuming that there is no change in fiscal or monetary policy, the deficit results in an excess supply of dollars in the foreign exchange market, reducing the value of the dollar relative to foreign currencies—that is, it raises the exchange rate. As the exchange rate rises, both the EE and IS curves move to the right. The effect of a rightward movement in the IS schedule is to shift the domestic equilibrium point to the right of Y_0. This movement and the rightward movement of EE continues as long as there is disequilibrium in the foreign exchange market. But will the EE curve move fast enough to "catch up" to the rightward moving domestic equilibrium point? the answer is "yes" because the EE curve moves faster than the IS curve in response to a changing exchange rate. In response to a change in e, each curve shifts by the following amounts:

$$\Delta Y_{\text{IS}} = [+(x_2 + \gamma_3)/(1 - b + \gamma_1)]\Delta e$$
$$\Delta Y_{\text{EE}} = [+(x_2 + \gamma_3)/\gamma_1]\Delta e$$

[3] For example, see Robert A. Mundell, "The Appropriate Use of Monetary and Fiscal Policy for Internal and External Stability," *IMF Staff Papers,* Vol. 9 (March 1962), pp. 76–79. However, doubt is cast on these conclusions by David J. Ott and Attiat F. Ott, "Monetary and Fiscal Policy: Goals and the Choice of Instrument," *Quarterly Journal of Economics,* Vol. 82 (May 1968), pp. 313–25.

As long as $b < 1$, the denominator of the former will be larger than the latter, making $\Delta Y_{IS} < \Delta Y_{EE}$. Consequently, a move toward a flexible exchange rate in this instance restores balance-of-payments equilibrium with a benefit of increased employment. This is accompanied, however, by a higher domestic price level. Also too, many argue that flexible exchange rates contribute to uncertainty and therefore inhibit world trade.[4]

Case 2. In the second case we have overfull employment and a balance of payments surplus as represented in Figure 14–6. The equi-

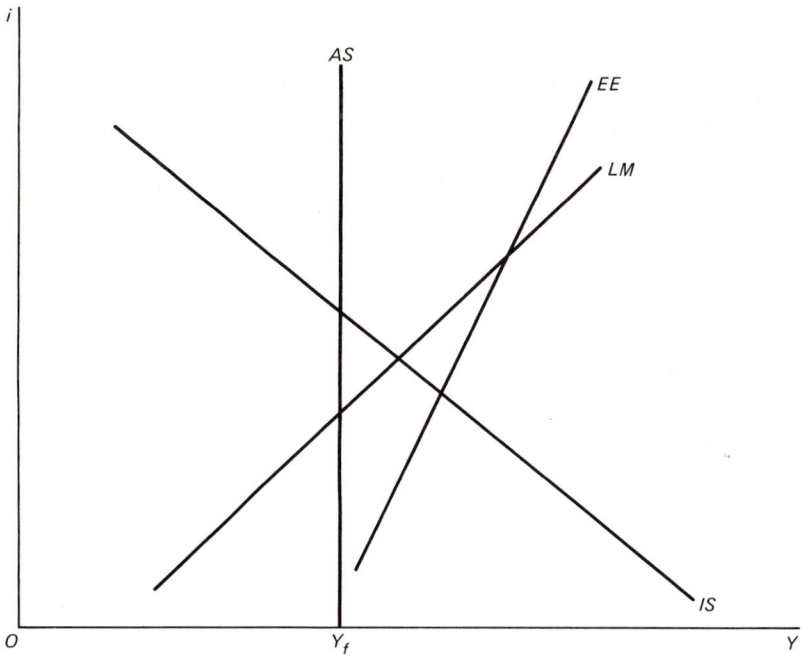

FIGURE 14–6
Overfull Employment and a Balance of Payments Surplus

librium level of aggregate demand is to the right of full employment. Since the economy's output cannot exceed full employment, this situation is accompanied by a continually rising domestic price level. With fixed exchange rates and in the absence of any policy measures, the

---

[4] This is not the place to go into all the "ifs," "ands," or "buts" of exchange rate variations. The interested student should consult Kindleberger, *International Economics,* pp. 322–37.

rising price level will shift the LM schedule to the left; it will shift the IS schedule to the left and will shift the EE curve to the left. As all three curves move to the left, they will eventually converge on the AS schedule.

There is, of course, no guarantee that the EE schedule will intersect at the same point as the other three schedules. A comparison of the price multipliers of the IS and EE curves indicates that the EE curve will shift to the left faster than the IS schedule for a given price increase. But this simply means that when the intersection of IS and LM converges on the aggregate supply schedule we may have either a deficit, equilibrium, or a surplus in the balance of payments. If a deficit results at full employment, a contractionary policy can be employed in the same way as the first case. The cost of restoring external equilibrium is some unemployment. If the intersection of IS, LM, and AS takes place with a balance-of-payments surplus, then expansionary fiscal or monetary policy can be used. The cost is a still higher price level.

A third alternative can be employed and that is to go to flexible exchange rates. If a flexible exchange rate is employed, given the excess demand for dollars, the value of the dollar will rise relative to other currencies, and this lowers the exchange rate. With a falling exchange rate, the EE schedule will move to the left as will the IS schedule. There is also in this case no guarantee that the schedules will all converge at full employment. Convergence may take place at less than full employment.

Use of Nonmarket Changes

1. The more frequently used nonmarket changes that affect balance of payments equilibrium involve the use of tariffs and/or quotas. Tariffs can be interpreted as a rise in the price of foreign goods relative to domestic goods. They therefore reduce the terms of trade. The effect of such reduction is to shift the IS schedule to the right and shift the EE to the right, faster than the IS schedule. A rightward shifting IS schedule increases aggregate demand, and this implies that the domestic price level will also rise. An increase in the domestic price level will shift the AS schedule to the right and shift the LM schedule to the left. Equilibrium occurs in the balance of payments at a higher income and interest rate level than initially.

Quotas produce a similar result except that quotas in this case may be interpreted as a shift in the import function since quotas are generally leveled on imports. A downward shift in the import function will shift the IS and EE schedules to the right. The resulting changes are the same as in the case of a tariff.

There are, of course, objections to the use of tariffs and quotas. One objection is that it cannot be assumed that other countries will not retaliate to the unilateral imposition of tariffs and quotas. To avoid such retaliation, changes in tariffs and quotas are usually done in consultation with other countries through a bargaining process.

A second objection is that nonmarket methods that influence the balance of payments usually result in trade taking place at non-Pareto optimal terms. The marginal value of imports will be higher than the marginal costs of producing those imports since relative prices are no longer used as an equilibrating mechanism.

Often too, a balance-of-payments deficit is interpreted to mean that the country incurring the deficit is "living beyond its means" since it is purchasing more from the rest of the world than it is selling to the rest of the world. The imposition of tariffs and quotas may restore balance-of-payments equilibrium without reducing the level of domestic economic activity. It does have the effect of imposing stringent conditions on foreign countries. For example, a tariff placed upon goods purchased from England will reduce England's exports of goods to the United States, thus reducing aggregate demand in England's product market. The effect will be deflation and increased unemployment in England. Thus the imposition of tariffs by the United States forces adjustments to take place in England's economy, rather than in the U.S. economy, to the detriment of the English economy.

2. Where fixed exchange rates are in effect, devaluation or revaluation can also be considered a nonmarket change. In this case, the exchange rate is raised (devaluation) or lowered (revaluation) by fiat. The analysis of the effect on domestic and external equilibrium is the same as in the case of flexible exchange rates except that the change is a once-and-for-all change rather than a continuous change.

The major objection to devaluation, in particular, is that it is politically unpopular. All too many people interpret devaluation as a disgrace which reflects economic weakness and a decline in the power of the nation's currency. However, the net export of capital plus unilateral transfers from the United States during the post–World War II period could hardly be interpreted as a sign of economic weakness. Nations with severe internal problems simply cannot export large amounts of capital and foreign aid while maintaining relatively full employment, as the United States did. The resulting dollar glut may have provided downward pressure on the dollar and resulted in devaluation, but it would be foolish to interpret this as an economic defeat.

For countries whose currencies are "overvalued," a move to flexible exchange rates would be the equivalent of devaluation. However, the major objection to flexible exchange rates is the fear of instability. Rate movements may be intensified by changing domestic conditions and by the activities of speculators. Unpredictable and perhaps violent rate movements may make bankers and import-export firms reluctant to engage in trade. The effect is to retard, rather than facilitate, world trade.

Supporters of flexible rates argue that speculative and hedging operations dampen, rather than intensify, rate movements and permit a faster adjustment from equilibrium to equilibrium. Moreover, with balance-of-payments concerns removed by flexible rates, policy makers can handle domestic problems more effectively.

A compromise may be effected by use of the "crawling peg." This approach involves frequent, but small, adjustments instead of the present infrequent and large adjustments. Thus adjustment is accomplished more rapidly than under present arrangements but without the possibility of instability.

A CAVEAT ON PARTIAL EQUILIBRIUM ANALYSIS

This chapter must be concluded with a warning. Although the model in this chapter may appear to be complex to the student, in reality it is too simple. The model allowed for income, price, and interest rate effects in the domestic economy but ignored foreign income, price, and interest rate effects. Put another way, this model was to the world economy what the simple model of Chapter 3 was to the domestic economy. Such partial equilibrium analysis can be misleading and, in the extreme, erroneous. A complete analysis of policy should take account of the influence of the policy, through the trade sector, on foreign incomes, prices, and interest rates. But that is beyond the scope of this chapter and even of this book.

SUMMARY NOTES

1. The balance of payments consists of two major accounts: the current account and the capital account.

2. The balance of trade, which involves the purchase and sale of currently produced goods and services, enters into the equilibrium condition for the product market.
3. The balance of trade (exports minus imports) is assumed to vary inversely with the domestic price level and domestic income. It also varies directly with the price of foreign currencies in terms of the dollar (the exchange rate).
4. The capital account balance (capital outflows minus capital inflows) is assumed to vary inversely with the ratio of domestic to foreign interest rates.
5. Abstracting from transfer payments, external equilibrium requires that the current inflow (outflow) of dollars be offset by the capital account outflow (inflow) of dollars.
6. Monetary and fiscal policies designed to restore balance-of-payments equilibrium are designed to alter its domestic determinants (income, price level, and the interest rate). Direct policies include tariffs, quotas, and exchange rate manipulations.

DISCUSSION QUESTIONS

1. In the chapter, the EE curve was drawn with a steeper slope than the LM curve. Examine the slope formulas for each to determine what conditions are required to make the EE curve steeper than the LM curve.
2. With the LM curve steeper than the EE curve, analyze the effects of fiscal and monetary policy measures in both the unemployment-BOP deficit case and the full-employment-BOP surplus case.
3. Some elements in the balance of payments can be called endogenous, in the sense that they are responsive to income, relative prices, and the exchange rate. Other elements, unresponsive to those variables, can be called exogenous elements. Using data for the past ten years, separate the balance of payments into its exogenous and endogenous components. On average, has the endogenous balance been a deficit or surplus? Has the exogenous balance reinforced or offset the endogenous balance?
4. Analyze the effects of fiscal and monetary policies where the economy is experiencing unemployment coupled with a balance-of-payments surplus.

15

Dynamics and Growth

STATIC AND DYNAMIC ANALYSIS
Some Concepts

THE MATERIAL in this book, up to this point, has been concerned with static macroeconomic concepts. This type of analysis is usually called *comparative statics*—involving, as it does, a comparison of static equilibrium points. The process by which the economy moves from one equilibrium point to the next is given minor consideration. However, even the static models used in the book thus far contain dynamic elements. In fact all economic models contain dynamic elements. A dynamic element is simply a statement, explicit or implicit, about the way in which economic variables change over time. In discussing the response of the basic model to a change in some exogenous variable, we implicitly describe a dynamic process. We did give the dynamic adjustment process a little more explicit treatment in our discussion of adjustment mechanisms in Chapter 6, but a complete static model would contain statements or equations that describe the adjustment process as well as equations that describe the behavior of each sector and the equilibrium conditions.

Actually the difference between a static model and a dynamic model is really the point of emphasis. As an analogy, suppose we took a baseball which was resting on the top of a table and pushed it off the table so that it fell to the floor. A static analysis would involve the taking of two pictures. The first picture would be of the ball as it rested on top of the table and the second picture would be of the ball as it rested on the floor. The dynamic counterpart would be a moving picture showing the motion of the ball as it leaves the top of the table, falls to the floor, and eventually comes to rest. The static model concentrates on the positions of rest (the equilibrium positions), while the dynamic model concentrates on the motion during the period of disequilibrium.

Nevertheless the conclusions we reached using the comparative statics analysis are not really meaningful without some due consideration of the dynamic process by which we move from one equilibrium to the next. In fact, we noted this in our discussion of stability in Chapter 13. In one instance in that discussion, the intersection of the IS, LM, and AS curves—which denotes an equilibrium position—was not meaningful. An analysis of the adjustment process showed that we would never reach the equilibrium position indicated by the intersection of the curves. Thus comparative statics tells an incomplete story. The complete story can only be told if we include dynamic analysis.

The idea that there is some dynamic adjustment in every comparative statics analysis has been called the *correspondence principle*.[1] While the preceeding chapters in the book have concentrated on comparisons of equilibrium points, this chapter will discuss the dynamic process in more detail.

Plan of the Chapter

Dynamics can be used in both growth and nongrowth models. We shall look at each of those in turn. As a starting point we shall begin with a comparative static model of the type that we have been using in the book and consider in more detail the adjustment mechanism which drives us from one equilibrium position to the next. If our comparative statics conclusions are to be meaningful, the equilibrium points must be stable. By considering the dynamic adjustment process, we can derive the necessary and sufficient conditions for stability to hold—and thus for the static conclusions to be meaningful.

Another type of dynamic analysis in a nongrowth framework focuses almost entirely on the dynamic process and treats the static equilibrium conditions only incidentally. In this type of model we trace the path from one equilibrium point to the next. The analysis is usually

---

[1] This term originated with Paul A. Samuelson in *Foundations of Economic Analysis* (Cambridge, Mass.: Harvard University Press, 1947).

conducted by means of a period analysis in which time is explicitly considered. This type of model is usually employed in describing economic fluctuations or business cycles.

The third type of dynamic analysis involves growth. Growth models are long-term or long-run dynamic models which show how the economy's productive capacity changes over time. The economy's productive capacity usually changes as a result of changes in the resource base (labor and capital) or technological change or both. Growth models are useful for long-run planning for developed economies and also for determining the necessary conditions for growth for underdeveloped economies.

The chapter will close with a brief discussion of policy issues.

DYNAMICS WITHOUT GROWTH

Complete specification of our basic model requires explicit statements about the way in which key variables adjust over time. Rather informally, in Chapter 6, we indicated that we expect the price level to vary directly with excess demand in the product market, and the interest rate to vary directly with excess demand in the money market. In other words, the price level rises in the face of excess demand and falls in the face of excess supply in the product market; and the interest rate rises in response to excess demand in the money market and falls in response to excess supply. These statements can be expressed algebraically as follows:

$$dP/dt = f(Y_d - Y_s)$$

where $f' > 0$; and

$$di/dt = g(M_d/P - M_s/P)$$

where $g' > 0$.

In their simplest form, dP/dt and di/dt are made proportional to excess demand in the respective markets, so that f and g are simply positive constants. As such, the magnitudes of f and g regulate the speed of adjustment. The larger f and g, the faster P and i respond to excess demand.

Whether or not the equilibrium positions defined by the model are stable depends both on the form of the structural equations and the form of the adjustment mechanisms.

As an illustration, consider the simple model of Chapter 3 which concerns only the product market. The equations of that model consist of the consumption function, the investment function, and the equilibrium condition.

$$C = C_0 + bY_D$$
$$I = I_0 - ai$$
$$Y = C + I + G$$

Under the assumptions made in Chapter 3, the level of income adjusts in response to excess demand. The adjustment mechanism can then be written:

$$\frac{dY}{dt} = f(C + I + G - Y)$$

where f is a positive constant. Substituting the consumption and investment functions gives us,

$$\frac{dY}{dt} = f(C_0 + bY_D + I_0 - ai + G - Y).$$

Making use of a Taylor series expansion, this can be written as:

$$\frac{dY}{dt} = \frac{\partial f(\ldots)}{\partial Y}(Y - Y^*) = f(b-1)(Y - Y^*)$$

where Y^* is the equilibrium value of Y, given the values of the parameters and exogenous variables of the model. A general solution for Y for some time period t takes the following form:

$$Y_t = Y^* + (Y - Y^*)e^{f(b-1)t}$$

In order for Y_t to approach the equilibrium value Y^* as time progresses, the exponential term must approach zero as t increases toward infinity. This will occur if $f(b-1) < 0$. Since f is a positive constant, $(b-1)$ must be negative, and this is the case as long as $b < 1$. Thus stability in the simple model requires that the marginal propensity to consume be less than one. This condition is both necessary and sufficient. However, it is not necessary in the more complex IS-LM-AS model.

The mathematics of the analysis for the basic model are somewhat involved, using systems of differential equations.[2] However we can note that our basic model will exhibit stable equilibria if the IS curve slopes downward. Recall that the LM curve unambiguously sloped

---

[2] For an application to a Keynesian system, see Samuelson, *Foundations of Economic Analysis*, pp. 276–83.

upward but that the IS curve slope was ambiguous, depending upon two things. First, if investment is responsive to changes in income, the sum of the marginal propensity to invest and the marginal propensity to consume may exceed one, and thus the IS curve would slope upward rather than downward. In addition, if consumption is responsive to the interest rate and if it turns out that the income effect outweighs the substitution effect, the IS curve could be upward sloping. This would happen if the positive relationship between consumption and the interest rate outweighed the negative relationship between investment and the interest rate.

While a *sufficient* condition for stability is that the IS curve slope downward, the downward sloping IS schedule is not a *necessary* condition. That is, it is possible to have stable equilibria with an upward sloping IS schedule. In fact we observed this in a somewhat informal sense in the discussion of stability of Chapter 13.

While the correspondence principle is important in comparative statics analysis, more attention has been directed towards the use of dynamics in developing models of economic fluctuations. In models of this type, time is introduced explicitly so that the period-by period change in the variables can be observed. Generally, the model involves the use of lags; variables such as consumption are not assumed to respond to a stimulus instantaneously in the same time period.

As an example, consider a simple model of the type discussed in Chapter 3. In order to stick to basics we shall also assume that there is no government sector; therefore government spending and taxes will not enter into the equations. We assume that consumption is a function of lagged gross national product and that investment is a function of changes in consumption. With specific values for the parameters, the model can be written as follows:[3]

$$C_t = 100 + 0.7 Y_{t-1} \tag{15-1}$$

$$I_t = 50 + 1.3(C_t - C_{t-1}) \tag{15-2}$$

$$Y_t = C_t + I_t \tag{15-3}$$

Note that investment consists of two parts: a constant or autonomous component and an induced component. The autonomous component can be assumed, in this case, to represent the amount spent

---

[3] One of the earliest models of this type is that found in Paul A. Samuelson, "Interactions Between the Multiplier Analysis and the Principle of Acceleration," *Review of Economics and Statistics*, Vol. 21 (May 1939), pp. 78-88.

15 / Dynamics and Growth

for capital replacement which is independent of the level of economic activity. The induced component arises as the business sector attempts to adjust the capital stock in response to changes in consumption. In other words, if the demand for consumer goods increases, the capital stock will have to be adjusted upward in order to produce the amount of consumer goods now demanded. Financial factors are, of course, ignored in this model as is the possibility of substitution between capital and labor in the productive process. Since consumption is itself a function of income the investment equation can be written as follows:

$$\begin{aligned} I_t &= 50 + 1.3(C_t - C_{t-1}) \\ &= 50 + 1.3(100 + 0.7Y_{t-1} - 100 - 0.7Y_{t-2}) \\ &= 50 + 0.9(Y_{t-1} - Y_{t-2}) \end{aligned} \quad (15\text{--}4)$$

For reference, call the coefficient on the change in income (0.9) simply the *accelerator*.

Current GNP in each period is then the sum of current consumption and current investment.

$$\begin{aligned} Y_t &= C_t + I_t \\ &= 100 + 0.7Y_{t-1} + 50 + 0.9(Y_{t-1} - Y_{t-2}) \\ Y_t &= 150 + 1.6Y_{t-1} - 0.9Y_{t-2} \end{aligned}$$

or

$$Y_t - 1.6Y_{t-1} + 0.9Y_{t-2} = 150 \quad (15\text{--}5)$$

Equilibrium in the model occurs when the variables are no longer changing from period to period. That is, when income in the current period is equal to income in the previous period which is equal to income two periods back. If we substitute the same income level into equation (15–5), we can solve for the equilibrium level of income.

$$\begin{aligned} Y - 1.6Y + 0.9Y &= 150 \\ 0.3Y &= 150 \\ Y &= 500 \end{aligned}$$

Suppose now that we disturb this initial equilibrium and follow the path of income, over time, in response to that disturbance. A period-by-period analysis can be conducted with the use of Table 15–1. The time period is listed in the first column. The change in income from two periods back to the previous period is listed in the second column. This will enable us to compute easily the current level of

TABLE 15–1
The Multiplier-Accelerator Model

Time	$Y_{t-1} - Y_{t-2}$	C_t	+	I_t	=	Y_t
0	0	450.00		50.00		500.00
1	0	450.00		60.00		510.00
2	10.00	457.00		69.00		526.00
3	16.00	468.20		74.40		542.60
4	16.60	479.82		74.94		554.76
5	12.16	488.33		70.94		559.27
6	4.51	491.49		64.06		555.55
7	−3.72	488.88		56.59		545.47
8	−10.08	481.83		50.93		532.76
9	−12.71	472.93		48.56		521.49
10	−11.27	465.04		49.86		514.90

investment. Current consumption, current investment, and their sum (current GNP) are listed in the remaining three columns.

At the outset, the equilibrium level of the income is $500 billion and this is divided between consumption of $450 billion and investment of $50 billion. Note that since income has not been changing, investment is only equal to the amount necessary for capital replacement—the autonomous component of $50 billion. Now suppose, for undetermined reasons, expenditure on capital replacement increases from $50 to $60 billion. In the period, consumption remains at $450 billion. Investment is now $60 billion, and income for the first period is now $510 billion.

In the second period, because of the increase in income of $10 billion, consumption rises to $457 billion and investment rises to $69 billion. Total income in the second period is $526 billion. Income continues to increase, but eventually at a decreasing rate. In the fourth period, the increase in income is less than the increase in the third period, and, as a result, investment begins to decline in the fifth period. The increment in income for each succeeding period is less and less until income actually begins to decrease, the turning point occurring at period 6. From period 6 through period 10 income declines.

The table can be continued, of course, for many, many periods. Given the parameters selected in this example, income will oscillate but gradually converge to a new equilibrium level. The oscillations will gradually dampen until they are completely eliminated. The new equilibrium level of GNP is $533.33 billion.

However this type of model is not always characterized by convergent or dampened oscillations. Other values for the marginal propensity to consume and for the accelerator coefficient can yield different results. In fact, depending upon the values of the parameters selected, the oscillations can explode or the system can be made to diverge from equilibrium continuously. Table 15–2 lists four ranges for the accelerator and the type of behavior that parameters selected within these ranges will impart to the system. A quick calculation by the reader will show that the values of the parameters selected in our example will yield dampened oscillations.

TABLE 15–2
Parameter Ranges for the Multiplier-Accelerator Model

Range of Accelerator	Path of Income
$v < (1 - \sqrt{s})^2$	Steady decline
$(1 - \sqrt{s})^2 < v < 1$	Damped oscillations
$1 < v < (1 + \sqrt{s})^2$	Explosive oscillations
$v > (1 + \sqrt{s})^2$	Steady growth

Note: v is the accelerator and s is the marginal propensity to save $(1 - b)$.

Source: R. G. D. Allen, *Macroeconomic Theory: A Mathematical Treatment* (New York: St. Martin's Press, 1967), p. 338.

The above model is the basic forerunner of modern models of economic fluctuations or business cycles. The very structure of the model leads to oscillations or explosive behavior when the system is disturbed by some random element. However while the dampened oscillatory behavior may seem realistic enough, ever increasing oscillations or explosive behavior, either in the upward or downward direction, seems unrealistic simply because income cannot rise without limit nor is it likely to fall without limit. In the former case, income can do no more than rise to the full-employment level. Thereafter it can rise only as fast as a growing resource base permits it to rise. In the latter case, it is probable that investment will not fall without limit. A lower limit undoubtedly prevails which is necessitated by some absolute minimum capital replacement. In any case, gross investment cannot fall below zero. Once investment stops decreasing, the fall in income will slow down. Given a slowdown in the fall of income, investment will once again begin to rise, and the cycle will reverse.

Thus the cycle becomes bounded, and fluctuations in economic activity vary between the full-employment ceiling and the floor dictated by the minimum investment level.[4]

---
[4] The bounded cycle of this type was introduced by John R. Hicks in *A Contribution to the Trade Cycle* (Oxford: Clarendon Press, 1956).

The important element of the above illustration is the assumption that the structure of the economy itself generates oscillations or business cycles in response to some random disturbance. What the model does not provide is a theory that explains the sources of the disturbances. For example, in our illustration we assumed that autonomous investment spending increased by $10 billion without any explanation of the cause of such increase. The model might be expanded to include a theory of business expectations which might help explain why changes suddenly take place in investment spending. Disturbances might also be introduced through the consumption function, through changes in consumer behavior. Finally we could assume that disturbances also originate in the money market through ill-timed fiscal or monetary policy. However the idea that the very structure of the economy itself reinforces disturbances by generating cyclelike behavior is a central element of modern business cycle theory.

ECONOMIC GROWTH

Some Terms and Definitions

For our purposes, we define growth as the long-term change (usually increase) in the economy's productive capacity. The productive capacity of the economy is defined to be that output that could be produced if all of the economy's resources were fully and efficiently employed. Thus most models of economic growth examine the determinants of the long-term trend in output, given full employment.

Economic growth is important, especially in the face of a growing population. Without a trend increase in total output, per capita income would decline steadily as the population increases. Even with a stable population, zero income growth means stable per capita income and a stable standard of living. Under conditions of no growth per capita income it is impossible for some groups to advance themselves economically without other groups losing. Thus it is likely that in a no-growth society conflicts between groups of unequal income will be intensified. With a growing economy, it is possible for all groups to enjoy a steady increase in the standard of living. This issue is especially crucial for underdeveloped economies.

The notation in the discussion that follows is essentially the same as that employed previously in the book. The symbols for output, labor, capital, and so on are the same as before. However since growth involves change in these variables we will of necessity talk of growth rates expressed as a percentage change in the variable per unit of time. We will be interested in the growth rate of income, the growth rate of the labor force, and so on. We denote the *percent change* in the variable by placing a dot over the symbol used previously. For example, the percent change in income is expressed by the following:

$$\dot{Y} = (dY/dt)(1/Y)$$

A similar interpretation applies to the other variables.

In one sense, growth models may be viewed as long-run versions of the short-run static and dynamic models discussed up to this point. In the short-run models, investment or capital accumulation takes place but is assumed to be so small relative to the total stock of capital that the stock of capital is taken as a given. In the long run, this assumption is not valid as long as net investment is nonzero. The long-run effect will be to alter the stock of capital and thus change the productive capacity of the economy. By a similar reasoning it may be appropriate to assume that the labor force is given in the short run, but that same assumption is not reasonable for the long run. Thus the long-run growth models are distinguished from short-run models primarily by the observed change in both the stock of capital and the labor force.

To start our discussion of growth models, consider a fairly elementary type.

A Simple Growth Model

The simplest growth model is based upon the work of Roy Harrod and Evsey Domar.[5] The Harrod-Domar type models assume that labor and capital, the two factors of production, must be employed in fixed proportions. In other words, the model does not allow for substitution between the two factors of production. Thus output can be expressed as a function of one factor alone, assuming that there is a sufficient amount of the other factor to maintain the fixed factor proportion requirement. Output then is assumed to be a constant proportion of the stock of capital. A second assumption is that for the long run, consumption is proportional to income. Finally, in order to stick to

---

[5] Evsey Domar, "Capital Expansion, Rate of Growth, and Employment," *Econometrica*, Vol. 14 (April 1946), pp. 137–47; Roy F. Harrod, "An Essay in Dynamic Theory," *Economic Journal*, Vol. 49 (March 1939), pp. 14–33.

basics, we assume that there is no government sector and no foreign sector. The model contains three equations: a production function, a consumption function, and an equilibrium condition as follows:

$$Y = K/\sigma \qquad (15\text{--}6)$$
$$C = bY \qquad (15\text{--}7)$$
$$Y = C + I$$

The parameter σ is often called the *capital-output ratio*.

Assuming that producers intend to produce the current level of output, the desired and necessary stock of capital is given by the following:

$$K = \sigma Y$$

Current net investment is the change in the stock of capital per unit of time which may be written as follows:

$$I = dK/dt = \sigma dY/dt \qquad (15\text{--}8)$$

Assume at the outset that labor and capital exist in the required proportions so that both must be fully employed in order to produce the current level of output. In equilibrium, which is now full-employment equilibrium, current output must be equal to aggregate demand consisting of current consumption and investment expenditures. Substituting the behavioral relationships into the equilibrium condition we can derive the following:

$$Y = C + I$$
$$K/\sigma = bY + \sigma dY/dt,$$

divide both sides by Y:

$$K/\sigma Y = b + \sigma \dot{Y},$$

but

$$K/Y = \sigma.$$

Thus we have

$$1 - b = \sigma \dot{Y}$$

and,

$$\dot{Y} = (1 - b)/\sigma \qquad (15\text{--}9)$$

We conclude that the equilibrium (full employment) rate of growth in output is equal to the marginal propensity to save divided by the capital-output ratio. For example, if the marginal propensity to consume is 0.9 and the capital-output ratio is 4, the equilibrium growth rate will be 2.5 percent.

In equilibrium, the growth rate of consumption and saving is equal to the growth rate of income. This follows from the assumption that consumption is proportional to income. If equilibrium is to be maintained, investment must grow at the same rate as saving, and this rate of growth is also the same for the stock of capital. Thus in long-run equilibrium, the growth rates of income, consumption, saving, investment, and the stock of capital are all equal to the marginal propensity to save divided by the capital-output ratio.

It is also important to note that if full employment of labor is to be maintained, the labor force must grow at the same rate as all the other variables. Harrod has called this growth rate the *warranted growth rate*. If the growth rate of the labor force exceeds the warranted growth rate, unemployment will gradually increase, since capital and labor must be employed in fixed proportions. On the other hand, if the labor force grows at a slower rate than the warranted growth rate, capital will become increasingly unemployed. It is not likely that the business sector will continue to invest while idle capital exists, and thus full-employment equilibrium is once again broken. As long as capital and labor cannot be employed in varying proportions, the growth rates of all the relevant variables must be equal or else disaster will result.

The Harrod-Domar model also implies that the warranted growth rate depends upon the capital-output ratio and the marginal propensity to consume. Presumably the capital-output ratio is determined by technology. An improvement in technology that lowers the capital-output ratio will raise the warranted growth rate. The warranted growth rate is also increased by an increase in the marginal propensity to save (a decrease in the marginal propensity to consume).

This model is limited because most of modern production theory permits substitution between factors of production, especially in the long run, to which growth models apply. Thus it was only a matter of time after the introduction of the Harrod-Domar model that others would introduce models with variable factor proportions.

The Neoclassical Approach

The neoclassical production function was introduced into growth economics by Robert Solow.[6] The neoclassical production function

---

[6] Robert M. Solow, "A Contribution to the Theory of Economic Growth," *Quarterly Journal of Economics*, Vol. 70 (February 1956), pp. 65–94.

exhibits three important characteristics for our purposes: (1) The factors of production can be substituted for each other; (2) the function exhibits diminishing marginal product to each factor of production; and (3) the production function is homogeneous of the first degree. The last characteristic simply means that if each factor of production is changed by the same percentage, total output will also be changed by that percentage. In other words, if capital and labor are each doubled, output will double. Another way of saying this is that the production function exhibits constant returns to scale. The Cobb-Douglas production function introduced earlier in this book fulfills these characteristics. We will use this function as the basis for the following discussion.

As long as capital and labor can be substituted freely for one another the capital-output ratio will not be constant for the neoclassical production function. This can be seen by a slight rearrangement of the Cobb-Douglas production function.

$$Y = AK^x N^{1-x}$$

Note that K^x can be written as $K(K^{x-1})$ which is also equal to K/K^{1-x}. By substitution

$$Y = A(N/K)^{1-x} K$$

or

$$K = (1/A)(K/N)^{1-x} Y$$

It can be seen from the above that the capital-output ratio varies directly with the capital-labor ratio. The higher the capital-labor ratio, the higher the capital-output ratio.

Now consider the long-run characteristics of a growth economy which employs a production function of the type indicated above. It can be shown that in long-run equilibrium the capital-labor ratio approaches a constant value and, further, that the growth rates of output, capital, and labor will be equal. Finally the output-labor ratio or output per worker also approaches a constant. To demonstrate this, we first convert the production function into output per worker form by multiplying capital and labor in the production function by $1/N$:

$$Y/N = A(K/N)^x (N/N)^{1-x}$$
$$y = Ak^x \qquad\qquad (15\text{--}10)$$

where $y = Y/N$ and $k = K/N$.

Note that output per worker increases as capital per worker increases, but at diminishing rate since the parameter x is less than one.

The function is plotted in Figure 15–1. Now the rate of change in capital per worker (that is, $\dot{k}$) is given by the following:

$$\dot{k} = \dot{K} - \dot{N} = dK/dtK - dN/dtN$$

We continue to assume, as we did in the Harrod-Domar case, that consumption is proportional to income. Further, equilibrium requires that total output be equal to aggregate demand. The equilibrium condition can be rearranged by substituting the consumption function into the equilibrium condition.

$$Y = bY + I$$
$$I = (1 - b)Y$$

Since $dK/dt = I$, we can substitute the equilibrium condition into the expression for the change in capital above (dK/dt). Assume also that the growth rate of labor is a constant which is determined by noneconomic forces or forces outside of the model. Thus the expression for the percent change in capital per worker becomes the following:

$$\dot{k} = (1 - b)Y/K - \dot{N}$$

Divide Y and K by $\dot{N}$.

$$\dot{k} = (1 - b)y/k - \dot{N} \qquad (15\text{–}11)$$

If capital per worker has reached an equilibrium, then its value will no longer be changing and its rate of change is equal to zero. By substituting $\dot{k} = 0$ in equation (15–11), we obtain the following expression:

$$(1 - b)y/k - \dot{N} = 0$$
$$(1 - b)y/k = \dot{N}$$
$$y = \dot{N}k/(1 - b) \qquad (15\text{–}12)$$

The last expression gives us combinations of output per worker and capital per worker for which the rate of change in capital per worker is zero. This relationship has been plotted in Figure 15–1 along with the per worker production function (15–10). Note that since the rate of growth in the labor force and the marginal propensity to consume are both assumed to be constants, this relationship is a straight line through the origin. It is upward sloping under the assumption that the growth rate in the labor force is positive and that the marginal propensity to consume is positive but less than one.

Long-run equilibrium occurs when the actual output per worker and capital per worker values are equal to those values that are con-

FIGURE 15-1
The Neoclassical Growth Model

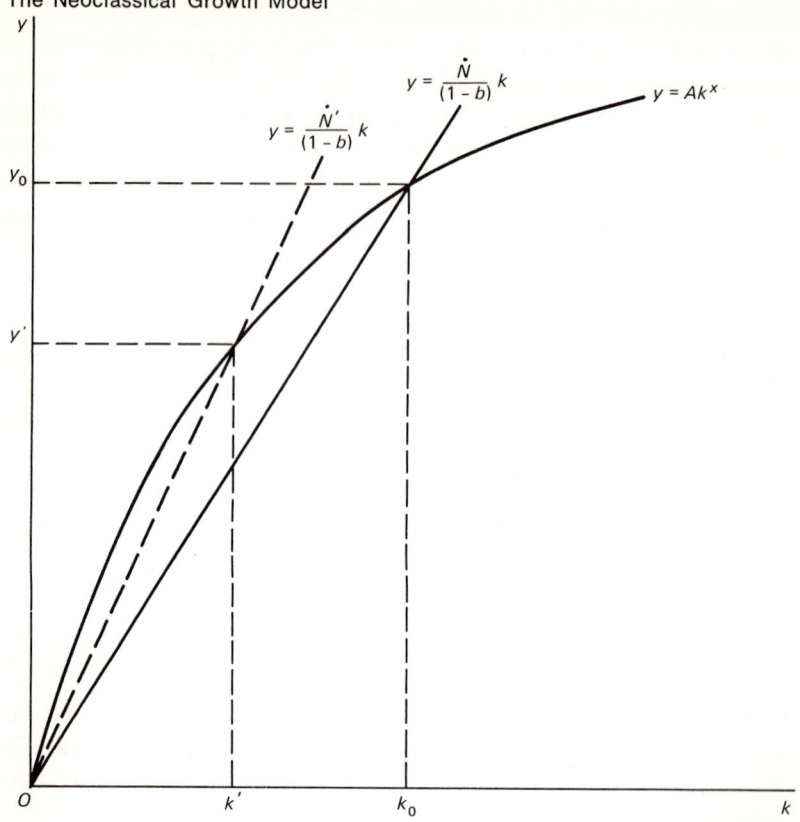

sistent with no further change in the capital-labor ratio, at (y_0, k_0). At that capital-labor ratio, both capital and labor will be growing at the same rate, which is equal to the exogenous growth rate in the labor force. Since the aggregate production function is homogeneous of the first degree, if capital and labor are growing at the same rate, output will also be growing at that rate. Thus the growth rates of output, capital, and labor are the same and are all determined by the growth rate in the labor force, a conclusion that departs from the Harrod-Domar conclusions. In addition, since output and labor are both growing at the same rate, per worker output is a constant in long-run equilibrium.

Two other results that differ with Harrod-Domar conclusions should also be noted. First, as can be seen from Figure 15-1, a change in the growth rate of the labor force changes the growth rate of total output and also changes the equilibrium per worker output. For example, an increase in the growth rate of the labor force to N' increases the growth rate of total output but reduces the equilibrium output per worker (to y' in Figure 15–1). Output per worker decreases because the aggregate production function employed exhibits diminishing returns. However the new equilibrium does take place at full employment, and this conclusion differs from the Harrod-Domar case. Second, a change in the marginal propensity to consume changes per worker output but does not change the growth rate of total output. For example, an increase in the marginal propensity to consume (decrease in the marginal propensity to save) lowers per worker output in equilibrium but does not effect the growth rate of total output which is determined solely by the growth rate of the labor force. This conclusion is also at variance with the conclusions of the Harrod-Domar model.

Throughout this analysis it has been assumed that technology is constant. While this may be a reasonable assumption in the short run, it is not in the long run. A change in technology can be interpreted as a shift in the production function, given the quantity of capital and labor employed. This shift can be seen by changing the coefficient, A. An increase in A pivots the production function upward. Inspection of Figure 15–1 will indicate that if we pivot the production function upward continuously—say, as a result of a constant rate of increase in A—the equilibrium per worker output and capital-labor ratio will gradually increase. Given the constant rate of change in the labor force, an increase in per worker output comes through an increase in total output. Thus in the context of this neoclassical growth model, the growth rate of total output is affected by the growth rate of the labor force and by the growth rate of technology. It is not affected by changes in the saving or consuming habits of the private sector. In fact, technological change has become an important element in the discussion of the sources of economic growth, a subject to which we now turn.

SOURCES OF ECONOMIC GROWTH

The conclusions of the neoclassical growth model are long-run conclusions and are based upon the assumption of no technical developments that alter the shape of the production function. In fact technical progress does take place in the long run, so that an examination of growth rates in total output indicates that such changes cannot be explained completely by the changes in capital and labor alone. Specifically, the growth rate in total output is greater than can be explained by the growth rates in capital and labor.

The Cobb-Douglas production function provides a framework for examining the contribution to the growth rate in output of technological change. The production function can be decomposed into rates of change as follows. The production function is:

$$Y = AK^x N^{1-x}$$

Taking logs of both sides,

$$\log Y = \log A + x \log K + (1 - x) \log N$$

Differentiate with respect to time.

$$d(\log Y)/dt = d(\log A)/dt + x d(\log K)/dt + (1 - x)d(\log N)/dt$$

Since $d(\log Y)/dt = \dot{Y}$ and so, on, we have,

$$\dot{Y} = \dot{A} + x\dot{K} + (1 - x)\dot{N} \qquad (15\text{-}13)$$

Changes in A are assumed to be due to technical development. Given data on the growth rates in output, capital stock, and labor, and independent estimates of the parameter x, we can determine the contribution of technological change as a residual. Rearranging equation (15-13), we obtain the following:

$$\dot{A} = \dot{Y} - x\dot{K} - (1 - x)\dot{N}$$

As an illustration of the approach, consider the data listed in Table 15–3. The table lists the growth rate in capital and labor for a number of years as well as the growth rate in output. The growth rate in A is obtained by deducting from the growth rate in output the weighted contributions of capital and labor (with $x = 0.25$). The average for the series is listed on the bottom line. Over the period, the annual rate of increase in total output has averaged about 2.9 percent, of which approximately 1.0 percent was contributed by capital and labor and the remaining 1.9 percent contributed by technological change.

This is essentially the approach taken by Edward Denison and Richard Nelson.[7] Robert Solow obtained similar results by fitting a produc-

---

[7] Edward F. Denison, *The Sources of Economic Growth in the United States and the Alternatives Before Us* (New York: Committee for Economic Development, 1962) and "Sources of Postwar Growth in Nine Western Countries," *American Economic Review*, Vol. 57 (May 1967), pp. 325–32. Richard R. Nelson, "Aggregate Production Functions and Medium-Range Growth Projections," *American Economic Review*, Vol. 54 (September 1964), pp. 575–606.

TABLE 15–3
Estimating the Contribution of Technical Change to the Growth Rate of Total Output

Year	$\dot{N}$	$\dot{K}$	$\dot{Y}$	$-\ 0.75\dot{N}$	$-\ 0.25\dot{K}\ =$	$\dot{A}$
1951	1.07	2.16	7.61	0.80	0.54	5.27
1952	0.21	3.29	3.00	0.16	0.82	2.02
1953	0.74	3.93	4.39	0.56	0.98	2.85
1954	–1.05	2.51	–1.42	–0.79	0.63	–1.26
1955	2.88	5.97	7.34	2.16	1.49	3.69
1956	1.34	4.89	1.83	1.01	1.22	–0.40
1957	–1.33	3.02	1.43	–1.00	0.75	1.68
1958	–1.66	1.88	–1.16	–1.25	0.49	–0.40
Average	0.27	3.46	2.88	0.16	0.86	1.86

$\dot{N}$ = percent change in index of available man-hours. Available man-hours is an index of man-hours employed divided by 1 − unemployment rate.
$\dot{K}$ = percent change in real capital stock.
$\dot{Y}$ = percent change in real GNP.
Sources: Man-hours and GNP data were obtained from the *Economic Report of the President, 1973*. Capital stock data were obtained from Raymond W. Goldsmith, *The National Wealth of the United States in the Postwar Period* (Princeton, N.J.: Princeton University Press, 1962), Table A–5, pp. 117–18.

tion function to the data.[8] His estimated annual rate of change in the technical progress index was about 1.5 percent.

Perhaps the chief difficulty with the approach employed here is that technical progress is assumed to be neutral and disembodied. It is neutral because technical progress does not change the optimal (profit-maximizing) mix between capital and labor. In other words, the parameter x is not changed by the introduction of technical progress. Technical progress is here disembodied because it can take place in the absence of any change in the stock of capital or the quantity of labor.

It seems, of course, likely that technical developments can be, and in fact probably are, introduced through new capital equipment and through improvements in the quality of the labor force. In other words, new technological developments are introduced into the aggregate production function by employing additional capital of higher quality than the existing stock of capital and by expanding the labor force with individuals that are more highly trained than existing individuals. In fact, Solow experimented with embodied technical progress by assuming that all technical developments are introduced through

---

[8] Robert M. Solow, "Technical Change and the Aggregate Production Function," *Review of Economics and Statistics*, Vol. 39 (August 1957), pp. 312–20.

changes in the stock of capital.[9] As might be expected, the estimated contribution of the capital stock increased sharply over the case where technical progress was assumed to be disembodied.

However, whether introduced independently of new capital or as a part of new capital, technical progress appears to be an important element in economic growth. Government policy designed to improve the rate of economic growth can be directed at altering the rate of technological change as well as altering the resource base.

POLICY ISSUES

Policies for the Developed Economy

Government policy in the dynamic context is intended to smooth out fluctuations in economic activity and promote long-term growth. The policies necessary to accomplish the former objective are the same as those we discussed in connection with the static basic model. The major difficulty is in the timing of policy. If economic policy is to be compensatory, if it is to offset fluctuations in the private economy, the policy must be properly timed. For example, given the lags in policy effect, policy makers must be careful that an antiinflationary policy does not take effect in the following recession. If so, fluctuations will be accentuated rather than attenuated.

Until forecasting techniques can be improved to a fine degree, compensatory policy can still be introduced through the use of automatic stabilizers such as unemployment compensation. A properly designed automatic stabilizer will take effect when it is needed.

Long-term growth can be promoted through policies that affect the quality and quantity of the resource base for the economy and through policies that affect technological progress. For example, in the neoclassical model that was discussed earlier, no indication was given as to why or how equilibrium was to be maintained. There is nothing in the model to indicate the forces that bring the growth rate of the

---

[9] Robert M. Solow, "Technical Progress, Capital Formation, and Economic Growth," *American Economic Review*, Vol. 52 (May 1962), pp. 76–86. Denison discounts the importance of the embodiment issue in "The Unimportance of the Embodied Question," *American Economic Review*, Vol. 54 (March 1964), pp. 90–94. See also Moses Abramovitz, "Review of Denison," *American Economic Review*, Vol: 52 (September 1962), pp. 762–82. For an analysis of the implications of embodied technical progress, see Edmund S. Phelps, "The New View of Investment: A Neoclassical Analysis," *Quarterly Journal of Economics*, Vol. 76 (November 1962), pp. 548–67.

capital stock into equality with the growth rate of the labor force or bring the growth rates of saving and investment into equality. The model simply indicates that as a matter of long-term equilibrium, these growth rates must be equal. Government policy may be directed toward insuring the adjustment to long-run equilibrium. Monetary policy, for example, can be employed to keep rising interest rates from retarding the growth rate of investment and the capital stock.[10] Fiscal policy can be employed through altering the tax rate structure so as to prevent the marginal propensity to save from falling—which, as we have seen earlier, would reduce equilibrium output per worker. Specific fiscal policies can also be employed to promote the rate of technical progress. The government might provide funds or subsides to promote research and development which tends to improve the quality of capital. Increased spending on education might be used to improve the quality of the labor force.

Policies for the Underdeveloped Economy

Economic growth is crucial for countries in which per capita income is uncomfortably low. Yet the vigorous pursuit of policies employed by developed economies may not be completely appropriate for the underdeveloped economy. The existing capital stock of an underdeveloped economy may be too primitive to take advantage of the technological state that the developed countries already enjoy. Moreover, lack of developed financial markets and other constraints may prevent the economy's capital stock from adjusting to its long-run equilibrium level.

Frustrated in its attempt to make use of modern technology and improve the rate of capital formation, the policy maker in the underdeveloped economy may attempt to raise per capita income by promoting policies that retard the growth of the population and, therefore, the labor force. One of the implications of the neoclassical model is that a reduction in the growth rate of the labor force raises the equilibrium level of per worker output. It also tends to reduce the

---

[10] Recent attempts to treat the monetary sector explicitly include Harry G. Johnson, "A Neoclassical One-Sector Growth Model: A Geometrical Exposition and Extension to a Monetary Economy," *Economica,* Vol. 33 (August 1966), pp. 265–87; Miguel Sidrauski, "Inflation and Economic Growth," *Journal of Political Economy,* Vol. 75 (December 1967), pp. 796–810; and James Tobin, "Money and Economic Growth," *Econometrica,* Vol. 33 (October 1965), pp. 671–84.

growth rate of total output. A once-and-for-all reduction in the growth rate of the labor force results in a once-and-for-all increase in the long-run equilibrium level of per worker output but lowers the growth rate of total output to the same level as the lowered labor force growth rate. If improvement in per worker output is the main goal, such a policy may be appropriate.

Unfortunately some writers speculate that the growth rate of the labor force in underdeveloped countries may not be an exogenous variable but may be a function of per worker (or per capita) output. Moreover the relationship may be a direct one, so that increases in per worker output result in increases in the growth rate of the labor force. In this case an upward shift in the production function—say, due to technological change—would in the first instance tend to raise per worker output, but the increase in per worker output in turn raises the growth rate of the labor force, thus negating the initial effect of the technological improvement. Under such circumstances, some underdeveloped economies appear to be trapped at a low level of per worker output. The possibility has been investigated by such writers as Harvey Leibenstein and Richard Nelson.[11] Both hypothesize that over some range of per worker or per capita output, induced changes in the growth rate of the labor force negate any improvement in per capita income. At some sufficiently high per capita output level, the induced changes in labor force growth rates will no longer negate any improvements. To achieve the higher level some "critical minimum effort" must be made either through improvements on a massive scale in the stock of capital or in the state of technology or both. To many underdeveloped countries, the possibility of either event may seem quite remote.[12]

Whether applied to the developed or the underdeveloped economy, the growth models discussed here imply that output is constrained only by the stock of capital and of labor and the state of technology. Sufficient raw materials or "natural" resources are assumed to exist. But we are rapidly discovering, especially in the United States, that

---

[11] Harvey Leibenstein, *Economic Backwardness and Economic Growth* (New York: John Wiley and Sons, 1963); Richard R. Nelson, "A Theory of the Low-Level Equilibrium Trap in Underdeveloped Economies," *American Economic Review,* Vol. 46 (December 1956), pp. 894–908.

[12] In some cases the "great escape" may be accomplished through a sustained shift from the low-productivity agrarian sector to the higher-productivity industrial sector. For a case study of Japan, see Frank Zahn, "Sectorial Labor Migration and Sustained Industrialization in the Japanese Development Experience," *Review of Economics and Statistics,* Vol. 53 (August 1971), pp. 283–87.

this assumption may be flawed. If we deplete certain raw materials for which substitutes have not yet been found, growth may be constrained regardless of the growth rates of capital and labor. Growth may have to wait for technology to discover substitutes or new ways to exploit existing raw materials.

Even so, rapid growth may no longer be desirable. Expansion of the capacity to convert raw materials into finished goods may come at the expense of clean air and water and a scenic environment. Since these things yield positive utility or satisfaction, the trade-off between environmental quality and manufactured products must be recognized in policy discussions. For many people, the marginal satisfaction of manufactured goods now equals, or has fallen below, the marginal satisfaction yielded by a pleasant environment. If the feeling is sufficiently widespread, a deemphasis of growth is implied.

On the other hand, it is not clear that growth, per se, is responsible for environmental decay. A stationary state (in which production exists for replacement only) using primitive technology can also result in unacceptable levels of pollution. Even human wastes, improperly disposed of, can have a devastating effect on water quality, for example. In fact, growth itself generates the resources that can be used to clean up the environment. Perhaps the problem is not growth, but a misallocation of the fruits of growth.

In any case, the issues are substantial and promise to be a significant part of future policy concerns.

SUMMARY NOTES

1. Dynamic analysis examines the way in which economic variables change over time. Static analysis, by contrast, examines the characteristics of equilibrium points.
2. Growth models are long-run dynamic models in which the central feature is the change in the economy's productive capacity.
3. In Harrod-Domar (fixed factor proportion) type growth models, the equilibrium growth rate of total output depends on the capital-output ratio and the marginal propensity to save.
4. In neoclassical growth models with variable factor proportions, the equilibrium growth rate of total output is determined by the growth rates of technological progress and the labor force. A change in the marginal propensity to save affects the equilibrium output per worker but not the growth rate of total output.

5. Technological progress has been as important to growth in the United States as the growth of the labor force and the capital stock.

DISCUSSION QUESTIONS

1. With the aid of Figure 15–1, analyze the effect of an increase in the marginal propensity to consume on the growth rate of total output and the equilibrium values of output per worker and capital per worker.

2. The nature of the fluctuations in business cycle models is determined by the lag structure of the model as well as by the parameter values. Let the investment equation used in the chapter be replaced by the following:

$$I_t = 50 + 1.3(C_{t-1} - C_{t-2}).$$

Using a table similar to Table 15–1, trace the time path of income and compare with the results obtained in the chapter.

3. With the IS curve upward sloping as in Figure 13–1 (Chapter 13), analyze the effect of an increase in the monetary base. What conclusions do you draw about stability?

4. Repeat the analysis of the previous question, using not the IS-LM-AS model but the IS-LM model of Chapter 4. Do your conclusions differ from those of the previous question?

16

Inflation

INTRODUCTION

IN THE MINDS of most people, inflation is one of the top two domestic problems facing the United States. In fact, in recent years, it has tended to rank as the top problem, ahead of unemployment. Special problems deserve special treatment, and therefore we shall devote this entire chapter to the discussion of inflation. Economists unfortunately are divided about the causes and processes of inflation. We will, in this chapter, examine two basic causes of inflation and three of the more popular mechanisms by which inflation becomes apparent. However it is difficult to talk about inflation without also discussing unemployment. In the minds of most economists and many layman there exists a permanent trade-off between inflation and unemployment. Consequently we shall devote a section to a discussion of the inflation-unemployment trade-off. Finally we shall round out the chapter with a discussion of the policy issues that are involved.[1]

For our purposes inflation can be defined as a rise in the general price level. Many writers distinguish among varying degrees of inflation. At slow price rise is sometimes called *creeping inflation*. At the

---

[1] To become thoroughly immersed in the subject, the student should read Martin Bronfenbrenner and Franklyn D. Holzman, "Survey of Inflation Theory," *American Economic Review,* Vol. 52 (September 1963), pp. 593–661. A shorter survey is by Harry G. Johnson, "A Survey of Theories of Inflation," in *Essays in Monetary Economics,* ed. Harry G. Johnson (Cambridge, Mass.: Harvard University Press, 1967), pp. 104–42.

other end of the spectrum, an extremely rapid price increase is called *hyperinflation. Galloping inflation* lies someplace in between. Analytically, it is often necessary to make a distinction between slow or creeping inflation and hyperinflation. The *rate* of inflation is simply the percent change in the price level per year.

Inflation is presumed to be bad because it produces undesirable effects for many individuals. Three effects might be noted here. The empirical evidence which bears on these will be discussed at the end of the chapter. First, inflation is said to result in a redistribution of income in an undesirable way. Many economists have argued that wage changes lag behind price changes, so that an increase in the price level would not be accompanied by a proportionate increase in the wage rate. The effect is that profits rise faster than wages, thus shifting real income from wage earners to profit earners. Since wage earners are assumed to be at the low end of the income distribution and profit earners at the upper end, this amounts to a redistribution of income from lower-income to higher-income groups.

Second, it is often argued that price increases hurt creditors and benefit debtors. It does this because loans are usually fixed in nominal terms. A rise in the price level depreciates the principal of the loan. For example, suppose I borrow $100 for one year at a 5 percent rate of interest. At the end of the year I will pay my creditor $105. If there is no change in the price of goods, then I will borrow $100 worth of purchasing power and repay $105 worth of purchasing power. On the other hand, suppose that during that period of time the price level of goods rises by 10 percent. At the end of the year I will repay a loan of $105 in nominal terms, each dollar of which has depreciated by 10 percent. It is as though I had borrowed $100 and repaid $95 in a world of unchanging prices. This kind of scenario, of course, benefits me, the debtor, and hurts the person from whom I borrowed the original $100, namely, the creditor. Thus the price rise—that is, inflation—shifted real income from the creditor to the debtor.

A third problem of inflation applies to the extreme case of hyperinflation. As we discussed in an earlier chapter, money can be used as a store of value. However its use as a store of value is conditional upon money's stability in terms of purchasing power. If I place $1,000 in the bank and keep it there during a period of rapid inflation, its command over goods will depreciate rapidly. In other words, in terms of real goods it becomes less and less valuable. This becomes particularly crucial in periods of hyperinflation when prices may be rising at the rate of 100 percent per week, or even per day. Under such circumstances no one wants to hold money as a store of value. Thus it is often argued that hyperinflation leads to monetary collapse. Given a sufficiently rapid rise in prices, people would no longer want to hold money, and the economy would revert to a barter economy in which goods were exchanged directly for other goods.

At this point the reader may ask, "If certain groups expect to be hurt by inflation, won't they take action to avoid being hurt?" The answer is generally "yes." For this reason we shall make a distinction between expected and unexpected inflation. The disadvantages of inflation occur when the inflation is unexpected. For when the inflation is unexpected, protective reactions will not be forthcoming. On the other hand, if inflation is fully expected, the real variables of the system such as unemployment, real income, and so on may behave as though there were no inflation. This will be more fully discussed later in this chapter. For now, however, we turn to the ultimate causes of inflation.

THE SOURCE OF INFLATION

The Keynesian, Excess Demand, or Inflationary Gap Approach

Perhaps the simplest approach to the cause of inflation is to say that inflation arises as a result of excess demand. Two questions immediately pose themselves: What caused the excess demand? Will the inflation that results be perpetual or will it be self-correcting? An elementary Keynesian approach, based on the simple model of income determination developed in Chapter 3, argues that the cause of the price rise in the first place is an autonomous increase in one or more of the components of aggregate demand at full employment. If the system converges to a point at which the new level of aggregate demand, in nominal terms, is equal to nominal income, the inflation will be self-correcting. If we can find no level of nominal income for which aggregate demand and nominal income are equal, the inflation will continue without limit.[2]

To put this in more concrete terms, consider the following situation: Suppose the economy is at full-employment equilibrium. At full em-

---

[2] One of the earliest analyses of inflation using this approch is Arthur Smithies, "Behavior of National Money Income Under Inflationary Conditions," *Quarterly Journal of Economics*, Vol. 56 (November 1942), pp. 113–29.

ployment, output or real income is at a maximum and cannot be increased. Suppose now that government expenditures are increased in real terms. This means that real aggregate demand will exceed the full-employment level of output and the price level will therefore rise. But note what happens. For the government to maintain its real expenditures at a new, higher level, it must increase its nominal expenditures as fast as the price level rises. Thus if prices start to rise at 5 percent per year, nominal government expenditures must also continue to increase at 5 percent per year in order to maintain the new level of real government expenditures. Therefore nominal aggregate demand will continue to rise.

Now consider the effect on the private sector. Equilibrium can be reestablished if real private saving can rise sufficiently to negate the increase in real aggregate demand. This, of course, means a reduction in real private consumption expenditures equal to the increase in real government expenditures, with the effect that command over real goods is shifted from the private sector to the government sector.

We have previously assumed in our analysis earlier in the book that real private saving depends only upon real private income. Real income in the present example is fixed. How therefore can real saving increase? One way is for us to drop the assumption of no money illusion on the part of the household sector. It may be that households do not really distinguish between increases in nominal income and increases in real income. Thus real and nominal savings may both rise in the face of an increase in nominal income.

A more sophisticated approach is to observe that our saving function is an aggregate relationship, incorporating the behavior of all persons in the private sector whether their incomes originate through wages, profits, or rent. It may be that a simple aggregation is not appropriate for all income levels. Suppose we make two assumptions. First, assume that the marginal propensity to consume out of profits is lower than the marginal propensity to consume out of salaries and wages. Second, assume that in an inflationary situation, nominal wage rates will rise, but not as fast as prices. Now if the total wage bill does not rise as fast as total sales, the share received by profit earners will increase. Thus real income is shifted from wage earners to profit earners. Under the assumption that profit earners have a lower marginal propensity to consume than wage earners, the aggregate marginal propensity to consume will fall, or, what is the same thing, the aggregate marginal propensity to save will increase. Thus as the inflation progresses and the marginal propensity to save increases, not only will nominal saving rise but real saving will rise also. Moreover, real saving may rise sufficiently fast, or real consumption fall sufficiently fast, so that the inflation becomes self-correcting as resources are shifted from the private sector to the government sector. Thus the inflation acts like a tax on the real resources of the private sector.

The situation may be illustrated with the use of Figure 16–1. The

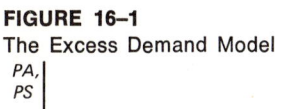

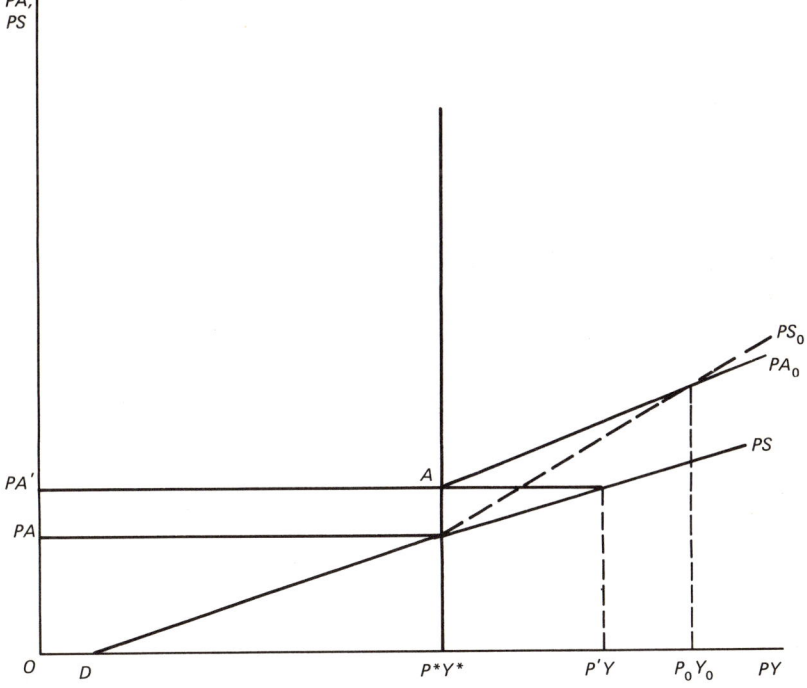

FIGURE 16–1
The Excess Demand Model

model shown there is a variation of the income expenditure model of Chapter 3. Rather than use the $Y = C + I + G$ equilibrium condition, the figure uses its formal equivalent, saving equals investment. However all variables in Figure 16–1 are expressed in nominal terms. Real income (Y) times the price level (P) is nominal income, and this is plotted on the horizontal axis. Similarly, nominal saving is plotted on the vertical axis along with nominal autonomous expenditures (PA). For purposes of this illustration, investment and government expenditures are grouped together under the category "autonomous expenditures." Taxes, which we will assume to be constant, are included in saving. Equilibrium occurs when $PA = PS$.

Suppose at the initial price level the nominal value of autonomous expenditures is OPA. With the saving function DPS, equilibrium occurs at nominal income P^*Y^*. Assume that to the left of P^*Y^* all changes in nominal income are due to changes in real income, with no price change. To the right of P^*Y^* all changes in nominal income are due only to changes in the price level since full-employment level of output cannot be exceeded. Assuming no money illusion on the part of the household sector, real saving increases up to P^*Y^*, and thereafter real saving remains constant and nominal saving increases only as fast as the price level.

Put another way, after P^*Y^* nominal saving is proportional to nominal income, since real saving and real income are fixed. Now suppose the government sector increases its expenditures, raising nominal autonomous expenditures from PA to PA'. This increase in aggregate demand cannot raise real output but does raise the price level, equilibrium being restored at $P'Y$. Inspection of Figure 16–1 will indicate that the ratio $PA'/P'Y$ is equal to the ratio PA/P^*Y^*. Thus an attempt by the government to raise its real expenditures by a once-and-for-all increase in nominal expenditures is frustrated because its share of nominal income has not changed. In order to increase its real expenditures, the government sector would have to raise its nominal expenditures and thereafter continue to increase its nominal expenditures as fast as the price level rises. Graphically this means raising its nominal expenditures from PA to PA' and thereafter, as nominal income rises due to the price level increase, along the line APA_0. But note that the line segment APA_0 diverges from the original saving function. Thus the excess aggregate demand is not resolved, and prices continue to rise without limit.

However suppose that one of the assumptions suggested above about the household sector prevails, so that the aggregate marginal propensity to consume decreases in the face of inflation. This has the effect of pivoting the savings function upward, perhaps to PS_0. If so, equilibrium may eventually be restored. In the diagram, PS equals PA at nominal income level P_0Y_0. The determining factor is whether or not the marginal propensity to consume in the aggregate decreases under inflationary conditions.

The assumptions of money illusion or differential propensities to consume are not necessary if the tax structure is progressive with respect to nominal income. Normally an income tax structure makes the nominal tax a function of nominal income. If the tax rises faster than nominal income, the tax is progressive. Now suppose as before that nominal income increases (due to a price increase) and that the tax rate is progressive. Total nominal taxes will increase at a faster rate than nominal income, and therefore nominal disposable income and *nominal consumption* will increase at a slower rate than nominal income. Thus real consumption will fall, and real saving plus taxes will increase. When real consumption has decreased by the amount of the increase in real government expenditures, the inflationary excess demand is eliminated.

Perhaps the major criticism of this type of analysis of inflation is that monetary factors are ignored. No account is taken of the effect that rising nominal income has on money demand, on interest rates, and ultimately on private investment expenditures. This is in contrast with the next approach we will consider which concentrates almost exclusively on monetary factors.

The Quantity Theory Approach

The fundamental relationship in the quantity theory approach is the demand for money.[3] Recall from our discussion in earlier chapters that the demand for real money balances varies inversely with the rate of interest and directly with real income. The quantity theory adds to that relationship, as a cost of holding money, the rate of inflation. If the price of commodities is rising at, say, 10 percent per year, the value of money balances in depreciating at the rate of 10 percent per year; and such cost must be considered when determining the utility-maximizing level of cash balances to hold. If we include the rate of inflation in the money demand equation and assume that the demand for real money balances has an income elasticity of one, we can write the money demand equation as follows:

$$M/P = (k - g_1 i - g_2 \dot{P})Y$$

For purposes of this discussion, assume that the real rate of interest (i) and real income (Y) are constant. The equation can be arranged

---

[3] The essays by Milton Friedman and Phillip Cagan in *Studies in the Quantity Theory of Money*, ed. Milton Friedman (Chicago: University of Chicago Press, 1956) are especially appropriate to this discussion.

to show the desired ratio of real balances to real income (which is the same as the ratio of nominal balances to nominal income) as follows:

$$M/PY = k - g_1 i - g_2 \dot{P}$$

In Figure 16–2 the desired ratio of money to income is plotted against the rate of inflation, for a given i.

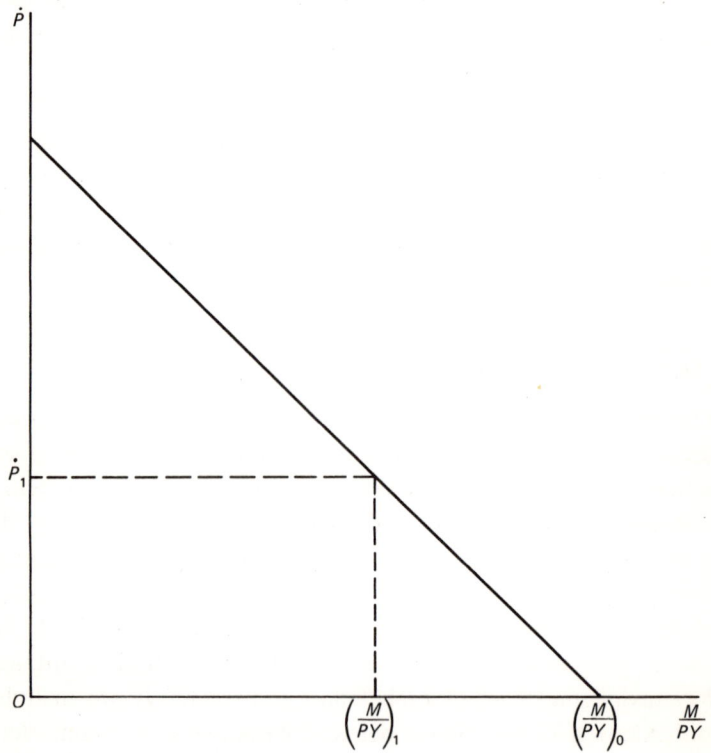

FIGURE 16–2
Money Demand under the Quantity Theory

The initial impetus to inflation in the quantity approach would be an increase in the supply of nominal money. Suppose the supply of nominal money is increased so that individuals are left holding larger nominal money balances than they desire, given the level of real income, prices, and interest rate. They will, in a quantity theory world, attempt to rid themselves of the undesired money balances by purchasing real goods. This bids up the price of real goods. Suppose the price level rises at an annual rate equal to $\dot{P}_1$ in Figure 16–2. Given the higher cost of holding money balances, individuals will revise their desired money-to-income ratios downward to M/PY_1. However once this revision has been made, the new ratio of money to income can be maintained only if nominal money holdings rise as fast as prices. Thus if $\dot{P}_1$ corresponds to a 10 percent rate of inflation, individuals would have to increase their nominal money balances at the rate of 10 percent per year in order to maintain the fixed ratio of money to income. Individuals can attempt to do this by not permitting their nominal consumption expenditures to rise as fast as nominal income, the increased nominal savings being used to add to their nominal money balances. This has the effect of reducing real consumption expenditures.

On the other hand, the agency that issues the money balances—namely, the government—is a recipient of an increase in real income. In effect, purchasing power is shifted from money holders to the issuers of money. Of course the purpose of increasing the supply of money may be to finance an antipoverty program, for example. Consequently the ultimate transfer of real income is from the holders of money to the beneficiaries of the expansionary monetary policy in the fashion of a combined tax and transfer payment.

However, note that aggregate nominal money holdings cannot be increased as fast as prices rise unless the aggregate nominal money supply is increased at the same rate. Thus the requirement in a quantity theory world for inflation to be sustained is for the money supply to increase continuously, at least as fast as the price level is rising. This is the crux of the issue. Without money there is no overall price level. The price level is *defined* to be an index of commodity prices *in terms of money!* A barter economy has no general price level. (Of course money need not be made of paper or precious metals. In different times and at different places cigarettes, rice, salt, etc. have served as money.) It follows that the exchange rate between goods and money depends on the quantity of goods relative to the quantity of money and its rate of turnover (velocity). To the quantity theorist, any explanation of inflation must show how the supply of money or its velocity is affected.

In fact, the Keynesian approach implies that an autonomous increase in aggregate demand indirectly increases velocity. In the extreme case of a liquidity trap in money demand, velocity can be increased without limit. The quantity theorist, on the other hand, rejects the idea that money demand can be reduced without limit (the condition for increasing velocity without limit). Therefore sustained inflation can only be accomplished through an increasing money supply.

These two general theories attempt in a broad way to get at the ultimate cause of inflation and its resolution. The specific means by which inflationary pressures are felt in the economy is a subject to which we now turn.

MECHANISMS OF INFLATION
Demand-Pull

The three mechanisms discussed here—demand-pull, cost-push, and sector-shift—are sometimes cited as theories of inflation. However none of the three really traces inflationary pressure back to some ultimate exogenous influence. The demand-pull approach takes an increase in aggregate demand as a given and attempts to show how that increase in aggregate demand impinges on various markets. Demand-pull inflation is something we are already familiar with from our discussion of the basic model. We discovered, for example, that an increase in aggregate demand—say, due to an increase in government expenditures—is felt directly in the product market, thus bidding up the price of commodities. The repercussions are subsequently felt back in the labor market where the rising price level makes it profitable for producers to hire more labor and produce more output. The net effect of such changes is that the price level rises and unemployment decreases. From this we can deduce, at least in our basic model, that there is an inverse relationship between the price level and the rate of unemployment in the face of shifts in aggregate demand. This conclusion crucially depends upon our assumption that the nominal wage rate is rigid in the face of changes in the level of economic activity. A little later in this chapter we shall drop that assumption with some interesting consequences.

Cost-Push

Most people interpret cost-push inflation as wage-push inflation. That is, they visualize a process by which wages are pushed up, perhaps due to union pressure, and then the higher wages are passed on to the consumer through higher prices, by action of the producers.

This is comparable in our basic model to an autonomous increase in the nominal wage rate for whatever reason. At the initial equilibrium this constitutes a rise in the real wage rate, inducing profit-maximizing producers to cut back their output. Given the level of aggregate demand, a fall in output results in a deficient supply or an excess demand, with the result that the price level begins to rise. The fall in output is, of course, accompanied by an increase in the level of unemployment. Thus in the face of cost-push inflation we would observe a direct or positive relationship between the price level and the rate of unemployment. As a matter of fact, analysis with the basic model suggests that one way to distinguish cost-push from demand-pull is to observe the relationship between the price change and the level of unemployment. If inflation is accompanied by a decrease in unemployment, the inflation may be demand-pull; and if the inflation is accompanied by an increase in unemployment, the inflation may be called cost-push. This technique has been used in the past to identify periods of cost-push and demand-pull inflation.[4]

The demand-pull mechanism seems obvious enough in periods of economic expansion when growing demand is pressing on limited resources. The cost-push explanation was developed in an attempt to explain why prices might continue to rise even when the economy fell into a recession. In 1959 Charles Schultze proposed another explanation for the upward creep in prices during periods of recession.[5]

Sector-Shift Inflation

We would not expect the composition of aggregate demand to remain constant over time. As time progresses, consumer preferences change, and the demand for certain products increases while that for others may decline in relative terms. The same applies to the composition of government demand. In a competitive economy we should expect the prices of those products experiencing an increase in demand to go up, and we should expect the prices of products whose demand is slackening to fall. Thus if total aggregate demand has not changed

---

[4] For example, see Franklyn D. Holzman, "Inflation: Cost-Push and Demand-Pull," *American Economic Review*, Vol. 50 (March 1960), pp. 20–42.

[5] Charles L. Schultze, *Recent Inflation in the United States*, Study Paper No. 1 in *Study of Employment, Growth, and Price Levels* (Washington: United States Congress, Joint Economic Committee, 1959). For an evaluation and policy recommendations, see Lloyd G. Reynolds, "Wage-Push and All That," *American Economic Review*, Vol. 50 (May 1960), pp. 195–204.

but rather only its composition has changed, there is no necessary reason in a competitive economy why the overall price level should rise or fall.

However we do not live in a perfectly competitive economy. The production of many products in the United States is done under conditions of monopoly and oligopoly. For example, the automobile industry contains only a few firms which dominate the entire domestic market. Similarly some factor markets are dominated by single sellers. Steel workers and automobile workers do not compete with one another for job vacancies or for wage increases. One characteristic of oligopolistic markets is that the sellers do not take the price of the product as a given, but instead are able to control the price by adjusting their own outputs. In the face of a reduction in demand, it may be that a firm in an oligopoly situation would rather absorb the reduction in demand by a reduction in output rather than permit the price level to fall.

This type of price control forms the basis for the sector-shift theory of creeping inflation. As the demand increases for some products, their prices will rise; but as the demand decreases for certain other kinds of products, their prices will not fall if the industry structure that produces those products can be characterized by oligopoly or monopoly. Thus an increase in the price of products for which the demand has increased is not offset by a decrease in the price of products for which demand has decreased. The net effect is an upward bias to the price level as consumers shift their preferences from one product to another.

The basic appeal of the sector-shift concept is that it seems more realistic than alternative explanations that assume a competitive economy. A disadvantage of the theory is that it requires that the profit-maximizing assumption be dropped for firms operating under oligopolistic structures.

All three models, demand-pull, cost-push, and sector-shift attempt only to explain how demand pressure or supply pressure is felt on prices and wages. They do not explain the origin of demand or supply pressures nor do they examine the conditions that are necessary to permit a sustained increase in demand or restriction in factor supply. Whichever mechanism is operative, a basic requirement for sustained inflation is either that velocity rise without limit due to a continuous fall in the demand for money or that the supply of money be increased continuously, say, by the monetary authorities. The former condition seems unlikely, but the latter condition has been the sustaining factor for hyperinflations in the past.

INFLATION VERSUS UNEMPLOYMENT: THE CRITICAL TRADE-OFF

A Look at the Phillips Curve

From our basic model we can deduce a trade-off between the price level and the rate of unemployment in the face of changes in aggregate demand. The basic model implies that increases (decreases) in aggregate demand result in price increases (decreases) and reductions (increases) in unemployment. The idea of an association between prices and unemployment was first given empirical content by A. W. Phillips.[6] Although Phillips examined the relationship between the rate of unemployment and the rate of change in nominal wage rates, the more popular interpretation of the Phillips curve is a relationship between the rate of unemployment and the rate of price change. As an illustration, consider Figure 16–3 which plots the rate of change in prices against the rate of unemployment for the U.S. expansion phase during the 1960s. A "freehand" Phillips curve has been drawn through the data points.

The Phillips curve has been interpreted by many economists to represent a permanent trade-off faced by the policy makers. If the curve is stable and movements along the curve are predictable, then lower unemployment can only be purchased at the expense of higher rates of inflation. Put another way, one must tolerate higher rates of unemployment if one expects to eliminate inflation or reduce it to tolerable levels. There are, however, some difficulties in using the Phillips curve. One difficulty is in defining full employment. If full employment is defined to be a situation in which the number of job vacancies is equal to the number of job applicants, the sector-shift discussion earlier would imply that there would be some positive rate of inflation at that level of unemployment. For even if aggregate demand and supply conditions provided enough jobs for all those who were willing to go to work, shifts in the composition of demand would

---

[6] A. W. Phillips, "The Relation Between Unemployment and the Rate of Change of Money Wage Rates in the United Kingdom, 1862–1957," *Economica,* Vol. 25 (November 1958), pp. 283–99. Trade-offs among rates of inflation, unemployment, and profits were estimated by George L. Perry, *Unemployment, Money Wage Rates, and Inflation* (Cambridge, Mass.: The M.I.T. Press, 1966).

FIGURE 16–3
Phillips Curve, 1962–1969

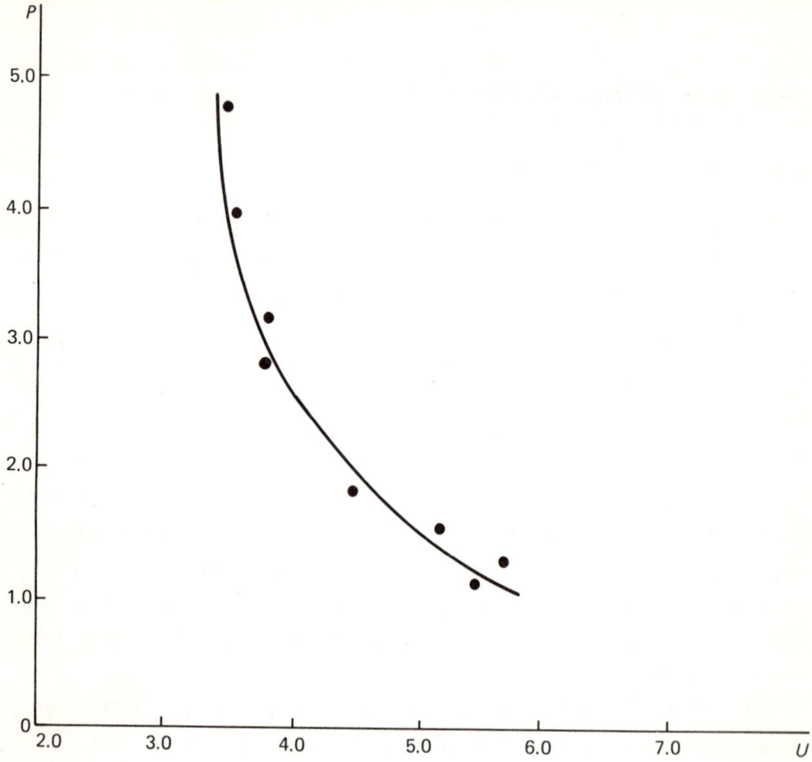

Source: *Economic Report of the President, 1973.*

imply an upward movement in the price level. On the other hand if full employment were defined as a situation in which prices were stable, the Phillips curve relationship indicates that this would be at an intolerably high level of unemployment.

A more crucial criticism of the Phillips curve approach is that it does not represent a permanent trade-off between inflation and unemployment but rather is a short-run disequilibrium phenomenon. Let us now consider this further.

An Alternative View of the Phillips Relationship

To anticipate the conclusions of this section, the alternative view of the Phillips curve argues that it is a short-run phenomenon that only occurs in periods of disequilibrium. In the long run, the analysis implies that there is no trade-off between inflation and unemployment and that the long-run Phillips curve is a vertical line at the "natural" rate of unemployment. The natural rate of unemployment is that rate that exists because of imperfections and frictions in the labor markets.[7]

We can illustrate the idea with our basic model. For this purpose we drop the assumption employed up until now that the nominal wage rate is rigid. Instead of having a rigid nominal wage rate, we assume that workers attempt to adjust their nominal wage to take account of changes in the price level. Specifically, if labor expects the price level to increase, it will want to increase its nominal wage rate so as to maintain the same real wage rate held previously. Otherwise workers will reduce the amount of labor offered. However it is important to note that the *expected* price level may not be the same as the *actual* price level in any given period. For example, if labor expects the price level to rise by 5 percent during the current year, it will push for increases in the nominal wage rate of 5 percent. However, if the actual price level increases by 6 percent, the real wage rate in actuality will fall during the year. The falling real wage rate will, in turn, encourage producers to expand output. As output is expanded, unemployment falls. However as labor revises its expectations of price increases to conform with actuality and subsequently pushes for still higher nominal wage rates, the real wage rate once again begins to rise toward its former level, and unemployment increases with output falling. Equilibrium is restored when the real wage rate, output, and unemployment return to their initial level. This occurs when expected and actual price changes coincide.

The process can be illustrated in sequence with the aid of Figure 16–4. The labor supply and demand curves in the figure are expressed in nominal terms.[8] Thus an increase in the price level shifts the labor demand schedule to the right, and an increase in the expected or perceived price level shifts the labor supply schedule to the left. We assume that since producers are selling the products, they know what

---

[7] The "natural" rate of unemployment was introduced in Milton Friedman, "The Role of Monetary Policy," *American Economic Review*, Vol. 58 (March 1968), pp. 1–17. A summary of the two views of the Phillips curve is found in Roger W. Spencer, "The Relation Between Prices and Unemployment: Two Views," *Review*, Federal Reserve Bank of Saint Louis, Vol. 51 (March 1969), pp. 15–21.

[8] A slightly different graphical approach to the same problem may be found in Samuel A. Morley, *The Economics of Inflation* (Hinsdale, Ill.: The Dryden Press, Inc., 1971).

the price level is. Workers, on the other hand, do not know what the actual price is until well after the fact. Consequently the price variable that is important in the labor supply curve is the expected price level for the given period. The upward sloping curves in Figure 16–4 are *short-run* curves. *Long-run* labor supply is inelastic with re-

FIGURE 16–4
Labor Market Adjustments

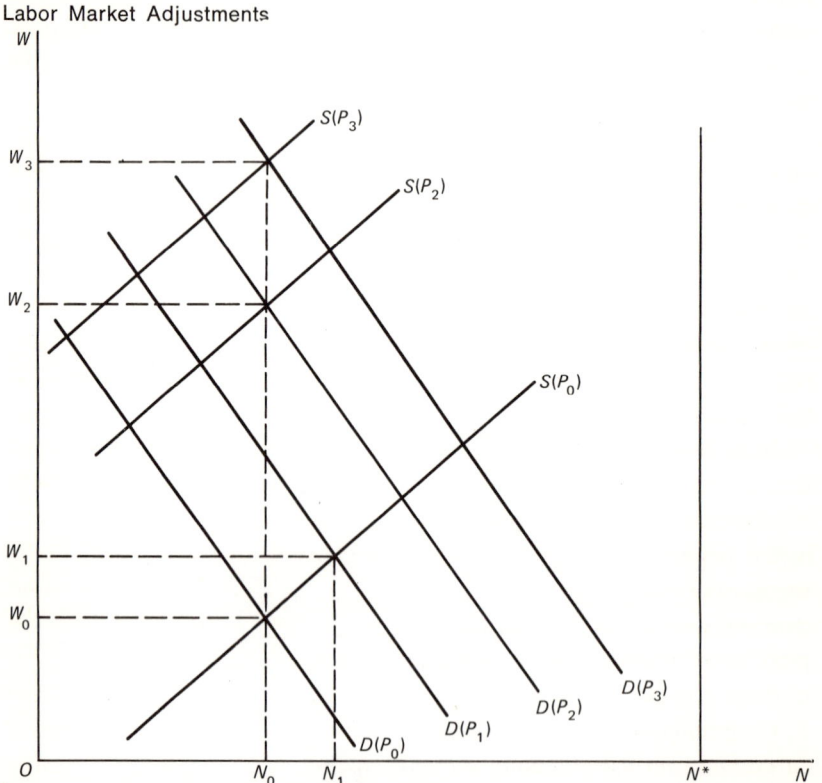

spect to wage rates and prices and is fixed at N^*. Long-run labor supply is defined to be the quantity of labor offered when each worker is able to satisfy his occupational and geographical preferences. If a worker's preferences are satisfied, he is assumed to want to retain his job even if the real wage rate paid him varies. In the short run, increases (decreases) in the real wage rate will induce him to accept (leave) a less than satisfactory job. Unemployment, then, is *voluntary* and is equal to the gap between N^* and the amount of labor actually employed.

Suppose we start initially in equilibrium with supply and demand curves subscripted zero, at nominal wage rate W_0 and labor employed equal to N_0. The real wage rate is W_0/P_0. Now suppose there is an increase in aggregate demand in the product market due to an increase in government expenditures financed by borrowing from the private sector. The price of goods rises during this first period, say, to P_1. This shifts the demand curve to the right to $D(P_1)$. Moreover, suppose that government expenditures continue to increase so that prices increase year after year at the same rate. Demand curves for the three periods following the initial period are drawn in the figure under this assumption.

Now in period 1, following the initial period, the price level is P_1, and the demand curve that prevails is $D(P_1)$. However, labor, having experienced no previous inflation, expects the price level in period 1 to be the same as in the initial period. Thus it remains on supply curve $S(P_0)$. The nominal wage rate rises as a result of the increase in labor demand to W_1. However this increase is not sufficient to offset the increase in the price level, with the result that the real wage rate falls and employment increases from N_0 to N_1. Unemployment falls (from $N^*\text{-}N_0$ to $N^*\text{-}N_1$) and output increases.

In period 2, the demand curve again shifts the same percentage that it did in period 1. However in period 2, labor has become aware of price changes. Let us assume that labor has observed the increase in the price level in the first period and correctly expects an identical increase in the price level in the second period. Not only must labor demand an increase in the nominal wage rate sufficient to offset the price increase in period 2, but it must demand an additional increase in order to "catch up" with the price increase that prevailed in period 1. Consequently it shifts its supply curve to $S(P_2)$. The new supply curve is a schedule of nominal wage rates that labor demands, given that the price level it expects to prevail—and in fact the price level that will prevail—in the second period is P_2. With the period 2 demand and supply curves, the nominal wage rate rises to W_2, and employment falls back to N_0. Unemployment in the process increases and output falls. For the third period and subsequent periods, assume that labor correctly anticipates the price increase that prevails and thus makes adjustments in its supply curve, shifting the supply curve to the left by the same amount that the demand curve shifts to the right. In the third period, the nominal wage rate rises to W_3, and the level of employment remains unchanged, as does the level of unemployment.

The essential feature of this model is that the Phillips curve is a disequilibrium relationship, occurring only when labor incorrectly anticipates the extent of price changes. When labor's anticipations coincide with actual price changes, the level of employment indicated by N_0 is consistent with any rate of inflation. One, perhaps objectionable, feature of the model is that all unemployment is voluntary. This stands in contrast to the widely held view that unemployment is generally involuntary.

The model has an important implication for policy. The analysis implies that the policy makers cannot select a point on the Phillips curve and expect it to persist indefinitely. In order for a lower level of unemployment to be maintained, actual price changes must advance ahead of labor's expectations. Thus not only must prices rise, but they must rise at an increasing rate. This, in turn, means that an expansionary policy measured by an increase in government expenditures or an increase in the money supply must proceed at an ever increasing pace. For example, in order to maintain a level of unemployment that is below the natural level of unemployment, the money stock must increase at an increasing rate. Such a policy, if pursued, would ultimately lead to hyperinflation.

In the face of this possibility, the behavior of the money stock during the 1960s may not be surprising. When the Federal Reserve becomes convinced that inflation is beginning to get out of hand, it apparently retrenches by sharply reducing the growth rate in the money supply. Table 16–1 presents rates of growth in the money supply and the wholesale price index, and the unemployment rate for the years 1962–1972. Note that from 1962 to 1965 the growth rate in the money supply increased each year. Prices accelerated over that period of time, reaching an annual growth rate of 3.4 percent in 1965. Unemployment during the same period declined from 5.5 percent to 4.5 percent. Perhaps the 1965 increase in the Wholesale Price Index was more than the Federal Reserve could tolerate, for it reduced the growth rate in the money supply by more than half in 1966. The effect on prices was felt immediately, for the wholesale price index growth rate slowed to 1.7 percent in 1966 and further slowed to 1 percent in 1967. Unemployment, which had been declining steadily, leveled off between 1966 and 1967, as we would expect. But in 1967, the Federal Reserve once again resumed a rapid growth rate in the money supply, with growth rates of 6.6 percent in 1967 and 7.8 percent in 1968. As expected, the Wholesale Price Index began to rise more rapidly at 2.8 percent in 1968 and 4.8 percent in 1969. Unemployment con-

TABLE 16–1
Unemployment Rates and Rates of Change in
Prices and the Money Supply, 1962–1972

Year	U (percent)	$\dot{P}$ (percent)	$\dot{M}$ (percent)
1962	5.5	0.0	1.4
1963	5.7	−0.1	3.7
1964	5.2	0.4	4.5
1965	4.5	3.4	4.7
1966	3.8	1.7	2.2
1967	3.8	1.0	6.6
1968	3.6	2.8	7.8
1969	3.5	4.8	3.2
1970	4.9	2.2	5.4
1971	5.9	4.0	6.2
1972	5.6	6.5	8.2

$\dot{P}$ = percent change in the Wholesale Price Index.
$\dot{M}$ = percent change in the money stock (narrow definition).
U = unemployment rate.
Source: *Economic Report of the President, 1973*.

tinued to decline in the face of this acceleration in the price level. Again in 1969, the Fed apparently renewed its concern about rapid price increases and reduced the growth rate in the money supply by more than half, down to 3.2 percent. As we should expect, the rate of growth in prices slowed by more than 50 percent in 1970 down to 2.2 percent, and in the following year unemployment began to climb again, reaching 4.9 percent by the end of the year. Because of the rise in unemployment and the apparent success in slowing down the rate of price increase, the Fed once again, in 1970, began to accelerate the money supply, increasing it at a 5.4 percent rate in 1970 and successively higher rates in 1971 and 1972. The impact on the Wholesale Price Index was expected. The rate of inflation in that index rose to 4.0 percent in 1971 and to 6.5 percent in 1972. With the acceleration in the Wholesale Price Index, unemployment began to drop again from 5.9 percent in 1971 to 5.6 percent in 1972.

Thus it would seem that although our analysis may imply that the money supply must be increased at an increasing rate in order to maintain a given level of unemployment, the monetary authority does not seem to be willing to act in this fashion. We find that prices accelerate for a time until the rate of increase becomes intolerable, then the monetary authority applies the brakes until the level of unemployment becomes intolerable, and then we reverse the process again.

The analysis of this section is only one element of a new approach toward macroeconomics. Some writers in recent years have departed from the comparative static analysis that has characterized this book and instead have begun to focus their attention on periods of disequilibrium. Disequilibrium is defined as a state where expectations and actuality differ. We shall continue this discussion of disequilibrium macroeconomics in the next chapter. For now, however, we shall discuss some policy issues pertinent to the issue of inflation.

POLICY ISSUES

Empirical Evidence on the Effect of Inflation

Public policy in the United States has generally been directed against inflation on the grounds that inflation produces detrimental effects on the economy. We mentioned three possible effects earlier. Specifically, inflation is said to redistribute income; it is said to benefit debtors at the expense of creditors; and if allowed to continue unchecked, it is said to lead eventually to monetary collapse. In looking at the effects of inflation, one should clearly distinguish between expected inflation and unexpected inflation. If inflation is expected, presumably individuals will attempt to protect themselves and the effect of expected inflation may be nil. On the other hand if inflation is unexpected, individuals do not have a chance to protect themselves and the problems attributed to inflation may indeed occur.

With respect to the issue of income redistribution, a recent study by Edward Budd and David Seiders concluded that unexpected inflation does indeed redistribute income.[9] Budd and Seiders found that unexpected inflation redistributed real income from the lower income groups and the very highest income group to the middle income groups. However, the authors were careful to distinguish between expected inflation and unexpected inflation and concluded that expected inflation would have a nil effect on income redistribution. In fact the redistribution that did take place under conditions of unexpected inflation was very small—smaller than the authors had expected.

The same study indicated that real wealth is redistributed from upper income groups to lower income groups in the face of unexpected

---

[9] Edward C. Budd and David F. Seiders, "The Impact of Inflation on the Distribution of Income and Wealth," *American Economic Review*, Vol. 61 (May 1971), pp. 128–38.

inflation. Given that the upper income groups are more likely to be creditors and the lower income groups are likely to be debtors, this is consistent with previous notions about the effect of inflation on creditor/debtor relationships. Again if inflation is expected, both creditors and debtors will make adjustments in anticipation of such inflation. Creditors will attempt to protect themselves by charging a higher interest rate than they would have required under conditions of no inflation. Debtors will be willing to pay higher interest rates than under conditions of no inflation. Thus the nominal (or market) interest rate will rise. Assuming that the expectations of debtors and creditors are identical, the nominal interest rate will rise by the amount of the expected inflation.

Finally the evidence seems clear that hyperinflation will destroy the use of money as a store of value but not necessarily as a medium of exchange. Colin Campbell and Gordon Tullock found that during the hyperinflation in China from 1927 to 1949, currency was still used as a medium of exchange even though it was not used as a store value.[10] Campbell and Tullock concluded that the reason for this was because the inflation was fully anticipated, and all nominal values (nominal wages, nominal interest rates, etc.) were adjusted accordingly. Thus hyperinflation need not lead to total collapse of the monetary system, although in many cases it has.

The Implied Policies

If the analysis of the previous section has any validity, two prongs for policy are suggested. First, any rate of inflation (within reason) is acceptable if it is steady and fully anticipated. Unemployment, output, and the other real variables of the system should be unaffected by fully anticipated inflation.[11] Policy makers should therefore avoid sudden or erratic changes in the policy variables in order to avoid unexpected changes in the rate of inflation.

---

[10] Colin D. Campbell and Gordon C. Tullock, "Hyperinflation in China, 1927–49," *Journal of Political Economy*, Vol. 62 (June 1954), pp. 236–45.

[11] The conclusion may not be completely true. If real money balances belong in the consumption function, anticipated inflation will raise the nominal interest rate by less than the expected rate of inflation. The real interest rate will therefore fall. For analyses of this effect, see Robert A. Mundell, *Monetary Theory* (Pacific Palisades, Calif.: Goodyear Publishing Co., Inc., 1971), Chap. 2; and Martin J. Bailey, *National Income and the Price Level*, 2d ed. (New York: McGraw-Hill Book Co., 1971), Chap. 4.

Second, the "natural" rate of unemployment should be attacked not by policy induced variations in aggregate demand but by policies designed to remove imperfections in the system. For example, labor mobility can be improved by improving the flow of job information, by removing monopoly elements in the labor and product markets, and by removing the restraints imposed by racial and sex discrimination.

Again, these conclusions are based on the assumptions of the previous section. It should be noted here that the weight of the evidence indicates that nominal wage rate adjustments do not lag behind price adjustments.[12] Moreover, the natural rate of unemployment is not a widely accepted concept. A majority of economists would probably argue that a significant portion of unemployment is due to deficient aggregate demand. Further, they would argue that such unemployment can be eliminated permanently by appropriate policies to increase aggregate demand. In any event, without agreement on the theory, there is little chance of agreement on the policy options. However, it remains to examine the evidence in the context of models like the one in this chapter. But that we defer to the discussion of macroeconomic disequilibrium models in the next chapter.

There remains the issue of price controls of the type employed recently under President Nixon's "New Economic Policy." Opinion varies, but in the author's mind price controls can do as much to stop inflation as Prohibition did to terminate the drinking habits of the American public. Congress might just as well pass a law requiring the sun to decrease its energy output. The best that controls can do is to temporarily induce the public to revise its inflationary expectations downward. No downward revision can be sustained if inflationary pressures are not abated, and that requires a moderation of expansive policy, whether fiscal or monetary.

SUMMARY NOTES

1. Inflation is the percent change in the price level per unit of time, ranging from creeping (slow) inflation to hyperinflation (extremely fast).

---

[12] See, for example, Bronfenbrenner and Holzman, "Survey of Inflation Theory," pp. 647–49; Budd and Seiders, "Impact of Inflation"; and R. A. Kessel and Armen A. Alchian, "The Meaning and Validity of the Inflation-Induced Lag of Wages Behind Prices," *American Economic Review*, Vol. 50 (March 1960), pp. 43–66.

2. The two major approaches to inflation and its resolution are the Keynesian (excess demand) and quantity theory approaches.
3. Inflationary pressure may be translated into price increases through demand-pull, cost-push, or sector-shift processes.
4. Regardless of the mechanisms involved, sustained inflation requires a continuous fall in the demand for money or a continuous rise in the supply of money or some combination of the two.
5. Two views of the unemployment-inflation trade-off exist: the permanent trade-off view and the short-run disequilibrium view. The latter view argues that the trade-off exists only when inflation is unexpected.
6. Empirical evidence generally supports the idea that the adverse effects of inflation occur when inflation is unexpected rather than expected.

DISCUSSION QUESTIONS

1. Discuss the differences in the implications for policy of the excess demand approach to inflation versus the quantity theory approach.
2. Make an attempt to classify periods of inflation as demand-pull or cost-push by comparing changes in the rates of inflation and unemployment as suggested in the text.
3. What was the growth rate of the money stock and the change in velocity for the periods identified in question 2?
4. Refer to your answers to questions 2 and 3 in Chapter 5. In what ways are your answers consistent and in what ways inconsistent with the alternative view of the Phillips curve discussed in this chapter?

17

Recent Developments in Macroeconomic Theory

CRITIQUE OF THE BASIC MODEL

THE BASIC MODEL used through most of this book may be criticized on several grounds. For one thing, the model is highly abstract and aggregated. Consequently any statistical counterpart that is to be used for purposes of prediction and policy making should involve some disaggregation and the inclusion of variables in addition to the ones presently contained in the various equations. But this criticism is true of any theoretical model that attempts to identify basic forces.

Criticism may also be levied at specific aspects of the model. For example, the assumption of rigidity in the nominal wage rate appears to be highly unrealistic in view of the fact that the nominal wage rate fluctuates with the business cycle. However this assumption was made to incorporate the concept of unemployment into the model. We saw in the previous chapter that an alternative method that does not rely on price or wage rigidity could also be used to incorporate unemployment into the model.

One implication of this model (and variations on the theme) is that given the state of technology and the stock of capital, fluctuations in employment imply fluctuations in the real wage rate in the opposite direction. In other words, over the course of the business cycle the real wage rate and the level of employment should vary *inversely*. However sufficient evidence exists that the real wage rate and employment vary *directly* over the course of the business cycle.[1] If one adjusts for changes in productivity due to technological and capital stock changes, the relationship between the real wage rate and employment in recent years seems more or less random. For example, from 1961 to 1965 the real wage rate adjusted for changes in productivity varied inversely with the level of employment. From 1966 to 1972 the relationship between the two was direct.[2]

However, the strongest recent criticism of the basic model concerns the fundamental theoretical assumptions made about disequilibrium adjustments in the model. We assumed, consistent with traditional neoclassical analysis, that prices begin to adjust instantly in response to excess demand. In response to the initial price change, producers adjust their output and so on. But consider this: The model assumes perfect competition among both buyers and sellers of goods and labor services. Now in the theory of perfect competition, each individual producer and buyer takes the price as given. All decision units are price takers. An individual producer believes he can sell as much as he desires, and an individual buyer believes he can buy all he wishes at the prevailing market price. Adjustments for individual buyers and sellers are made by adjusting quantities purchased or sold, since each believes that he has no control over the price. If demand changes, who then is it that changes the price level? Certainly it is not the individual producers, for we have assumed that they are price takers. Certainly it is not the individual buyers, for we have also assumed that they are price takers. Information about the new market clearing price structure is not, in reality, transmitted instantaneously to all units. Perfect information is an *assumption* of competitive models, not a *conclusion* reached through the process of deduction.

It may be appropriate, therefore, to reverse the adjustment mechanism. If aggregate demand falls such that individual producers find that they are no longer able to sell all they wish to sell at the prevailing market price, they will reduce the quantities produced rather than lower the price. In effect, we previously assumed that prices change instantaneously and quantities adjust more slowly. Now we may reverse that and assume that quantities change instantaneously but that

---

[1] For a recent study, see R. G. Bodkin, "Real Wages and Cyclical Variations in Employment," *Canadian Journal of Economics,* Vol. 2 (August 1969), pp. 353–74.

[2] Data for these conclusions were obtained from the *Economic Report of the President, 1973,* Table C–32, p. 230.

prices are sticky. It is this reversal of the adjustment process that distinguishes Keynes from his predecessors, at least according to Robert Clower and Axel Leijonhufvud.[3] According to these writers, the trouble with modern Keynesian models such as our basic model is that they incorporate neoclassical assumptions into a Keynesian framework. The neoclassical approach is to compare static equilibrium points. With the neoclassical adjustment mechanism, unemployment can be introduced only by building restrictions into the labor market (such as the rigid nominal wage rate). However, the real contribution of Keynes (according to Clower and Leijonhufvud) is an examination of *disequilibrium* states rather than a comparison of static equilibria. In this spirit, then, we shall examine in the next section some approaches to unemployment as it occurs during disequilibrium in macroeconomic models.

DISEQUILIBRIUM APPROACHES

A common feature of disequilibrium models is the assumption of friction in the process of adjusting from one equilibrium to another. Two types of friction will be discussed in this section. First, friction may arise in the way in which markets clear, in the sense outlined above. That is, in perfectly competitive markets prices may be sticky in response to changes in demand conditions because individual producers believe that they have no control over prices but can only adjust their outputs. Second, friction may arise in the labor markets as a consequence of lags in the supply of labor behind price and wage rate changes. Put another way, suppose there is a sudden change in wage rates or prices. If suppliers of labor do not believe that the wage or price changes are permanent or normal, they may behave differently than the case in which such wage and price changes are believed to be normal or permanent.

---

[3] See Robert W. Clower, "The Keynesian Counterrevolution: A Theoretical Appraisal," in *The Theory of Interest Rates,* ed. H. Hahn and F. P. R. Breckling (London: Macmillan & Co., Ltd., 1965), pp. 103–25; and Axel Leijonhufvud, *On Keynesian Economics and the Economics of Keynes* (New York: Oxford University Press, 1968). A summary work is A. G. Hines, *On the Reappraisal of Keynesian Economics* (London: Martin Robertson and Co., Ltd., 1971). The essays in Edmund S. Phelps et al., *Microeconomic Foundations of Employment and Inflation Theory* (New York: W. W. Norton and Co., Inc., 1970) are also relevant to this discussion.

Market-Clearing Friction

Much of the work with models incorporating market-clearing friction has been done recently by Robert J. Barro and Herschel Grossman and has been built upon the work of Clower and Leijonhufvud.[4] In this approach, firms are assumed to be maximizing profits; and households, which are the suppliers of labor, are assumed to be maximizing utility. The profit-maximizing demand for labor is shown in Figure 17–1A, as is the utility-maximizing supply of labor. Full employment may be defined as the market-clearing quantity of labor, N^*, which would prevail at real wage rate, $W^*/P^* = w^*$. In Figure 17–1B aggregate demand and supply are plotted against the price level (see Chapter 5 for derivation). The full-employment level of output is Y^* at price level P^*. Note that the aggregate supply curve, Y_s^*, is drawn for a given nominal wage rate, W^*.

Suppose there is a fall in aggregate demand in the product market, perhaps brought about by a reduction in government expenditures, shifting Y_D to $Y_D{}'$. Effective demand at P^* is now Y_0. At the initial price level, producers find that they can no longer sell as much as they were selling previously. Since as individual producers they are powerless to change the price level, they cut back on output so as to avoid an unprofitable build up of inventories, $(Y^* - Y_0$ per period). Given that labor is the variable factor of production in the short run, the cutback in output is accomplished by reducing the amount of labor employed. In Figure 17–1A this results in a reduction of labor employed from N^* to N_0. The real wage rate remains at w^* since there has been no change either in the price of goods or in the nominal wage rate. In short, because producers perceive that they are unable to make price adjustments, they are forced—in the face of a reduction in aggregate demand—to move off their own demand curves for labor and off their supply curves for goods.

Now sooner or later prices and nominal wage rates will begin to respond. Just how they respond is not completely clear, but Barro

---

[4] Robert J. Barro and Herschel I. Grossman, "A General Disequilibrium Model of Income and Employment," *American Economic Review,* Vol. 61 (March 1971), pp. 82–93. Robert J. Barro, "A Theory of Monopolistic Price Adjustment," *Review of Economic Studies,* Vol. 39 (January 1972), pp. 17–26. Herschel I. Grossman, "Money, Interest, and Prices in Market Disequilibrium," *Journal of Political Economy,* Vol. 79 (September/October 1971), pp. 943–61; and Herschel I. Grossman "Aggregate Demand, Job Search, and Employment," *Journal of Political Economy,* Vol. 81 (November/December 1973), pp. 1353–69.

FIGURE 17–1
A Disequilibrium Model

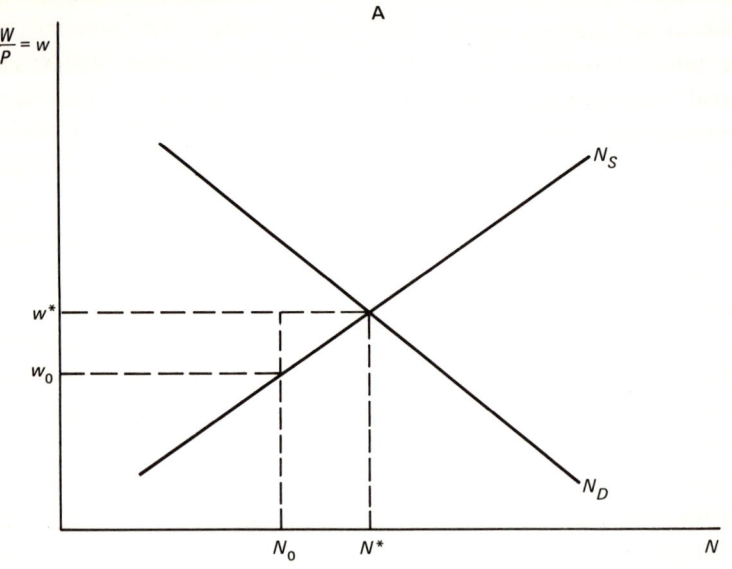

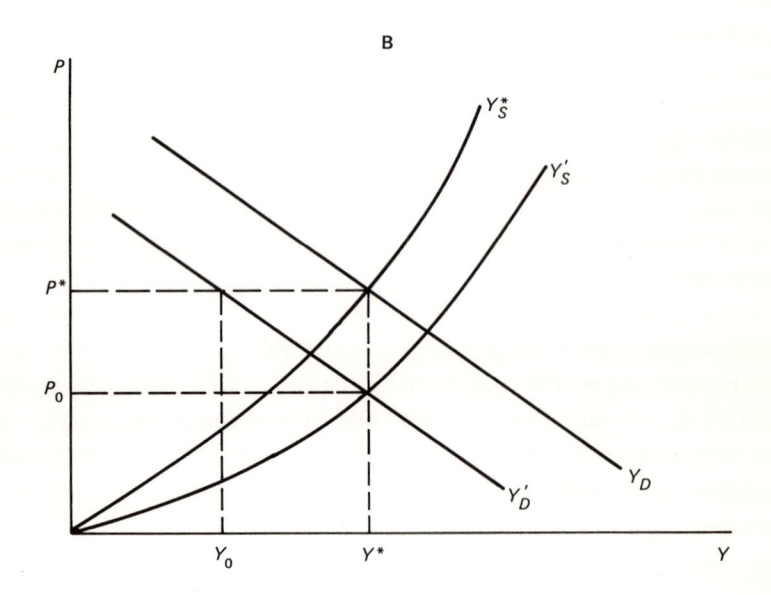

suggests that producers may act like monopolists during period of disequilibrium. However, suppose that nominal wage rates respond first. Since at w^* there is an excess supply of labor, the nominal wage rate falls—thus reducing the real wage rate until the market clears at real wage rate $w_0 = W_0/P^*$ and labor employed N_0. Thus we get an increase in unemployment $(N^* - N_0)$ accompanied by a reduction in the real wage rate, which is consistent with some empirical observations.

Note that the fall in the nominal wage rate pivots the intended or "notional" supply function to the right. Eventually prices will begin to fall and increase the quantity demanded. The fall in the price level also leads to a rise in the real wage rate. As the price level decreases and the quantity demanded increases, output moves from Y_0 toward the notional supply function. As output approaches the notional supply function, labor employed increases toward the full-employment level. Thus during this phase, output is expanding, employment is increasing, and the real wage rate is rising. A new equilibrium is eventually reestablished at output Y^* and employment N^*, with only the nominal wage rate and the price level lower (by the same percentage) than previously. The real wage rate at the new equilibrium is the same as it was at the previous equilibrium.

This analysis interprets unemployment as appearing during *disequilibrium*. It arises because prices do not respond instantaneously to excess demand or excess supply. Long-run equilibrium, occurring after all prices and wages have adjusted, is characterized by full employment. This contrasts with conventional models which feature equilibria at less than full employment.

The pattern of price, wage, and employment change in this model is also consistent with empirical observations. In this sense the model overcomes one of the defects of the basic model. Another feature of this model is that unemployment can be said to be involuntary—the lay-off decision is made by the employer. This characteristic distinguishes this model from the next model in which unemployment is voluntary.

Job Acceptance Friction

Delay in the acceptance of job offers during periods of disequilibrium may arise for two reasons. First, information about prevailing jobs and wage rates is costly because it is not universally available.

A worker who is faced with the choice of accepting a lower wage rate or seeking another position does not have at his fingertips all the information necessary to make a decision about the new position. Further, he might expect that some time spent in searching the labor market will reveal a position that pays higher wages than his present position. To find this job, however, he must leave his present position and search for the new position. In the interim he foregoes current wages. Given that the wage in his current job has the potential of falling enough and that the expectations about other positions are high enough, he will voluntarily quit his present position in order to search for a new, higher paying position. In the interim period he is voluntarily unemployed; or, as the originator of this concept, Armen Alchian, would suggest, he is employed in acquiring information.[5] He stops searching when the marginal wage gain from search is just offset by the marginal search cost.

A second source of job acceptance friction, associated with the work of Lucas and Rapping, involves the worker's subjective comparison of the actual real wage rate with the real wage rate that he considers to be "normal" or "permanent."[6] If the current real wage rate and the normal real wage rate deviate from each other, he will change his leisure-work time mix so as to continue to maximize utility. For example, if the current real wage rate rises above the normal wage rate, the individual will substitute work for leisure, on the grounds that the opportunity cost of leisure has risen above normal. As in the former case, variations in employment and, therefore, unemployment are voluntary.

In both cases a fall in aggregate demand leads to voluntary unemployment. For example, suppose aggregate demand falls, resulting in a reduction in the price of commodities. In order to continue to maximize profits employers will want to either cut back on the amount of labor hired or lower the prevailing nominal wage rate. Now neither the employer nor the employees know for sure whether the reduction in demand is part of a reduction in aggregate demand or whether it is simply a reduction in the demand for their own product. They are likely, at least initially, to assume the latter. In addition, employees

---

[5] Armen A. Alchian, "Information Costs, Pricing, and Resource Unemployment," *Western Economic Journal,* Vol. 7 (June 1969), pp. 107–29.

[6] Robert E. Lucas, Jr. and Leonard A. Rapping, "Real Wages, Employment, and Inflation," *Journal of Political Economy,* Vol. 77 (September/October 1969), pp. 721–54.

will not initially be aware of a general fall in the price level. Consequently in the situation described by Alchian, employees, believing that better wages exist elsewhere, will elect to voluntarily quit their jobs and search for higher paying employment rather than accept the wage cut.

In the Lucas-Rapping case, employees will perceive that the nominal wage cut would make the actual real wage rate below the normal real wage rate and will therefore elect to substitute more leisure for work. This will increase voluntary unemployment. Thus initially it appears as though unemployment occurs with an increase in the real wage rate, if after the fact we observe the actual changes.

Given that there is a reduction in aggregate demand, Alchian type employees will fail to find higher paying jobs and will therefore be forced to accept employment at the lower wages. Similarly, Lucas and Rapping type employees will revise their estimates of prices and wages until they conform with those that actually prevail. They will then shift away from leisure back towards work. Thus as lower nominal wage rates become established, the real wage rate falls toward its initial value and employment increases.

The pattern of movement in the real wage rate and employment is similar to the pattern shown in our basic model and shares that defect with the basic model. Another criticism may be levied at the job acceptance friction approach. All unemployment is treated as voluntary in the sense that the decision to quit work is left to the employee rather than the employer. This seems at variance with actual industry practice in which the employee is laid off by the employer without being offered the option to work for a lower nominal wage rate. In response, Alchian has argued that the practice of layoffs in the face of falling demand exists because employers have learned from past experience that employees would tend to quit anyway rather than accept lower wage rates.[7] Rather than go through the cost of renegotiating wages, layoffs are instituted, to the mutual satisfaction of both employee and employer.

The Equilibrating Process

Most, if not virtually all, of the current models of macroeconomic disequilibrium involve the use of expected or perceived values for

---

[7] Alchian, "Information Costs," pp. 118–19.

prices and wages. These perceived or expected prices and wages in disequilibrium deviate from actual prices and wages. It is this difference that makes employers and employees behave in ways that cannot be explained by simply observing actual prices and wage rates. Equilibrium in these models occurs when actual prices and wages are equal to expected prices and wages.

There remains the question as to how perceptions about prices are brought into conformity with reality. Most models make use of a device called "adaptive expectations." Briefly, this simply says that decision-making units adjust their expectations in the light of information about present and past values. In its simplest form, this period's expected price might be made equal to last period's expected price plus some fraction of the difference between last period's expected price and the current actual price. Denoting the expected price with an asterisk, this may be expressed as follows:

$$P_t^* = P_{t-1}^* + a(P_t - P_{t-1}^*)$$

where $0 < a < 1$. This is more often expressed in the following form:

$$P_t^* = aP_t + (1 - a)P_{t-1}^*$$

as long as a is a positive fraction, P_t^* will eventually converge on P_t, given a once-and-for-all change in P_t. Thus given a change in the actual price, decision-making units will keep adjusting their anticipated or expected price until the latter eventually converges on the actual price.

Disequilibrium models are still in their infancy. The formal apparatus has not hardened to the extent that traditional Keynesian models have. The interest in such models represents a revolution of sorts in the sense that basic neoclassical assumptions about the formation of prices are being challenged. On the other hand one might well argue that the analysis is still traditional in the sense that no changes are assumed or recommended in the basic institutions underlying the models. For example, private property is still a basic institution in the disequilibrium model. Firms still maximize profits. Households are still assumed to maximize utility. Wants are still insatiable and normative recommendations about changes in income distribution, the mix between public and private goods, and so on are not made. This contrasts sharply with a growing school of economic thought loosely classified as "radical economics."

RADICAL ECONOMICS

Growth of Radicalism[8]

Radical economics is not new in the United States and radical economists have made their voices heard in the past. Most of the ideas and concerns of the current crop of radical economists have a long history. Consequently, the current movement is more of a resurgence than a revelation. What does make current radicalism worthy of note is the extent of its cohesiveness among professional economists. Among professionals, two national organizations have sprung up, the New Order in Political Economy (NOPE) and the older and larger Union for Radical Political Economy (URPE). URPE publishes a professional journal, the *Review of Radical Political Economics*. In addition, radical papers have found their way into the annual meetings of the American Economic Association and into its journal, the *American Economic Review*. Student outlets such as the *American Economist*, published by Omicron Delta Epsilon, the international honor society in economics, have also featured articles by radical economists. Thus radical economics seems to be a rapidly growing branch of the discipline.

The reasons for the rapid growth of interest in radical economics are probably many and diverse but would no doubt include the following: (1) the perceived failure, in the United States, for full employment to exist without substantial military budgets; (2) continuing racial conflicts in both the North and South; (3) increased concern about the effects of pollution on the quality of life, and the possible link between the spread of pollution and the growth of American capitalism; and (4) the war in Vietnam, including the problem of military conscription.[9]

Disillusioned with reformist attempts to solve these and other problems, radicals have turned to the possibilities offered by fundamental and revolutionary change in American society.

---

[8] A good collection of radical and traditional contrasts is found in David Mermelstein, ed., *Economics: Mainstream Readings and Radical Critiques* (New York: Random House, 1970). For a survey, see Martin Bronfenbrenner, "Radical Economics in America: A 1970 Survey," *Journal of Economic Literature*, Vol. 8 (September 1970), pp. 747–66.

[9] These and other reasons are discussed in Bronfenbrenner, "Radical Economics America," p. 748.

The Nature of Radical Economics

While the radical movement is dominated by the so-called "New Left," the views of libertarians on the Right may also be heard.[10] However, there are some fundamental differences. New Left economists generally reject basic assumptions used in traditional economics. For example, traditional economists accept the concept of scarcity. Indeed, economics in the traditional sense may be defined as the study of the allocation of scarce resources that have alternative (competing) uses. For the New Left economist, scarcity is an artificial concept created by the advertising schemes of big business. Wants are not insatiable. Many go so far as to argue that all the basic needs, and more, of society can be satisfied by releasing the already existing productive powers of the economy.

Traditional economists assume that individuals maximize utility or satisfaction. New Left economists tend to reject this and instead assume motivations toward action that are basically racist, imperialistic, corrupt, and oppressive.

Traditional economists may concentrate much of their efforts on analyzing the characteristics of a perfectly competitive economy. Radicals on the Left tend to focus on monopoly power structures and the linkage between monopoly power and political power. Given assumptions about the institutionalized power structure and the assumed motivations of American society, radicals conclude that the existing American structure naturally leads to poverty, discrimination, and war.

However, libertarians of the Right generally accept the basic assumptions that traditional economists use. They also tend to accept private property as an institution which is necessary for the preservation of individual liberties and which is not inherently oppressive or corrupt. Their analyses tend to focus on the way in which governmental activities interfere with individual liberties as individuals pursue their economic goals. Thus the New Left economist sees monopoly capitalism using government as a tool to oppress workers, the poor, and minority groups. The Right Wing libertarian economist sees government as an interference that destroys the liberties of everyone.

No area of activity or belief is free from critical inspection by the

---

[10] A representative New Left view is Michael Zweig, "A New Left Critique of Economics," in David Mermelstein, ed., *Economics: Mainstream Readings,* pp. 25–31. On the Right is Angus Black, *A Radical's Guide to Economic Reality* (New York: Holt, Rinehart, and Winston, 1970).

radical economist. Basic values are often attacked by the introduction and demonstration of alternative life styles (for example, hippie clothes, long hair, drugs, etc.). To the radical, basic values which give rise to economic evils are in themselves evil and must be destroyed. Some radicals focus their efforts on constructing a new future through the use of such devices as communes. For a substantial number, the new future is to be based on democratic or libertarian socialism. The professional economist who happens to be radical is likely to concentrate his efforts on a critical analysis of existing institutions along the lines outlined earlier. Since change is the key to the restructuring of society, radicals tend to be active participants in the change process through such devices as community action groups, demonstrations, etc.[11]

With respect to economic analysis, radical concerns tend to be more microeconomic in nature than macroeconomic. Such concerns include problems of income distribution, business behavior under conditions of monopoly, discriminatory practices in pricing and hiring, and so on. Macroeconomic concerns tend to be concentrated on growth, or the necessity for it, and economic development of "Third World" nations as well as the international financial relationships between those nations and capitalist countries such as the United States.

Macroeconomic stabilization policies are seen as attempts to preserve the status quo. Radicals argue that stabilization policies are implemented to protect monopoly capitalism from depression induced revolution or, as John Gurley has put it, to maintain the growth of corporate profits.[12]

Radical economists, however, do not confine their analyses to economics. Their approach seems to be more interdisciplinary than is the case with traditional economists. In fact, the segregation of knowledge into identifiable disciplines is viewed as a device to promote irrelevant specialization and elitism. On these same grounds, the use of the conventional tools of economic analysis—specifically, equations and graphs—is generally shunned by the radical economists.[13] The

---

[11] Four representative "types" from the past are discussed by Daniel R. Fusfeld, "Types of Radicalism in American Economics," *American Economic Review*, Vol. 63 (May 1973), pp. 145–51.

[12] John G. Gurley, "How Fiscal and Monetary Policies Failed," *American Economic Review*, Vol. 62 (May 1972), pp. 19–23.

[13] There are exceptions. See Gerald E. Peabody, "A Primer on the Critique of Marginal Distribution Theory," *American Economist*, Vol. 17 (Fall 1973), pp. 23–27.

use of mathematics makes articles available only to professionals and not to the general public. This tends to preserve the class distinction between intellectuals and the people. The formal student-teacher relationship is also viewed as being reflective of the intellectual's intent to preserve the class structure. Thus courses in radical economics are more likely to be freewheeling seminars with everyone a teacher and everyone a student.

Unfortunately much of the present radical literature is long on rhetoric and short on analysis. Conclusions such as "the distribution of income in the United States is becoming increasingly unequal" are assumed rather than deduced from some theoretical framework. Very little in the way of testable hypotheses has been advanced. However as radical articles find their way into the traditional journals, these characteristics are likely to change. To the extent that this occurs, radical economics is likely to lose much of its "soul" and become just another branch of traditional economics.[14]

SUMMARY NOTES

1. Disequilibrium analysis interprets resource unemployment as arising from friction in the way markets clear or friction in the acceptance of job offers.
2. The market clearing friction approach assumes instant adjustment in quantities rather than in prices, reversing the neoclassical adjustment mechanism.
3. The job acceptance friction approach assumes that labor becomes voluntarily unemployed when wages and prices deviate from their normal or permanent values.
4. Disequilibrium is resolved when expectations about prices and wages, formed adaptively, are brought into conformity with actual prices and wages.
5. Radical economics is a rapidly forming branch of economics that calls into question the basic assumptions of traditional economics.
6. Radical economists tend to emphasize normative, rather than posi-

---

[14] Of course, traditional or "establishment" economists can be more or less radical. We suggest two works by traditional economists: Paul Baran and Paul M. Sweezy, *Monopoly Capital: An Essay on the American Economic and Social Order* (New York: Monthly Review Press, 1966); and John Kenneth Galbraith, *The New Industrial State* (Boston: Houghton Mifflin, 1967). Galbraith, it should be noted, is a past president of the American Economic Association.

tive, economics by criticizing society as presently structured and advocating alternative structures.

DISCUSSION QUESTIONS

1. The neoclassical adjustment mechanism can be reversed in the money market as well as in the product market. Do so and analyze the patterns of change in the face of a change in the monetary base. What is implied about the lag in effect of monetary policy?

2. Outline some government policies that are implied by the various types of disequilibrium models discussed in the chapter.

3. Suppose private property were abolished. What effects would this have on the behavioral relationships and adjustment mechanisms of our basic model?

4. Suppose private property were retained, but firms no longer wished to maximize profits and individuals no longer wished to maximize utility. What effects would this have on the basic model?

Index

A

Adjustment mechanism
 critique, 287–88
 labor market, 77
 money market, 77
 product market, 77
Aggregate demand
 components, 13, 37, 44
 in IS-LM model, 56
 in P,Y plane, 89–91
Aggregate supply
 derivation, 61–63
 elasticity, 158–59
 in P,Y plane, 89–91
 shifts in, 75–76
Alchian, Armen, A., 292–93
American Economic Association, 295
Ando, Albert, 119, 122, 125, 128–29
Assumptions
 behavioral, 15–16
 institutional, 15–16
Autonomous spending
 financing, 80–85
 multiplier, 46–47, 80, 86, 130, 199

B

Bailey, Martin, 163–64
Balance of payments
 accounting, 219–21
 capital account, 95, 218–21
 current account, 95, 219–20
 influence of

Balance of payments—*Cont.*
 exchange rates, 224–27
 income, 221
 relative interest rates, 222–24
 relative prices, 221–22
 policy objective, 95–96
Balance of trade, 95, 217–18, 227–29; *see also* Balance of payments
Barro, Robert J., 289
Baumol, William, 167, 170
Beals, Ralph, 131
Brady, Dorothy, S., 117
Bronfenbrenner, Martin, 176
Brunner, Karl, 178, 194–95
Budd, Edward C., 282

C

Cagan, Phillip, 194
Cain, Glen G., 155
Campbell, Colin D., 283
Chenery, Hollis B., 143
Circular flow, 8, 13
Clark, J. Maurice, 138
Clower, Robert W., 288
Cobb-Douglas production function, 139, 148–49, 151, 158, 199, 252, 256
Consumption, 8, 24, 37–40
 absolute income hypothesis, 113–16
 empirical evidence, 127–29
 and interest rate, 123–25
 life-cycle hypothesis, 122–23
 permanent income hypothesis, 120–22
 relative income hypothesis, 116–19
 and wealth, 125–27

D

de Leeuw, Frank, 194–95
Denison, Edward F., 256
Depreciation, 26–27; *see also* National income, accounting
Disposable income, 8, 13, 23; *see also* National income, accounting
Domar, Evsey, 249, 251
Duesenberry, James S., 116, 127
Dynamics; *see also* Economic growth
  accelerator, 245–48
  comparative statics, 240–41
  correspondence principle, 241
  stability, 242–44

E

Economic growth
  capital-output ratio, 250–52
  definitions, 248–49
  Harrod-Domar model, 249–51
  neoclassical, 251–55
  policies
    developed economy, 258–59
    objective, 94–95
    underdeveloped economy, 259–61
  sources, 255–58
  warranted growth rate, 251
Eisner, Robert, 144
Employment Act of 1946, 3–4, 92
Equation of exchange; *see* Quantity theory *and* Velocity
Euler's theorem, 149
Evans, Michael K., 129
External equilibrium
  function defined, 229–31
  IS curve and balance of trade, 227–29
  nonmarket changes
    devaluation, 237–38
    tariffs and quotas, 236–37
  policy effects, 232–36

F

Federal Reserve System
  balance sheet, 184–85
  borrowing from, 53
  open market operations, 53
  recent policy, 280–81
  required reserve ratio, 53
  reserve changes, 52–54
Feige, Edgar, 179
Fisher, Irving, 164–65
Flow of funds accounts, 29–32, 88–89
Friedman, Milton, 108, 119–21, 125, 162–63, 173, 175–76, 178
Friedman, Rose D., 117

G

Goldfeld, Stephen M., 145, 194–95
Government expenditures, 24, 43–44; *see also* Autonomous spending
  change in, 78–80
Gross investment, 9, 24
Gross national product; *see also* National income, accounting
  definition, 20
  shares in, 9, 10
Grossman, Herschel I., 289
Grunfeld, Yehuda, 145
Gurley, John, 162, 297

H

Hamburger, Michael J., 127, 179
Hammer, Frederick, 145
Hansen, Alvin, H., 54
Harrod, Roy F., 249, 251
Hess, Alan C., 194
Hicks, John R., 54
Hosek, William R., 194–95

I

Implicit price deflator, 32–33
Income determination
  IS-LM model, 56, 58
  simple model, 45–47
Indicators
  appropriate qualities, 203–4
  fiscal policy, 204–6
  monetary policy, 206–7
Inflation
  creditor-debtor relationship, 264, 282–83
  creeping, 263
  galloping, 264
  hyperinflation, 264–65, 283
  income redistribution, 264, 282
  mechanisms
    cost-push, 272–73
    demand-pull, 272
    sector-shift, 273–74
  policies, 283–84
  source
    Keynesian, 265–69
    quantity theory, 269–72
  trade-off with unemployment
    alternative view, 276–82
    Phillips curve, 275–76
Investment
  empirical evidence, 143–45
  inventories, 142–43
  present value, 40–43, 135–37

stock adjustment approach, 137–42
  crude accelerator, 138–39
  expected profits, 142
  liquidity or internal funds, 141–42
  neoclassical approach, 139–41
IS schedule
  derivation, 56
  empirical evidence, 197–99
  shifts in, 72–74
  slope of, 106–7, 200–203

J–K

Jorgenson, Dale W., 144
Keynes, John Maynard, 3, 113, 123, 165–67, 170, 179, 288
Kosters, Marvin, 155
Koyck, L. M., 143
Kuh, Edwin, 141
Kuznets, Paul W., 144
Kuznets, Simon, 117

L

Labor demand
  basic model, 63
  elasticity, 150–51
  neoclassical derivation, 148–52
Labor market, 63–67, 148–57; see also Labor demand *and* Labor supply
Labor supply
  basic model, 63–64
  empirical evidence, 154–55
  money illusion, 156–57
  utility maximization, 152–54
Lee, Tom Hun, 179
Leibenstein, Harvey, 260
Leijonhufvud, Axel, 288
LM schedule
  derivation, 55–56
  empirical evidence, 198–99
  shift in, 72–75
  slope of, 75, 106–7
Loanable funds market, 87–89
Lovell, Michael C., 144
Lucas, Robert E., Jr., 155, 292–93

M

Macroeconomic disequilibrium
  adaptive expectations, 294
  equilibrating process, 293–94
  information costs, 291–92
  job acceptance friction, 291–93
  market clearing friction, 289–91
  notional supply, 291
Market; see also *individual markets*
  factor, 9

Market—*Cont.*
  money, 14–15
  product, 9, 13–14
Marshall, Alfred, 165
Marx, Karl, 7
Mayer, Thomas, 145, 176
Meltzer, Allan H., 176, 178–79, 194
Meyer, John, 141
Model
  reduced form, 12
  stability, 200–203
  structure
    behavioral statements, 12
    definitions, 12
    equilibrium conditions, 12
  variables
    endogenous, 12
    exogenous, 12
Modigliani, Franco, 119, 122, 125, 128–29
Monetary base, 54
  change in, 80–81
  defined, 188
Money
  data on, 33
  definition, 161–64
  stock, 52, 195
Money demand; see also Quantity theory
  basic model, 49–51
  Cambridge school, 165
  empirical evidence, 174–80
  issues in, 160–61
  portfolio balance, 173, 179
  precautionary motive, 166, 170
  speculative motive, 167, 170–71
  transactions demand, 168–70
Money market; see Money demand *and* Money supply
Money supply
  balance sheets, 183–87
  basic model, 52–54
  currency ratio, 190
  empirical studies, 194–96
  excess reserve ratio, 191–92
  identity, 188–90
  liquidity trap, 192–94
  multiplier, 188–90
  time deposit ratio, 190–91
Multiplier; see Autonomous spending

N

National income
  accounting, 19–29
  conceptual problems
    double counting, 26–27

National income—*Cont.*
 illegal goods, 26
 imputations, 25
 definition, 22
 measures of, 21–24
Nelson, Richard R., 256, 260
Net national product definition, 21
New left, 296
New Order in Political Economy, 295
Nixon, Richard M., 3, 284

O–P

Omicron Delta Epsilon, 295
Patinkin, Don, 126, 128–29
Personal income definition, 23
Petty, Sir William, 19
Phillips, A. W., 275
Pigou, A. C., 126, 165
Policy
 conflict, 93–94, 96–97
 examples of change, 99–104
 fiscal defined, 97–98
 goals, 92–96
 lag in effect, 210–11, 258
 monetary defined, 98
 relative impact, 104–9, 197–99
 role of policy maker, 96–97
 tools, 97–99
Pollution
 accounting for, 27–28
 growth and, 261
Price stability objective, 93–94
Product market; *see individual components*

Q–R

Quantity theory, 85, 164–165, 173–174, 269–72
Radical economics
 growth, 295
 nature, 296–98
Rapping, Leonard A., 155, 292–93
Rasche, Robert H., 195
Reduced form equations
 basic model, 71
 defined, 12
Resek Robert, 145
Ricardo, David, 6
Rosen, Sherwin, 155

S

Saving, 8; *see also* Consumption *and* National income, accounting

Saving function, 38–40
Schultze, Charles L., 273
Scott, Robert Haney, 198–200
Sector
 business, 6, 8
 classification, 6–7
 foreign, 7, 9
 government, 7, 9
 household, 7–8
 interrelationships, 8–11
Seiders, David F., 282
Shaw, Edward S., 162
Siebert, Calvin D., 144
Smith, Adam, 164
Solow, Robert M., 251, 256–57

T

Tanner, J. Ernest, 129
Teigen, Ronald L., 178, 194–95
Terms of trade, 221–22
Tobin, James, 126, 167, 170, 172, 174–76
Transmission mechanism, 85, 108, 207–10
Tsiang, S. C., 170
Tullock, Gordon C., 283

U–V

Unemployment
 basic model, 64–67
 natural rate, 277, 280, 284
 policy objective, 92–93
 rate, 33
Union for Radical Political Economy, 295
Variable
 endogenous, 12, 71–72
 exogenous, 12, 72
Velocity, 85–86

W–Z

Wage rate; *see also* Inflation; Labor market; Macroeconomic disequilibrium
 autonomous changes, 75
 rigidity in nominal, 64, 77
Weber, Warren, E., 128
Weinrobe, Maurice D., 170
Wholesale price index, 32–33
Wright, Colin, 128–29
Zahn, Frank, 195
Zellner, Arnold, 127, 129